BIOMES OF THE EARTH

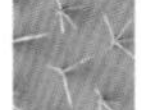  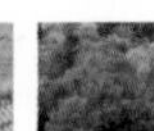 

# LAKES AND RIVERS

Trevor Day

Illustrations by
Richard Garratt

CHELSEA HOUSE PUBLISHERS
An imprint of Infobase Publishing

*From Richard Garratt:*
*To Chantal, who has lightened my darkness*

**Lakes and Rivers**



Chelsea House
An imprint of Infobase Publishing
132 West 31st Street
New York NY 10001

**Library of Congress Cataloging-in-Publication Data**
Day, Trevor.
Lakes and rivers / Trevor Day; illustrations by Richard Garratt.
p. cm.—(Biomes of the Earth)
Includes bibliographical references and index.
ISBN 0-8160-5328-6 (alk. paper)
1. Lake ecology—Juvenile literature. 2. Lakes—Juvenile literature. 3. Stream ecology—Juvenile literature. 4. Rivers—Juvenile literature. I. Garratt, Richard, ill. II. Title. III. Series.
QH541.5.L3D39 2006
577.6'4—dc22 2005011519

Chelsea House books are available at special discounts when purchased in bulk quantities for businesses, associations, institutions, or sales promotions. Please call our Special Sales Department in New York at (212) 967-8800 or (800) 322-8755.

You can find Chelsea House on the World Wide Web at http://www.chelseahouse.com

Text design by David Strelecky
Cover design by Cathy Rincon
Illustrations by Richard Garratt
Photo research by Elizabeth H. Oakes

Printed in China

CP FOF 10 9 8 7 6 5 4 3 2 1

This book is printed on acid-free paper.

# CONTENTS

CHAPTER 8
## THREATS TO LAKES AND RIVERS

# PREFACE

Earth is a remarkable planet. There is nowhere else in our solar system where life can survive in such a great diversity of forms. As far as we can currently tell, our planet is unique. Isolated in the barren emptiness of space, here on Earth we are surrounded by a remarkable range of living things, from the bacteria that inhabit the soil to the great whales that migrate through the oceans, from the giant redwood trees of the Pacific forests to the mosses that grow on urban sidewalks. In a desolate universe, Earth teems with life in a bewildering variety of forms.

One of the most exciting things about the Earth is the rich pattern of plant and animal communities that exists over its surface. The hot, wet conditions of the equatorial regions support dense rain forests with tall canopies occupied by a wealth of animals, some of which may never touch the ground. The cold, bleak conditions of the polar regions, on the other hand, sustain a much lower variety of species of plants and animals, but those that do survive under such harsh conditions have remarkable adaptations to their testing environment. Between these two extremes lie many other types of complex communities, each well suited to the particular conditions of climate prevailing in its region. Scientists call these communities *biomes.*

The different biomes of the world have much in common with one another. Each has a plant component, which is responsible for trapping the energy of the Sun and making it available to the other members of the community. Each has grazing animals, both large and small, that take advantage of the store of energy found within the bodies of plants. Then come the predators, ranging from tiny spiders that feed upon even smaller insects to tigers, eagles, and polar bears that survive by preying upon large animals. All of these living things form a complicated network of feeding interactions, and, at the base of the system, microbes in the soil are ready to consume the energy-rich plant litter or dead animal flesh that remains. The biome, then, is an integrated unit within which each species plays its particular role.

This set of books aims to outline the main features of each of the Earth's major biomes. The biomes covered include the tundra habitats of polar regions and high mountains, the taiga (boreal forest) and temperate forests of somewhat warmer lands, the grasslands of the prairies and the tropical savanna, the deserts of the world's most arid locations, and the tropical forests of the equatorial regions. The wetlands of the world, together with river and lake habitats, do not lie neatly in climatic zones over the surface of the Earth but are scattered over the land. And the oceans are an exception to every rule. Massive in their extent, they form an interconnecting body of water extending down into unexplored depths, gently moved by global currents.

Humans have had an immense impact on the environment of the Earth over the past 10,000 years since the last Ice Age. There is no biome that remains unaffected by the presence of the human species. Indeed, we have created our own biome in the form of agricultural and urban lands, where people dwell in greatest densities. The farms and cities of the Earth have their own distinctive climates and natural history, so they can be regarded as a kind of artificial biome that people have created, and they are considered as a separate biome in this set.

Each biome is the subject of a separate volume. Each richly illustrated book describes the global distribution, the climate, the rocks and soils, the plants and animals, the history, and the environmental problems found within each biome. Together, the set provides students with a sound basis for understanding the wealth of the Earth's biodiversity, the factors that influence it, and the future dangers that face the planet and our species.

Is there any practical value in studying the biomes of the Earth? Perhaps the most compelling reason to understand the way in which biomes function is to enable us to conserve their rich biological resources. The world's productivity is the basis of the human food supply. The world's biodiversity holds a wealth of unknown treasures, sources of drugs and medicines that will help to improve the quality of life. Above all, the world's biomes are a constant source of wonder, excitement, recreation, and inspiration that feed not only our bodies but also our minds and spirits. These books aim to provide the information about biomes that readers need in order to understand their function, draw upon their resources, and, most of all, enjoy their diversity.

# ACKNOWLEDGMENTS

I would like to thank the team that helped create this book: illustrator Richard Garratt, picture researcher Elizabeth Oakes, project editor Dorothy Cummings, and executive editor Frank Darmstadt, who commissioned and managed the project. A final thank-you goes to my partner Christina, who is unswerving in encouraging me in my work.

# INTRODUCTION

A biome is a major region on Earth's surface. It contains a distinctive community of plants and animals that are adapted to the climate and environmental conditions that exist there. Hot deserts, for example, contain plants and animals that are adapted to high temperatures and scarcity of water. Tropical rain forest organisms, on the other hand, thrive at similar temperatures but where rainfall is much higher. Most biologists recognize 10 biomes, nine of which refer to extensive areas of land surface. The 10th biome is often taken to be the oceans. However, the oceans are not really a biome in the same way that land-based biomes are defined, because between them the oceans straddle all climatic zones, from the polar to tropical regions. Lakes and rivers—the liquid freshwaters that settle or flow over the land—are like oceans in that between them they are found in a wide range of climatic zones. To omit oceans, or lakes and rivers, from a series about biomes would be a grave imbalance, such is their importance. Most of Earth's living space lies in the oceans, and the salty seas exert a profound affect on the climate of land-based biomes. Although freshwater ecosystems cover less than 3.5 percent of the land surface, they have an impact on other biomes that is out of all proportion to their size.

Chapter 1 clarifies some key differences between lakes and rivers and explains the nature of the water that is contained within them. Rivers are unique in connecting all the land-based biomes with the oceans.

Chapter 2 describes the physical geography of lakes and rivers. It considers how these freshwater systems were created, how lakes come to lie in landscapes and how rivers move through them, and how both shape the land surface.

Chapter 3 offers portraits of eight of the world's rivers and three of its lakes. These are chosen to reflect the diversity of major freshwater ecosystems. Each example reveals how the interplay of physical geography, climate, and human activity influences the biological communities that they contain. The examples also provide a context for the interaction between biological processes and human activities that are described in later chapters.

As chapter 4 explains, all larger freshwater animals and plants have evolved from forms that colonized lakes and rivers from the sea or via the land. Living in freshwater, with its scarcity of dissolved substances, poses particular challenges for organisms that evolved in the salt-rich environment of the sea. The chapter briefly considers the habitats found at different levels, from the water's surface to the river or lake bottom. Finally, the chapter systematically surveys the breadth of life found in present-day freshwater ecosystems.

Chapter 5, on ecology, explores different kinds of interaction between members of freshwater biological communities, especially competition and predation. The text describes two models of river function that explain how ecological processes shape the lives of the river's animals. The chapter finishes by discussing marginal wetlands, the intermittently water-covered land found at the edges of lakes and rivers.

Chapter 6 begins by considering the impact of lakes and rivers on human disease. It then goes on to give historical case studies of three rivers—the Nile, the Thames, and the Colorado. These examples reveal how the nature and extent of human impact on rivers has changed rapidly within a few decades. These impacts have altered the physical and chemical nature of these watercourses and continue to dramatically affect the lives of their inhabitants.

As chapter 7 makes clear, lakes and rivers provide many services people take for granted. They are highways for transporting goods, and they often serve as political boundaries, separating one country or province from another. People obtain vital domestic, agricultural, and industrial water supplies from freshwater ecosystems, and they also use them for waste disposal. Lakes and rivers supply food, especially in the form of fish, and many have a high recreational and amenity value. Some rivers provide hydroelectric power. If all the services that lakes and rivers provide are costed, acre for acre they are considerably more valuable than the land that borders them.

Exploiting lakes and rivers, as chapter 8 shows, has its environmental costs. People alter the rate at which water is cycled through lakes and rivers. They add harmful substances to freshwater, they harvest some of its creatures at an unsustainable rate, and they move animals and plants from one location to another, causing further disruption to habitats and the biological communities they contain. These negative impacts affect almost everyone, whether it is through the decline in water quality, the loss of food supplies, or the destruction of much of the world's natural beauty.

As the last chapter explains, keeping lakes and rivers healthy means managing their resources. In the last 30 years international laws have been created to protect and manage these freshwater ecosystems. But effective action still falls far short of good intentions. Managing freshwater ecosystems needs focused effort that draws upon sound scientific principles. Ecosystem management needs to be coordinated at different scales of organization, from international to local. Raising public awareness of the importance and fragility of freshwater ecosystems plays a vital role in their sustainable management.

As I hope this book makes clear, what happens in the air, on land, and in the sea, affects lakes and rivers. What happens in lakes and rivers affects us all.

# CHAPTER 1

# FRESHWATER, LAKES, AND RIVERS

Rivers run through channels in the landscape. Lakes fill hollows. They do so in all but the very coldest, hottest, and driest places on land. Together, lakes and rivers contain less than 1 percent of all the freshwater on Earth's surface. However, this tiny fraction is disproportionately important. Lakes and rivers are vital stores of freshwater that people utilize in many different ways.

Rivers shape the land. Seen from the air, the winding course of rivers and streams is one of the most distinctive features of a landscape. Rivers are among the most powerful natural forces that shape the land surface by gradually wearing it away. The wearing away and removal of rock and soil, called erosion, encompasses a wide range of physical, chemical, and biological processes (see "Erosion and transport," pages 41–45). Given enough time, a river can cut a swath through a mountain or plateau that is thousands of feet deep. The Colorado River has carved the one-mile (1.6-km)-deep Grand Canyon over several million years, with possibly one-third of this depth being carved within the last 700,000 years.

A river's flowing waters carry particles of rock to the ocean. In total, the world's rivers carry more than 20 billion U.S. tons (18 million metric tons) of land surface to the sea each year.

Many of the world's largest rivers are millions of years old. They have changed remarkably in that time. Today, they form networks of waterways that drain large portions of all continents except Antarctica.

By comparison, most lakes are very young. Lake Baikal in Siberia, probably the world's oldest lake, is contained in a basin with parts more than 25 million years old. Most lakes are only a few hundred or thousand years old, and on geological timescales, smaller ones are like puddles in the landscape that will soon shrink and disappear.

*A stream cascading through a deciduous forest in Bayerischer Wald National Park, Germany* (Konrad Wothe/Minden Pictures)

Water is precious. It is essential for life, and on water-scarce land surfaces, lakes and rivers are magnets for life-forms. When Lake Eyre in the South Australian desert swells with water after heavy rains, nearly 1 million waterbirds—pelicans, cormorants, gulls, terns, and black swans—fly hundreds of miles to establish colonies there. In East Africa's dry season, elephants, wildebeest, and antelope will trek several miles a day in search of water holes and drying riverbeds. For people, lakes and rivers form transport corridors, supply freshwater for drinking and for irrigating crops, and provide fish for food. The control of access to such resources shapes human history.

As streams and rivers carve into hills and mountains, they transport the eroded material downstream and deposit it as sediment (deposited particulate material), so creating particle-

### Technical terms

The scientific study of the physical and chemical characteristics of water on Earth's surface, and its distribution and utilization, is termed *hydrology* (from the Greek word *hydôr,* "water") and is carried out by *hydrologists.* Scientists who study organisms living in water are aquatic biologists (from the Latin word *aqua,* "water"). The study of freshwater systems is called *limnology* and is distinct from oceanography, which is concerned with marine systems. In freshwater, *lentic* systems are still waters, and *lotic* systems contain flowing water.

rich landforms elsewhere. Many rivers regularly overflow onto the lowlands surrounding their lower reaches. As well as posing a hazard to humans and wildlife, this flooding can be highly beneficial in depositing fertile sediment over large areas.

## Freshwater

The water in most rivers and lakes is called *freshwater* because it is low in salts. This makes it drinkable by people—although it is often not safe to drink because of chemical or biological contamination (see "Rivers, lakes, and human health," pages 152–157, and "Freshwater pollution," pages 205–207). Seawater, which is rich in salts, is not readily drinkable.

There is no absolute agreement among scientists as to the precise definition of freshwater. Most aquatic scientists maintain that freshwater contains three parts or fewer of dissolved salts in each 1,000 parts of freshwater by mass. This concentration is equivalent to a salinity of 3. *Salinity* is a measure of saltiness. Some scientists define freshwater as water having a salinity of less than 1, equivalent to one part per thousand (1 ppt) of dissolved salts.

What then is a salt? Technically, a salt is a chemical compound (a substance made of two or more elements chemically combined) that is formed when an acid reacts with a base.

The best-known salt—and by far the most abundant in seawater—is sodium chloride ($NaCl$), or table salt. In freshwater, other common salts include sodium carbonate ($Na_2CO_3$) and calcium carbonate ($CaCO_3$).

Just a tiny fraction of the water on Earth's surface—less than 100th of 1 percent (0.01 percent)—is liquid freshwater found in lakes and rivers. Most of Earth's surface water (about 97 percent) is salty and moves in the ocean. Of the 2.6 percent that is freshwater, about three-quarters is locked up as ice in glaciers and ice sheets, and nearly one-quarter lies in near-surface rocks as groundwater.

The tiny volume of water in lakes and rivers has an importance out of proportion to its abundance. This is partly because the water in rivers and freshwater lakes drains away and evaporates and is replaced by water flowing in. This makes the amount of water passing through lakes and rivers substantial. Likewise, water is cycled through lakes and rivers much more rapidly, in proportion to their volume, than it is through the larger water stores such as oceans and glaciers.

Scientists express the average amount of time a water molecule spends within a compartment or system on Earth's surface as the *residence time*. Put another way, the residence time

**The percentage of water in different compartments on Earth's surface and the residence times in each**

| Compartment | Percentage of total | Typical residence time |
|---|---|---|
| Oceans | 97.4 | Thousands of years |
| Ice caps and glaciers | 1.9 | Thousands of years |
| Groundwater (in rock) | >0.6 | Days to thousands of years |
| Soil moisture | 0.01 | Weeks |
| Freshwater lakes | 0.008 | Years |
| Saline (salty) lakes | 0.006 | Years to thousands of years |
| Atmosphere | 0.001 | 1–2 weeks |
| Rivers | 0.0001 | 2 weeks |
| Plants and animals | 0.00004 | 1 week |

is the time it takes for all the water in that compartment to be replaced. Streams and rivers have residence times of the order of days to weeks, freshwater lakes of the order of years, but oceans and glaciers take thousands of years before all their water is recycled.

The size of a system, and the pace at which water is recycled through it, affects the dilution of pollutants and their rate of removal. Because the amount of water in a river system is comparatively small, the impact of any pollution is likely to be great because the dilution effect is small. On the other hand, unless pollutants are trapped in sediments in and around the river system, pollutants may be flushed from the system fairly rapidly—although the freshwater community of organisms affected by the pollution may take many years to recover (see "Freshwater pollution," pages 205–207).

## Lakes

The word *lake* comes from the Latin *lacus,* meaning "hole" or "space." Lakes are moderate to large bodies of water that form where water collects in a dip in the ground. Ponds are usually considered to be small, shallow bodies of water, typically with an area of less than one acre (0.4 ha), in which sunlight penetrates to the bottom across the entire area. Lakes are larger and deeper, and sunlight may not penetrate all the way to the lake bottom.

Lakes' large size means they have several differences from ponds. Winds generate waves that erode the sides of the lake. Ponds are too small for winds to build such waves. In most lakes, sunlight does not penetrate to the lake bottom across the entire area. Consequently, the column of water from top to bottom is usually layered for at least part of the year. There is a deep layer at a distinctly different temperature from the surface layer. Between the two is a boundary across which the temperature changes steeply, called the *thermocline.* Such differences mean that ponds respond to environmental changes—particularly sunlight, temperature, and wind—in a rather different way than lakes do (see "The properties of lakes," pages 28–31). This in turn has an influence on the animals and plants that live there.

Among the smallest ponds are those that form in the forks of tree branches in tropical rain forests. These ecosystems in miniature commonly hold only a gallon or two of water and yet contain a wide variety of organisms, from microscopic algae—the major plants of this biological community—to tree frogs that lay their spawn there. At the other extreme, Lake Baikal in Siberia, the world's largest lake in terms of volume, holds the equivalent of 8 billion Olympic swimming pools of water.

Some of the biggest lakes lie inland far from the ocean, yet they are called seas. These inland seas are salty because of evaporation: Most of the incoming water leaves the lake by evaporating into the air, leaving salts behind. The Caspian Sea, the great inland sea of eastern Europe, is mostly brackish—that is, with salt concentrations between one (or three) and 20 parts per thousand (ppt). This means it contains salt concentrations between that of freshwater (typically less than 0.1 ppt) and full-strength seawater (averaging about 35 ppt). The Caspian Sea is one of the remnants of the Tethys Sea, a large, ancient sea whose major vestige today is the Mediterranean Sea. Today the Caspian's waters are replenished by major rivers such as the Ural and Volga.

The Dead Sea, lying between Israel and Jordan, receives water flowing into it from the Jordan River and the surrounding hills. Over the past 10,000 years, the Dead Sea has become intensely saline (salty) as it has shrunk in size. The concentration of salts in the Dead Sea is about nine times higher (320 ppt) than that found in the world's oceans (about 35 ppt). So salty is the Dead Sea that—as far as scientists know—nothing can live in its waters. It is truly a dead sea.

## Rivers

Rivers are moderate to large channels in the ground along which water flows. The channel containing the water usually has steeply sloping sides called banks. The name *river* comes from the Latin *ripa,* for "bank." The bottom of the river is the riverbed. The area on either side of a stream or river, where deeper soils are saturated with water, is called the *riparian zone*.

Small natural channels are usually called streams. Technically, the term *stream* can apply to a water channel of any size, but in general usage—as in this book—it applies to a small watercourse. There is no general agreement about the size at which a stream becomes a river. One rule of thumb is that if a fit, able-bodied young adult can leap across the watercourse, it is a stream; if not, it is a river.

Not all streams and rivers flow all the time, and some exist only seasonally. Some disappear or form a string of temporary ponds during the dry season.

Rivers and streams form a network of channels that drain water from a large area of land called the *drainage basin* (also called the *watershed* in the United States and the *catchment* in the United Kingdom). Within a drainage basin, the river

*North America's Continental Divide and the Colorado River's drainage basin*

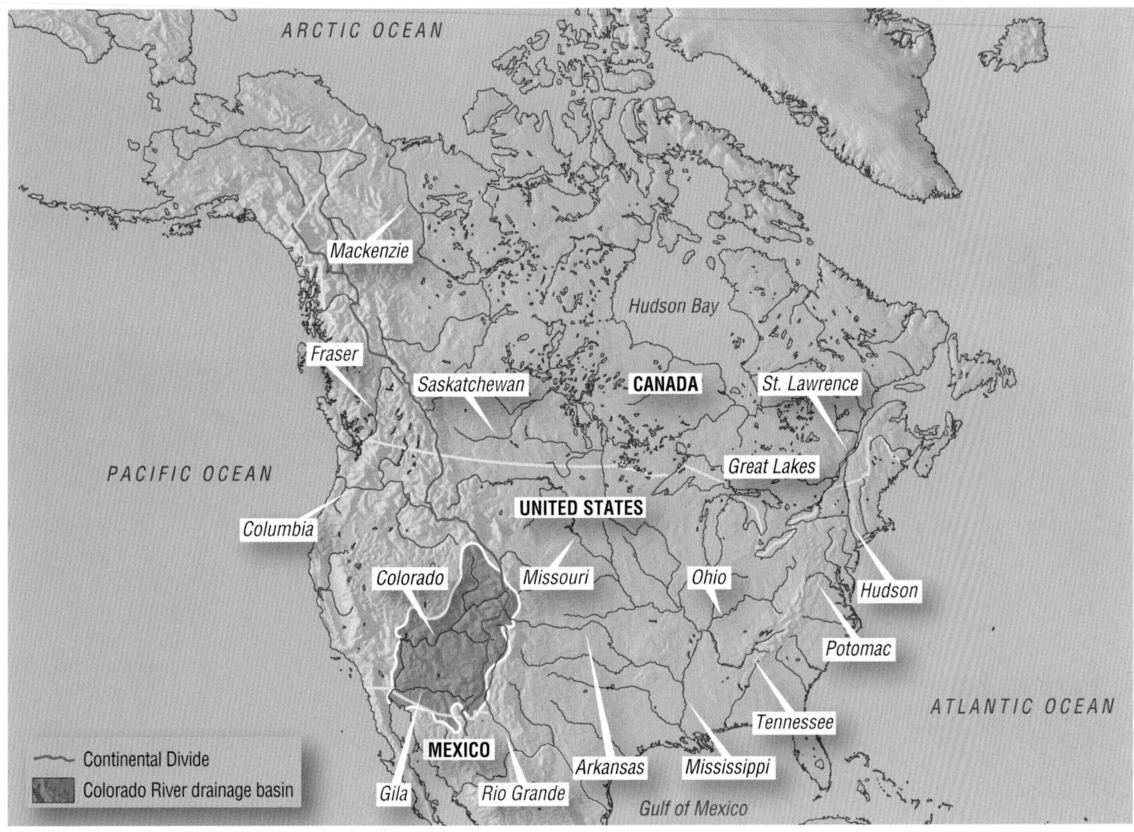

network usually looks like the branches of a tree, with many smaller channels, called tributaries, draining into a final main river. A drainage basin for a small creek can be less than an acre in area; that for the Amazon River exceeds 2.7 million square miles (about 7 million sq km).

Between one river system and the next is a high boundary called the *drainage divide.* In North America, the crest of the Rocky Mountains forms a giant drainage divide running roughly north-south: the Continental Divide (see sidebar). To the west, drainage basins carry water to the Pacific Ocean. To the east, the massive Mississippi River receives water from the Missouri and Ohio Rivers and other major tributaries and carries it to the Gulf of Mexico. The Appalachian Mountains in the east form a drainage divide roughly parallel to the eastern seaboard. To the west of this, the Ohio River empties into the Mississippi. To the east, the Hudson, Delaware, Potomac, James, Roanoke, and Savannah Rivers carry water to the Atlantic Ocean. North of the Rockies, in Alaska and in Canada's far north, icy rivers flow north into the Arctic Ocean.

River systems typically begin as streams in upland regions. The streams flow downhill under the pull of gravity. They merge into deeper and wider channels—rivers—and in many cases these eventually empty into the sea. Some river systems discharge into a lake or inland sea, such as the Volga and Ural Rivers, which empty into the Caspian Sea, and the Jordan River, which enters the Dead Sea. Some rivers disappear when they enter parched country. Some branches of river systems that drain California's Sierra Nevada end in the desert, where

### The Continental Divide of the Americas

The Continental Divide is a belt of high ground running from Alaska in the north to Cape Horn at the southernmost tip of South America. To the west of this boundary, rivers flow westward into the Pacific Ocean. To the east, they run eastward to the Atlantic Ocean or its marginal seas, such as the Gulf of Mexico and the Caribbean Sea. In Canada and the United States, the Continental Divide runs along the crest of the Rocky Mountains.

their water seeps away through porous sediments in the San Joaquin Valley floor.

The water that fills rivers comes from precipitation—water falling to Earth's surface—in the form of rain, snow, hail, sleet, frost, or dew. Very little of this water enters straight into a river. Most of the precipitation falls onto the surrounding land, where much of it evaporates (turns from liquid to gas) and returns to the air as water vapor. Of that which remains, much is water that runs off the surface in rivulets that merge to form streams that empty into rivers. This water reaches the river within minutes or hours. The remaining water soaks into the soil and may enter porous underlying rock, where it becomes *groundwater;* that is, water within rock beneath the ground (see "The hydrologic cycle," pages 21–25). Much of this groundwater takes weeks or months to move through the rock to reach a nearby river. This slower movement of water beneath the ground empties gradually into the river and maintains the river's flow between periods of rain.

After heavy rainfall, the volume of water in the river swells and the water level rises as surface runoff and moving groundwater fill the river. This occasionally causes flooding when the water spills over the banks and onto the surrounding land.

In some cases, the water falling onto the land can take thousands of years to reach a river. It may become locked in ice or snow and may have to melt before it can flow to the river.

In conclusion, the four main water inputs into a river are: direct precipitation, watershed runoff, groundwater, and the flow from upstream. The four major outputs are: evaporation, overflow onto the floodplain, flow downstream, and loss into groundwater (when the water table is very low following a drought). The balance of these inputs and outputs varies for different sections of the river and from one season to the next, so that water level and water flow in a river system vary considerably across space and time.

## Water's unique properties

The physical and chemical characteristics of water and of the chemicals dissolved in it provide the environment in which lake and river organisms live.

A water molecule is the smallest amount of water that exists. There are at least 1 billion billion water molecules in a drop of water balanced on a pinhead. How water molecules behave with each other and with other chemicals gives water its unique physical and chemical properties.

A water molecule ($H_2O$) is an atom of oxygen (O) combined with two atoms of hydrogen (H). The structure of a water molecule is unusual. In most molecules with three atoms—carbon dioxide ($CO_2$), for example—the atoms arrange themselves in a straight line. A water molecule, however, is shaped more like a boomerang or a banana. It is bent in the middle.

Although a water molecule is electrically neutral overall, it has separated electrical charges on its surface. The oxygen atom is slightly negative, and the two hydrogen atoms are slightly positive. Since opposite electrical charges attract, the slightly positive parts of a water molecule are attracted to the slightly negative part of another water molecule. This type of attraction is called hydrogen bonding. Combined with the fact that water molecules are bent, hydrogen bonding encourages water molecules to align with each other in geometric arrangements. This tendency creates the beautiful star-shaped patterns of ice crystals found in snowflakes. Hydrogen bonding also produces many of water's other unusual properties.

Without hydrogen bonding, water would be a gas like carbon dioxide at normal temperatures. Hydrogen bonding makes water molecules less likely to fly apart and form a gas. It is for this reason that most of the water on Earth is in a liquid form rather than as vapor. Water is also unusual among substances in that within the normal range of temperatures on Earth it exists in all three physical states: solid (ice), liquid, and gas (vapor).

At sea level, pure water freezes at 32°F (0°C) and boils at 212°F (100°C). If substances are dissolved in water—as in the case of freshwater—this lowers the freezing point slightly and raises the boiling point.

Water, like other liquids, gets denser as it cools—its molecules move closer together, making the same volume of water weigh more. So water at 39.2°F (4°C) is heavier (denser) than

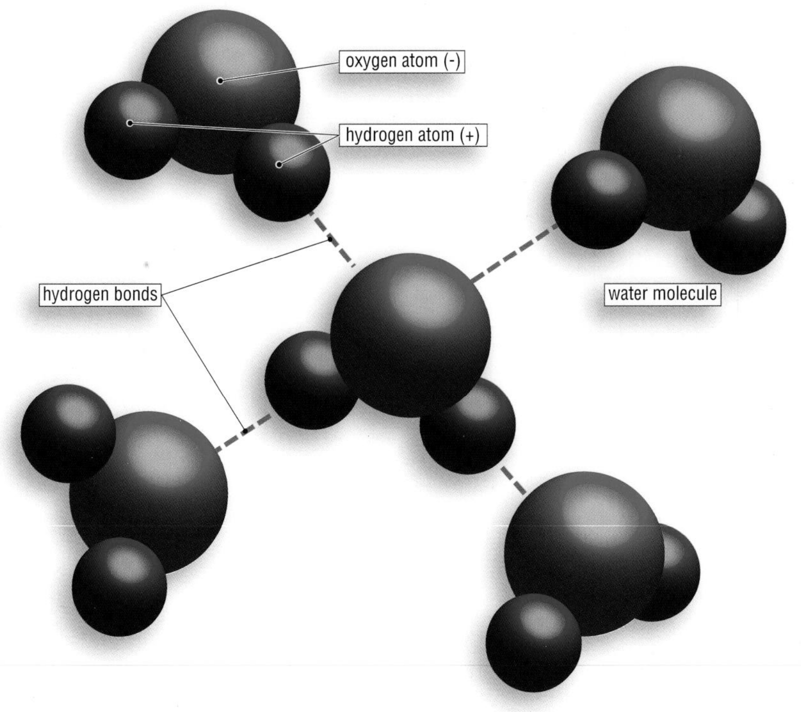


*Water molecules and hydrogen bonding. Electrostatic forces of attraction between oxygen and hydrogen atoms in adjacent water molecules are called hydrogen bonds. They produce many of water's unusual physical properties.*

water at 42.8°F (6°C) and tends to sink below it, while warm water tends to rise above cool. As cool water sinks and warm waters rises, this sets up convection currents—that is, mass movements of liquid caused by temperature differences. As water moves sideways to replace water that has sunk or risen, convection currents create vertical circulations of water that help distribute heat and mix water from different layers.

Most liquids sink when they freeze. Water, again, is an exception. Below 39.2°F (4°C), as water approaches its freezing point, it becomes less dense as hydrogen bonding creates an open framework of ice crystals. A material that is relatively less dense than that around it is effectively lighter than its surroundings. In both freshwater and seawater, ice floats. If it did not, lakes, rivers, and polar seas would freeze solid. In that case, only the warmer regions of the planet would have liquid water, and large areas of the planet would be more or less uninhabitable. In reality, when lakes freeze at the surface, water continues to circulate beneath the ice. The ice layer keeps warmer water away from the chilling air that might freeze it.

More substances dissolve in water than in any other liquid. Water is a good solvent—a liquid in which solids, called solutes, dissolve. One reason why this is so is the presence of separate electrical charges on the surface of water's atoms. Water molecules are attracted to and cluster around the charged atoms, called ions, found in salts such as sodium chloride (common salt).

Sodium chloride contains sodium ions ($Na^+$) and chloride ions ($Cl^-$) that, in their usual form, bond together to form salt crystals. When salt crystals are dropped in water, water molecules gather around the salt's ions, pulling them out of the crystal so they dissolve. Water has the same effect on other salts.

Given that water is such a good solvent and that it is present in such large quantities at normal temperatures, it is not surprising that water is the liquid in which life processes take place. Most organisms are at least 65 percent water; humans are about 62 percent water.

Gases, too, dissolve in freshwater, and their presence influences the distribution of life. Most organisms depend upon oxygen for the chemical reactions, called respiration, that release energy from food. Oxygen dissolves in freshwater, coming from two sources: the air above freshwater (from which it is absorbed) and freshwater plants, which release it in the process of photosynthesis (by which plants trap sunlight and use it to make food).

The attraction between water molecules means that it is difficult to break water droplets simply by stretching them. The surface of a droplet has a "skin" brought about by surface tension—mutual attraction between the water molecules at the droplet's surface. Water can "creep" through small holes and narrow cracks, because once some water molecules enter, others are dragged along behind.

All in all, due to water's ability to change physical state at near-normal temperatures and its capacity to flow around and creep through rock, water on Earth's surface is always on the move. Water circulates between the ground, sea, and air in the hydrologic cycle (see "The hydrologic cycle," pages 21–25).

## Freshwater's physical properties

Light is a major factor that governs the abundance and distribution of organisms in the freshwater world. Aquatic plants trap light energy and through the process of photosynthesis they convert light energy to chemical energy trapped in food molecules. Using light energy, plants combine water with carbon dioxide to make a wide range of complex, carbon-rich substances, including carbohydrates, fats (lipids), and proteins. Photosynthesis occurs in those parts of the plant—in complex plants, typically the stem and leaves—that contain the light-trapping green pigment chlorophyll. Dissolved carbon dioxide is usually plentiful in freshwater and so, of course, is water. So, lack of water and carbon dioxide rarely, if ever, limits a freshwater plant's ability to photosynthesize. However, lack of light does. Anything that blocks sunlight penetration in freshwater can limit photosynthesis. In addition, plants need nitrogen- and phosphorus-rich nutrients to manufacture their wide range of carbon-rich products. Scarcity of these nutrients limits plants' ability to photosynthesize. As the products of photosynthesis are the ultimate source of food for all freshwater organisms—including animals and microbes—the plant nutrient supply and the penetration of sunlight have a profound effect on the nature and abundance of organisms living in a stretch of water.

Among the products of photosynthesis, carbohydrates include glucose (which the plant breaks down to release chemical energy for a wide range of processes), starch (a stored form of glucose), and cellulose (a substance that forms the main component in the walls of plant cells). The fats or lipid products of photosynthesis form valuable stores of chemical energy; they are also vital constituents of the membranes that enclose plant cells and are widely distributed within them. Proteins, too, are major constituents of biological membranes. Biological catalysts called enzymes speed up chemical reactions in cells and determine the overall function of individual cells. Most enzymes are made of protein.

Animals, too, need carbohydrates, fats, and proteins, but whereas plants normally make their own, animals have to obtain them ready-made. When an animal eats a plant or another animal, it gains a supply of carbon-rich foods that it digests and then reassembles according to its own needs.

Ultimately, all organisms depend on plants and some forms of bacteria that make their own food from inorganic (not carbon-based) substances. Most of these organisms make their food using light energy, so light governs the availability of food. Light, of course, is also necessary for animals to see.

Water—even clear water—filters out light quite quickly. In clear freshwater, about 99 percent of the light that penetrates the water surface is filtered out by a depth of about 165 feet (50 m). Most lakes and rivers are much shallower than this, so in those with fairly clear water, the sunlight penetrates right to the river or lake bottom and plants can photosynthesize there. However, many lakes and rivers are far from clear, and substances dissolved in the water, or particles suspended in it, absorb much of the penetrating light. In these circumstances, most of the sunlight is filtered out within 16 feet (5 m) depth of water, and little or no photosynthesis occurs below this depth.

Water, of course, is much denser than air. At atmospheric pressure and close to water's freezing point of 32°F (0°C) freshwater is about 700 times denser than air. One result is that water supports the bodies of underwater animals and plants, and they generally need less internal support—such as a skeleton in the case of animals or a system of supporting fibers in plants—than their land-living relatives. On the other hand, because it is dense, water is much harder to move through than air. Animals have to expend considerable energy to swim through water. Their bodies, as in the case of fishes, are usually *hydrodynamic* (streamlined) to minimize drag (resistance to motion).

Water, like other liquids, becomes less dense (lighter per unit volume) as its temperature rises. This means that water becomes less buoyant—it provides less support—as it warms. However, water is unusual because it becomes less dense as its temperature nears freezing point. Water at about 39°F (4°C) is denser than water at temperatures below this, down to 32°C (0°C). Consequently, ice floats.

Fortunately for living things, water resists temperature change. It has a high *specific heat capacity;* specific heat is the quantity of heat required to raise the temperature of a unit mass of substance by one degree. It takes about five times as much heat energy to raise the temperature of a given mass of water by 1°F (0.55°C) as it does to warm the same mass of dry soil through the same temperature range. This means that the land warms and cools more rapidly than the water in lakes and rivers. Over the course of a day or the duration of a year, the temperature fluctuations in water are much less than those in air or on land. In temperate regions, air temperatures can fluctuate by as much as 27°F (15°C) in a single day, while the temperature of a small pool is unlikely to change by more than 5.4°F (3°C). This temperature-buffering effect helps animal and plant life to survive in freshwater throughout the year, from the icy conditions of winter to the baking heat of summer.

All freshwater fishes and invertebrates (animals without backbones) are *ectothermic* (from the Greek *ektos,* meaning "outside," and *therme* for "heat"). This means their body temperatures are largely determined by their environment. When the water chills, their bodies cool, and when it warms, their bodies follow suit. This in turn affects the rate at which biological functions take place. As a general rule, for temperate freshwater plants and ectothermic animals subjected to temperatures between 41°F (5°C) and 68°F (20°C), an 18°F (10°C) rise in temperature doubles the rate of chemical reactions within the body. Life processes—such as digestion, respiration, and movement—are faster at warmer temperatures within this range.

Birds and mammals, however, can regulate their temperature internally, usually keeping their body temperatures somewhere in the region of 100°F (38°C), considerably warmer than their usual surroundings. Birds and mammals are *endothermic* (from the Greek *endon* for "within"), and their body temperature alters little over the normal range of water temperatures between 41°F (5°C) and 68°F (20°C).

Water's temperature also affects its ability to hold dissolved substances. Solids that dissolve in water usually do so more readily at warm temperatures than cool ones. The opposite trend applies to gases that dissolve in water. Oxygen is twice as soluble in water near its freezing point than it is at 86°F (30°C). Oxygen is a constituent of air and vital to most organisms because they need it for respiration, and most freshwater organisms gain their oxygen by extracting it from the surrounding water. For fishes and invertebrates, high water temperatures can pose a problem. Warm water temperatures speed up life processes, causing animals to demand more oxygen, but at the same time the water contains less dissolved oxygen. Under such conditions, animals often move to cooler parts of the lake to avoid the oxygen-shortfall problem. If dissolved oxygen becomes scarce, fish may resort to gulping air at the water surface.

Wind exerts a great effect on lakes, particularly large lakes. Strong winds blowing in the same direction for any length of time generate a series of waves. These stir the water near the surface and help to oxygenate the water. Winds can be cooling or warming, and the wind enhances the rate at which heat energy is either added to the lake or removed from it. Winds also pile up water on the downwind side of the lake. All these wind-driven factors influence the distribution of organisms in the lake.

Winds generate water currents (flows of water). The stronger the wind, and the longer it blows in a given direction, the stronger the surface current it produces. Because water is so much denser than air and so difficult to shift, strong winds produce water currents that flow relatively slowly. When moving water piles up at the downwind side of the lake, it cannot flow back along the surface in the direction it has come, because the water flowing in behind it blocks the way. Instead, it moves either sideways or downward. This effect creates currents beneath the surface that flow in the opposite direction to the surface current. These subsurface currents rarely penetrate deeper than 65 feet (20 m) even in the deepest lakes (an exception is Lake Baikal: see "Lake Baikal," pages 79–83).

Other types of water currents arise because of water's tendency to rise when warm and sink when cool (except near water's freezing point). The most obvious effect occurs when cool air chills the lake's surface water, causing it to sink. This sets up convection currents, with cool water sinking and warm water rising in a circular pattern. Such movements can bring nutrient-rich water close to the lake surface, encouraging the growth of phytoplankton (microscopic drifting algae).

In rivers, water flow tends to be unidirectional (one-way) and much stronger than in lakes. Flowing water delivers oxygen and food, but water that is flowing too strongly will wash animals downstream. Different species of animals are adapted to survive in different speeds of water flow (see "Adaptations for life in running water," pages 95–96).

Water is heavy. Its density (mass per unit volume) is high—about 8.3 pounds per U.S. gallon (1 kg/L). Being so dense, a column of water exerts hundreds of times more pressure than an equivalent column of air. The air pressing down on Earth's surface is several miles thick, and the pressure it exerts is defined as 1 atmosphere. A column of water about 33 feet (10 m) high exerts a similar pressure. Descending from the water surface, where the pressure is 1 atmosphere, the pressure becomes 2 atmospheres by 33 feet (10 m) beneath the surface and 3 atmospheres by 65 feet (20 m) down.

The pressure inside an aquatic organism is about the same as that in the surrounding water. Most of an organism is liquid, and small changes in the depth at which an organism swims pose little problem. However, gases change markedly in volume with changes in pressure. A doubling of pressure will halve the volume of a gas, so the air-filled lungs of a human swimmer at the surface will decrease to half this volume when he or she dives to a depth of 33 feet (10 m). They will return to their original size when she surfaces.

Problems arise when animals living at high-pressure depths rise in the water column. Gases dissolved in the blood expand and tend to bubble out. This is not a problem if the ascent is slow, but if it is rapid, the gas bubbles can block small blood vessels, causing pain and even death. A condition called "the bends," in which the human body is wracked with pain, causing the diver to bend over in an attempt to relieve it, is produced in this way. The diver breathes pressurized air and when he rises in the water column too quickly, dissolved nitrogen bubbles out of the blood, causing recognizable symptoms, which, in severe cases, can prove fatal. The reduction in water pressure during ascent causes other problems. For example, when a fish is raised too quickly from deep water, the air in its swim bladder, a buoyancy control sac, expands and can burst.

Finally, the attraction between water molecules creates surface tension that gives water an obvious surface film, almost like a skin, at its boundary with air. Water has the highest surface tension of any liquid except the metal mercury. For some creatures, water's surface film is their habitat (see "On the surface," pages 96–97).

## Freshwater's chemical composition

Freshwater has much lower levels of dissolved salts than seawater (see "Freshwater," pages 3–5). Although the water in a stream—as well as that from springs which is sold as bottled drinking water—may look, smell, and taste pure, it contains upward of 25 different dissolved mineral ions that are present in readily measurable amounts. Chief among the minerals are calcium, sodium, magnesium, silica, potassium, and iron. If the water contains moderately high quantities of magnesium and calcium ions it is described as "hard." Such water does not foam readily. Its high calcium load is invaluable for organisms, such as crustaceans, that make their covering skeletons (exoskeletons) from calcium carbonate. "Soft" water, containing low levels of magnesium and calcium, foams readily but is less suitable for those organisms that make structures composed of calcium carbonate.

The pH scale is a measure of acidity or alkalinity of a solution, ranging from 0 to 14. A pH of 7 is neutral, a pH greater than 7 is alkaline, and a pH less than 7 is acidic. The pH scale is a measure of hydrogen ion ($H^+$) concentration, and each unit of pH is equivalent to a tenfold change in concentration. Low pH values correspond to high hydrogen ion concentrations, so a drop in pH from 6 to 4 corresponds to a hundredfold increase in hydrogen ion concentration.

Most freshwater organisms function best in waters with pH values close to neutral within the range 5.5 (slightly acid) to 8.5 (slightly alkaline). Rainwater is typically slightly acid (about pH 5.6). It becomes more acid when contaminated by large quantities of sulfur and nitrogen oxides that enter the atmosphere from the burning of fossil fuels such as gasoline, diesel, natural gas, and coal. Sulfur and nitrogen oxides dissolve in water to produce sulfuric acid and nitric acid, respec-

## The major chemical constituents of seawater, rainwater, and river water

| Chemical constituent | Seawater (typical concentration in parts per million, ppm) | Rainwater (typical range of concentrations in ppm) | River water (typical range of concentrations in ppm) |
|---|---|---|---|
| Calcium ($Ca^{2+}$) | 412 | 0.2–4 | 5–24 |
| Magnesium ($Mg^{2+}$) | 1,290 | 0.05–0.5 | 1–5 |
| Sodium ($Na^{+}$) | 10,770 | 0.2–1 | 3–7 |
| Potassium ($K^{+}$) | 380 | 0.1–0.5 | 1–2 |
| Chloride ($Cl^{-}$) | 19,500 | 0.2–2 | 3–7 |
| Sulfate ($SO_4^{2-}$) | 2,700 | 1–3 | 3–15 |
| Bicarbonate ($HCO_3^{-}$) | 140 | Highly variable | 26–80 |
| Silicate ($SiO_3^{2-}$) | 7 | 0 | 7–16 |

tively. Rainwater of pH 5 or less is commonly called acid rain. Lakes can become very acid (pH 5 or less) when they receive large inputs of acid rain.

In Europe and North America, acid rain produced by atmospheric pollution has been causing the acidification of some lakes in Scandinavia and eastern Canada to the point at which they are devoid of fish and almost all invertebrates (animals without backbones). Environmental legislation to curb the release of sulfur and nitrogen oxides has caused the problem to gradually lessen since the 1990s in North America and northwest Europe (see "Dealing with acidification," pages 223–225).

Some lakes are naturally acidic. Those that form in volcanically active regions, for instance, can dissolve high quantities of acidifying sulfur dioxide released from volcanoes. Likewise, the slow decomposition of plant material in high-latitude, peat-producing wetlands releases humic acids that acidify local lakes and ponds.

Highly alkaline ponds and lakes are relatively uncommon, but they form, for example, in volcanic regions where sodium-rich salts leach into water from lava and from soils rich in volcanic ash. Sodium carbonate ($Na_2CO_3$) and sodium bicarbonate ($NaHCO_3$) in these so-called soda lakes raise the water's pH to values of 10 to 11. The diversity of life is highly reduced in such alkaline waters, but those organisms that survive can thrive. In the soda lakes of East Africa's Rift Valley, blue-green algae (cyanobacteria) and copepods (tiny, shrimplike crustaceans) provide food for vast flocks of lesser and greater flamingos, respectively (see "On two or four legs," pages 117–127).

The levels of nutrients dissolved in river or lake water are key factors governing both the nature and abundance of the animal and plant community. Nitrates (a source of nitrogen) and phosphates (a phosphorus source) are key nutrients utilized by plants and some microbes in manufacturing a wide range of biological molecules, such as proteins and nucleic acids. Animals ultimately depend upon plants for their food, so if nutrients are in short supply, the production of both plant and animal material becomes limited. The nature of the animal and plant community also changes with increasing nutrient levels. A range of other chemical and physical factors changes in concert with the nutrient level. For example, very high nutrient levels—known as *eutrophic* conditions, from the Greek *eu* for "well," and *trephein,* "to flourish"—are commonly accompanied by high levels of decaying organic matter. Bacteria involved in the decay process can deplete oxygen levels in such water, causing distress to other organisms. River systems typically contain low nutrient concentrations in their upper reaches and higher concentrations in their lower reaches and, accompanying these differences, very different communities of animals and plants (see "How freshwater communities function," pages 133–139). In lakes, the fish community found in nutrient-poor lakes is usually quite different from that found in nutrient-rich ones. One common classification of lakes is based on dissolved nutrient level (see "Lakes through time," pages 31–35).

The mix of chemicals dissolved in river or lake water is governed in large part by the nature of the *substrate* (the underlying material) beneath the lake or river and the chemical composition of the rocks and soil in the watershed. Although rainwater contains low concentrations of dissolved solutes, as it flows through or over the ground it picks up particles and dissolves solutes that enter watercourses. Many of these chemicals are of natural origin, but some are contaminants produced by human activities (see "Freshwater pollution," pages 205–207).

In river systems, the concentration of solutes and suspended particles in the water typically increases from source to mouth. Sudden local increases in dissolved substances and suspended particles can occur after heavy rainfall. Fast-flowing runoff from the surrounding land and increased flow and turbulence in the river produce a pulse of dissolved solutes and suspended sediment and detritus (carbon-rich material from decomposing organisms).

## The hydrologic cycle

As described earlier, water is remarkable for many reasons, not least because it can exist as a gas, liquid, or solid across the range of temperatures commonly encountered on Earth's surface (see "Water's unique properties," pages 9–12). Physical-state changes from liquid to gas (evaporation) and back from gas to liquid (condensation) are major factors driving the cycling of water between land, sea, and air. The Sun's heat (solar radiation) is the prime source of energy driving the water cycle. It causes water to evaporate from Earth's surface, and its heating effect stirs the oceans and the atmosphere, transporting water and its stored heat from one place to another.

Warmed by solar radiation—especially infrared radiation, light with wavelengths slightly shorter than the visible spectrum of light—water evaporates from the sea surface and, from land surfaces and their associated lakes and rivers. Only pure water evaporates; minerals and other dissolved substances are left behind.

The rate at which water evaporates depends upon temperature. Evaporation increases as temperature rises because by absorbing heat energy more molecules have the energy to break free of the water surface and enter the gaseous state. Evaporation also depends upon the relative humidity of the air (see sidebar on page 22). When the air is absolutely saturated with water, evaporation ceases. When the air is dry—other factors aside—evaporation is likely to be rapid.

## *Humidity*

Humidity refers to the amount of water vapor in air. The mass of water vapor present in a given volume of air is called the absolute humidity. The amount of water vapor the air can hold changes markedly with temperature and pressure. At high temperatures and pressures, such as in tropical lowland rain forests, the air may be saturated (capable of holding no more water vapor) when it contains more than 30 grams of water per kilogram of air. In the cool, low-pressure conditions at the top of a mountain, the air may become saturated when it contains much less than five grams of water per kilogram of air. For this reason, *relative humidity* is often a more useful measure. Relative humidity is the mass of water vapor in a given volume of air compared to the amount the air could contain if saturated. When the air has a relative humidity of 100 percent, it is saturated with water vapor and cannot absorb any more. If the air is saturated at ground level, evaporation effectively ceases.

When water enters the air as a gas (water vapor), it often rises several hundred feet or more above the Earth's surface, where it cools. When the air becomes saturated with water—its relative humidity reaches 100 percent—water tends to condense around dust particles to form droplets or, in freezing conditions, ice crystals. The droplets or ice crystals become visible as clouds. As the droplets or crystals coalesce, they become large and heavy enough to drop out of the clouds as rain, or if frozen, as snow. Sometimes, powerful updrafts drive raindrops upward where they freeze before falling to Earth as hail (frozen rain). Clouds are readily pushed along by even light winds, so water that evaporates in one place can soon be carried hundreds of miles before falling back to Earth as precipitation.

When precipitation hits the land, some evaporates almost immediately and returns to the air as water vapor. Some soaks into the soil, where it is absorbed by plant roots and drawn up the stem. Most of this water is later lost by evaporation from the plant's leaves, a process called *transpiration.*

Of the water that remains on the land, some runs over the surface as *surface runoff* and gathers in streams, rivers, and lakes. Some sinks into the soil and stays there temporarily as the soil water store, and some penetrates to the rocks beneath to add to the temporary groundwater store. The balance between runoff, soil water, and groundwater formation varies depending on factors such as the type and amount of precipitation, the contours of the land, and the composition and layering of the soil and rock. Underlying rock such as chalk or other types of limestone is permeable to water (it allows water to pass through), and the water percolates readily into the ground. In the country, where limestone is the underlying rock, there may be relatively few ponds, lakes, and rivers above ground, although such features may occur in caves and fissures beneath the ground. Where the soil and rocks are impermeable clays, surface runoff may be greater, and streams, lakes, and marshes more common.

In the soil and in the rocks beneath the soil, water gathers and may saturate the ground up to a level—typically a few feet beneath the soil surface—known as the *water table*. The water table is not horizontal but follows approximately the contours of the land surface. The water table usually rises and falls with the changing seasons according to net effects of precipitation and evaporation. In most temperate

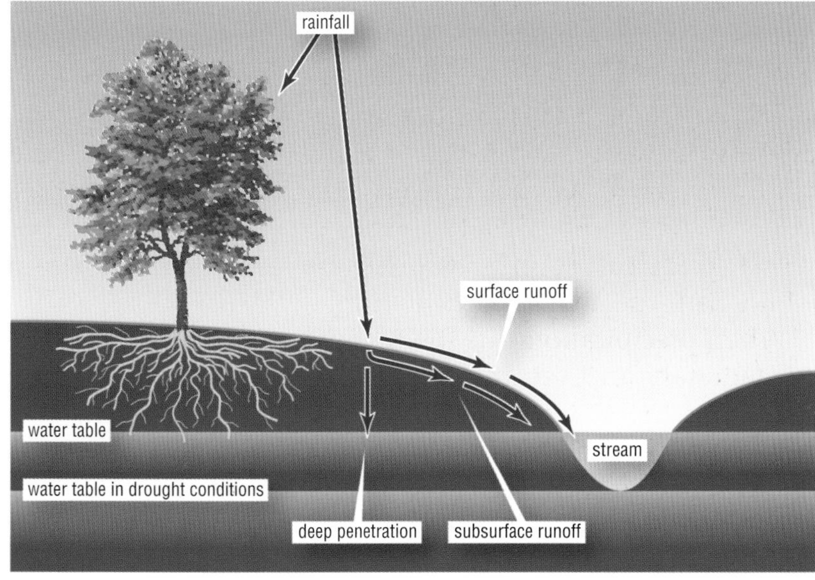


*Routes of water flow into a stream*

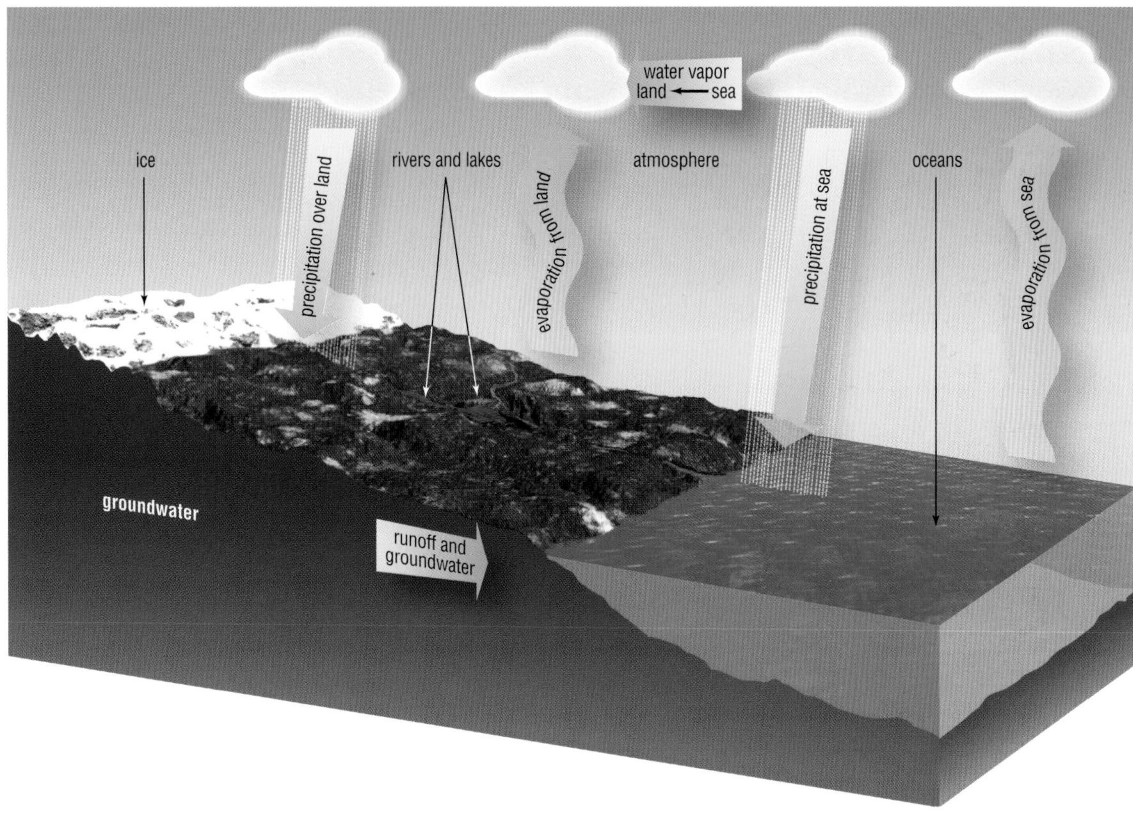


*The hydrologic cycle. Water circulates between sea, air, and land.*

regions, the water table is lower in summer and higher in winter.

Water moves sideways within the water table because the soil or rock contains an interconnected series of spaces. Soil and material beneath it such as sand or gravel have numerous tiny spaces called pores between the constituent particles through which the water can flow. Underlying rock, such as chalk or sandstone, contains larger spaces and cracks through which water can percolate. *Aquifers* are highly permeable layers of rock through which groundwater seeps in sufficient amounts to supply wells. Aquifers are an important reserve of freshwater for people in regions where little surface water—in the form of lakes or rivers—is available.

At any point in time, most of the water in the hydrologic cycle is held in storage in the oceans. Rivers play a role out of proportion to their size in carrying water from the land sur-

## *Water, life, and the hydrologic cycle*

Water is vital to all forms of life on Earth, and water in living organisms is an important component of the hydrologic cycle. Water speedily passes through organisms. Animals consume it in food and drink, and then expel it in urine, in solid waste, in exhaled breath, and across the body surface by evaporation. Land plants absorb water through their roots and release it across their moist, air-exposed surfaces in the process of transpiration. Only a tiny fraction of the freshwater on Earth's surface is resident inside living organisms at any moment (less than 0.0001 percent), but because of the high mobility of this water, it plays a disproportionately large role.

Water is an important medium in which chemical elements essential to life—carbon, sulfur, nitrogen, and phosphorus—are carried. Pollutants, too, dissolve or suspend in water and are swept along by it (see "Freshwater pollution," pages 205–207). And most forms of weathering and erosion require moisture in one form or another. Precipitation on land determines the distribution of life, both on land and in freshwater. Water vapor is a potent greenhouse gas (see "Climate change," pages 196–199), and its presence in Earth's atmosphere has kept the planet comfortably warm for the last 4 billion years. All in all, the history of Earth, and the history of life on Earth, is inextricably linked with the presence of water and its shifting state in the hydrologic cycle.

face to the sea. They are rapid channels of water movement rather than stores. Lakes, on the other hand, are temporary stockpiles of water. About two-thirds of all liquid freshwater on Earth's surface is stored in about 250 large lakes.

# CHAPTER 2

# PHYSICAL GEOGRAPHY OF LAKES AND RIVERS

Lakes and rivers form in a variety of ways. Their physical features and chemical makeup offer clues to their formation. These factors also influence the nature of the biological communities that live within these freshwater systems.

Diverse groups of scientists and engineers have developed ways of classifying lakes and rivers and the zones that exist within them. For example, geologists have described more than 100 different types of lakes based on how they formed, and ecologists use several different methods for classifying the various sections along the length of a river. Today, however, the emphasis of studies has shifted from description to explanation. Increasingly, scientists and engineers are interested in the processes that make lakes and rivers the way they are. They recognize that lakes and rivers lie on a continuum in terms of their physical, chemical, and biological characteristics, rather than falling into neatly separate categories (see, for example, "How freshwater communities function," pages 133–139). Each water body is unique.

## The creation of lakes

The dips or depressions that fill with water to form lakes arise in several ways. The five Great Lakes of eastern North America—Erie, Huron, Michigan, Ontario, and Superior—were created within the past 60,000 years when existing depressions in the landscape were further gouged out by advancing glaciers. Glaciers are rivers of snow, ice, and debris that flow slowly under the force of gravity, wearing down underlying rock in their paths. Within the past 15,000 years, as the climate warmed, glaciers left behind deeper depressions that gradually filled with melted water to create the present arrangement of the Great Lakes. When the climate warmed, glaciers no longer flowed so far south, but the debris they had dragged along remained. At their extreme southward extent the glaciers left behind arc-shaped piles of rubble called *moraines* that blocked major outflows to the south. New outflows developed to the east; in particular, the St. Lawrence River, which empties into the North Atlantic.

Across the world, glacial depressions are the most common type of natural still-water basins, and they account for many of the lakes in temperate latitudes. The existence of extensive glaciers and ice sheets during the last ice age (ending within the past 15,000 years) explains why Canada's landscape now contains several hundred thousand lakes and why the northern United States contains many more lakes than the southern part. Minnesota alone contains about 11,000 glacial lakes.

In the southern United States, lakes become common in limestone country—regions where the limestone bedrock is easily eroded by water flowing underground. Cracks in the rock enlarge to become channels that erode to form large underground chambers. Eventually, the layers of rock and soil above may collapse into the chamber, creating a sinkhole that is often 50 feet (15 m) deep or more. The sinkhole fills with water to become a pond or lake. The Florida peninsula is particularly rich in sinkhole lakes and ponds.

Much less common—but responsible for some of the world's largest lakes—are depressions where chunks of the Earth's rocky outer layer, the *crust,* have split and sunk. This subsidence is caused by movement of Earth's plates (the 20 or so plates of crust and underlying material that fit together on Earth's surface). Lake Baikal in Siberia, the world's deepest lake, arose in this way, as did the major Rift Valley lakes of East Africa, including Lake Tanganyika and Lake Nyasa. Most tectonic lakes are deep, but there are exceptions, such as East Africa's Lake Victoria, which descends to less than 265 feet (81 m).

Some lakes form in volcanic cones, such as Oregon's Crater Lake. This lake formed after a major volcanic eruption about 6,900 years ago, when the upper part of the volcanic cone collapsed into the evacuated magma (molten rock) chamber, creating a large bowl-shaped depression. Technically, depressions formed by such major collapses are called calderas rather than craters. Crater Lake is roughly circular, about six miles (10 km) across, and at 1,932 feet (589 m) deep is North America's second-deepest lake.

Some lakes form naturally when rivers deposit sediment to the extent that it eventually blocks the course of the river. The water remains trapped behind this natural barrier, and unless the barrier is breached, a lake or pond forms. Landslides or lava flows can dam a river valley, creating a lake almost overnight. In the 1910s, a rock slide in the Murgab Valley of what is now Tajikistan, Central Asia, blocked the river, creating a massive lake, Lake Sarez. Within a few years, the lake grew to a length of 38 miles (61 km) and a depth in excess of 1,657 feet (505 m).

Some animals dam rivers purposely to create regions with raised water level. Beavers construct dams out of logs and branches to keep the entrance of their home, called a lodge, flooded so that land predators cannot enter (see "On two or four legs," pages 117–127). Beaver ponds are common features in forested river systems in many parts of Canada and the United States.

Humans create artificial lakes when they dam rivers or when they dig quarries or mines that later fill with water. Artificially created and maintained lakes—strictly called *reservoirs*—often provide domestic and industrial water supplies, sometimes generate hydroelectric power, and usually create an attractive landscape that offers amenities for a wide variety of water sports.

## The properties of lakes

The physical and chemical properties of a lake depend upon many factors. Such conditions include the shape of the basin that contains the lake, the climate of the region, the nature of the water flowing into the lake (for example, whether it is rich or poor in nutrients), and the age of the lake (see sidebar). Despite these differences, there are generalizations that apply to many lakes.

Temperature has a great impact on the inhabitants of ponds and lakes. Many organisms thrive within a fairly nar-

## Saline lakes

Some rivers empty into warm, low-lying regions of continents from which water does not drain away but accumulates in lakes. The lakes act as giant solar stills, with water evaporating from the surface and leaving behind solutes. Over time, the concentrations of dissolved salts rise and the lake becomes salty (saline). The Dead Sea in the Middle East's Jordan Trench—the lowest-lying lake in the world—is also the world's saltiest.

Most saline lakes, including Utah's Great Salt Lake, are rich in common salt (sodium chloride) along with sodium bicarbonate and sodium sulfate. Saline lakes tend to fluctuate greatly in size with changing climatic conditions because they have inflow with little or no outflow. Lake Eyre in the desert of South Australia is the lowest basin on the Australian continent. This saline lake has fluctuated markedly in size in the last 100 years, depending on the annual rainfall of central Australia. Eyre's basin filled with water only three times in the 20th century, the last time in 1990. In most years, the salty lake occupies less than 20 percent of the basin. The Aral Sea of Central Asia, on the other hand, has progressively shrunk as people have extracted excessive amounts of water from its feeder rivers to irrigate cotton fields. The Aral Sea has diminished to less than half of its original surface area in the last 50 years, while the salinity of its waters has almost tripled (see "The Aral Sea disaster," page 194).

row range of temperatures. In temperate ponds and lakes, organisms become dormant, sluggish, or may die when their surrounding water chills to about 33.8°F (1°C) or when water temperature rises above 77°F (25°C). Ponds, being smaller and shallower than lakes, more closely follow the temperature of the air than do lakes. Due to its high specific heat (see "Freshwater's physical properties," pages 13–18), water warms up and cools down more slowly than the atmosphere does, and any air temperature changes tend to be followed only sluggishly by water in lakes and ponds. Nevertheless, in a hot summer, the temperatures in small, unsheltered ponds—subjected to the baking rays of the Sun—can rise to more than 77°F (25°C), threatening the health and survival of many of the pond's inhabitants. Fish, for example, require moderately high levels of oxygen, and warm water contains comparatively less dissolved oxygen than cool. On hot, sunny days, distressed fish can sometimes be seen gulping air at the pond surface.

In lakes in temperate climates, freshwater "turns over" as it warms and cools with the changing seasons. During the coldest parts of the winter, lake water freezes at the surface. The water just beneath the ice is chilly (about 34°F or 1°C), while deeper water is typically about 39°F (4°C). Freshwater at 39°F (4°C) is denser than water at lower temperatures, down to about 32°F (0°C), the temperature at which freshwater freezes. As a result, ice and chilly water float on top of slightly warmer water. The lake is stratified, with cold water lying above slightly warmer water with a steep temperature gradient (the thermocline) in between.

The daily duration and intensity of sunlight increases with the arrival of spring, and the lake's surface layer warms and any remaining ice melts. Spring storms help stir the lake's water so that the shallow and deep layers mix. By the middle of spring, most of the lake's water typically lies in the temperature range 39–43°F (about 4–6°C).

*Annual temperature cycle in an idealized temperate lake*

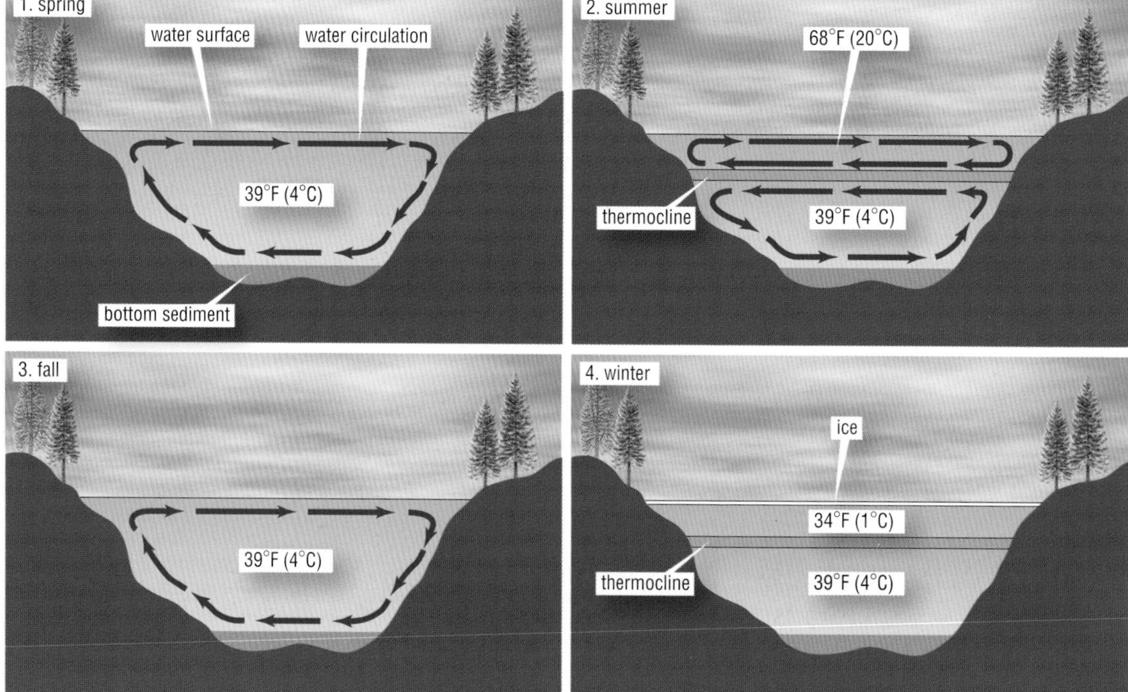

As spring gives way to summer, the days become longer, and the Sun is higher in the sky. Water at the lake surface warms as it absorbs increasing amounts of solar energy. By the middle of summer, the lake is once again two-layered, but now with less-dense warm water (temperature 59–68°F, or 15–20°C) floating above cool water (39–46°F, or 4–8°C), and with a thermocline lying between the two. The warm shallow layer is called the *epilimnion* (from the Greek root *epi,* meaning "upon," and *limne,* "lake") while the deeper, cool layer is the *hypolimnion* (from the Greek *hypo,* "under").

During the fall months, the air temperature drops and the epilimnion cools. Eventually, the temperature of the epilimnion becomes similar to that of the hypolimnion, and autumnal storms stir the water so that the two layers mix and break down. As winter begins, the lake's water drops to a fairly uniform temperature, typically within the range 39–46°F (4–8°C).

Seasonal temperature shifts in the water column have a major effect on the distribution, activity, and productivity of organisms. In summer, for example, temperatures and light levels in the surface waters may be favorable for the growth of microscopic plants, but the nutrients they require are trapped in the hypolimnion. This starves the microscopic plants of nutrients, curbing their potential growth. Breakdown of lake stratification in spring and fall serves to circulate nutrients throughout the water column, and many lakes experience an explosion of phytoplankton growth at these times (see "Plants adrift," pages 97–100).

## Lakes through time

Many of the small- to medium-size lakes that exist today will probably disappear within the next few hundred or thousand years unless people decide to maintain them. People could do this by constructing dams to keep the water in and dredging the lakes to counter the buildup of sediment. Left to their own devices, most lakes undergo a natural aging process that last hundreds or thousands of years and ends in the death of the lake. The surrounding land eventually claims the lake by filling it with mud, sand, or silt, while land plants invade the edges of the former lake and gradually spread toward its center.

When a lake first forms, it usually fills with clear freshwater that is low in nutrients such as nitrates (a source of nitrogen) and phosphates (providing phosphorus) and contains few dissolved salts. The lack of nutrients limits the mass and variety of plant life that is able to colonize the lake. Likewise, the absence of sediment on the lake bottom means that there are few rooted plants. Most of the early colonizing plants are phytoplankton, microscopic algae that float in the water. Animals, one way or another, depend on plants for their food, so the lack of plants limits the growth of animals. The lake supports a relatively small population of animals, and the fish that grow best are those, such as trout, that feed on animals that fall into the lake or land on its surface (flying insects, for example). A lake at this stage is called *oligotrophic* (from the Greek *oligos,* meaning "small" and *trophe,* "nourishment"). Lakes that form at high altitudes fill with precipitation or with runoff that has had little opportunity to erode particles and dissolve solutes from the surrounding landscape. Such lakes often remain oligotrophic throughout their lives.

In lowland areas, however, over tens or hundreds of years, the water draining into a lake brings with it dissolved nutrients and salts and particles that settle as sediment on the bottom of the lake. The accumulating sediment makes the lake shallower. Freshwater plants take root in the sediment at the edges (margins) of the lake, gaining nutrients from the sediment. The plants grow toward the surface, but most remain submerged. The water is moderately clear, and sunlight penetrates deeply, so rooted plants can readily photosynthesize (make their own food by trapping sunlight energy). A wide range of animals, including fishes, graze the phytoplankton and the rooted plants, keeping the plant growth in check.

Once the lake ages and becomes very rich in nutrients, with its water green for most or all of the year and its bottom thickly covered in sediment, it is said to be *eutrophic* (derived from the Greek for "well nourished"). Eutrophic lakes are usually defined as those that have a hypolimnion that is depleted of oxygen in summer. This effect is caused by high levels of organic matter that sink from the epilimnion and decay in the hypolimnion, encouraging bacterial growth that strips the water of much of its oxygen.

In aging lowland lakes, submerged freshwater plants such as broad-leaved pond weeds gradually become replaced by those with floating leaves, such as water lilies and water hyacinth. The process of plants colonizing the edges of the lake continues. The plants accumulate sediment around their roots and stems, and when they die back each winter, their rotted remains contribute further to the sediment. Emergent plants—those that grow from the lakebed and through the water surface—speed up the drying out of the lake. Because their leaves release water vapor drawn from the lake bottom, emergent plants vastly increase the surface across which evaporation takes place. Emergents include reeds and arrowhead plants (see "Freshwater plants," pages 102–107) that grow in the edges and shallows of the lake. Eventually, sediment accumulates sufficiently so that land-living plants, such as tussock sedges, grow in the accumulating water-saturated sediment at the edges of the lake, and they replace the freshwater plants. Submerged plants meanwhile colonize areas closer to the center of the lake, later to be succeeded by reeds and other emergent plants. Once emergent plants are growing across most of its area, the lake's days are numbered. Within a matter of decades it will most likely become wetland (soil that is saturated with water for at least part of the year) or even dry land. Most or all of the clear patches of water disappear.

The transition from lake to bog and from bog to firm ground, as a result of encroaching land vegetation, is evident on all continents in regions from temperate to tropical. Geologists find the remains of thousands of former lakes as sediment deposits filling depressions in the underlying rock.

The gradual replacement of one type of biological community by another in a given location, in an orderly series over time, is called an *ecological succession*. The disappearance of a lake and its replacement by forested dry land over hundreds or thousands of years is a good example of ecological succession.

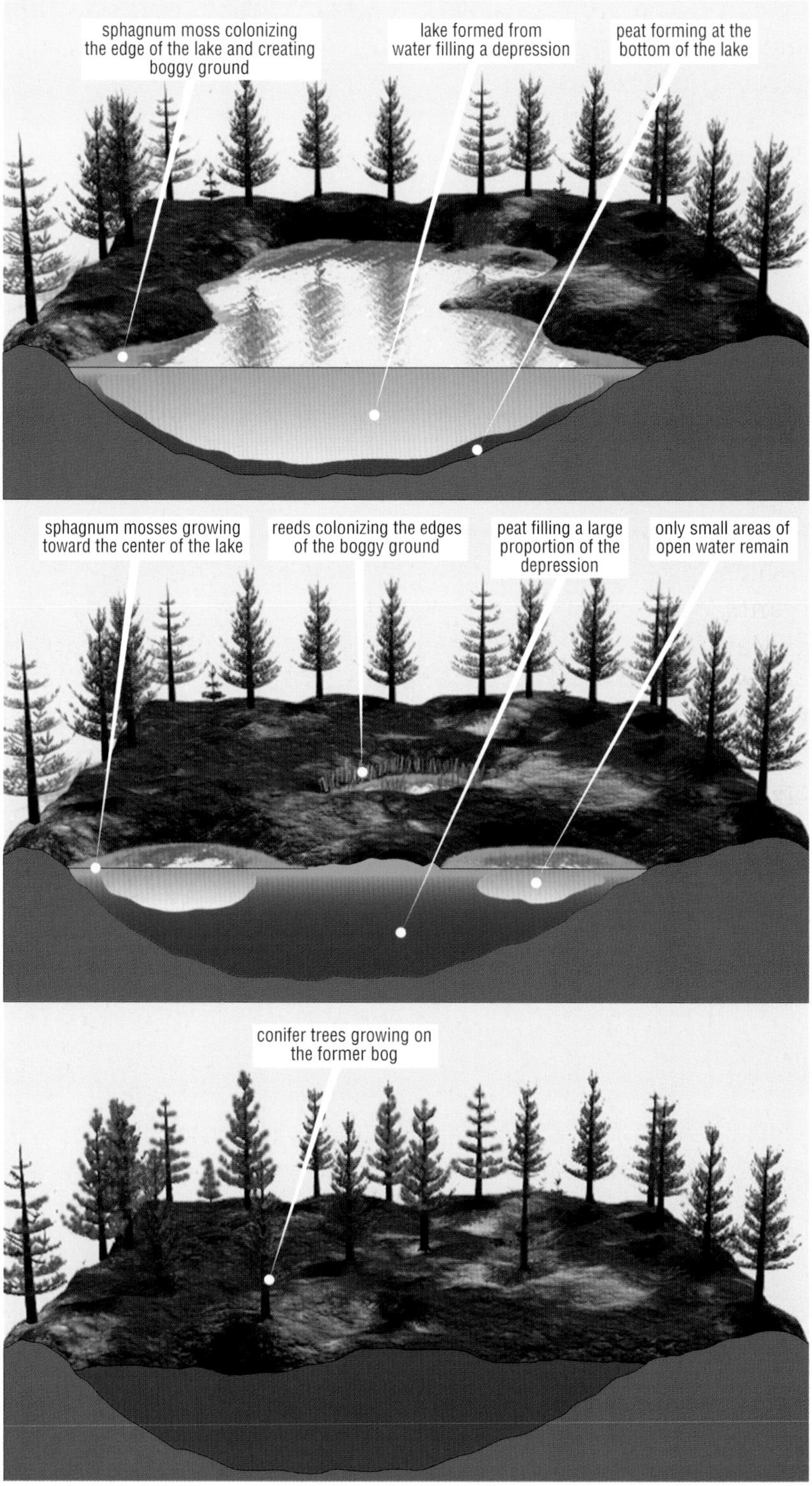

*Three stages in an ecological succession from lake to conifer forest*

In forested areas with cool temperate climates, sphagnum mosses are commonly the pioneer colonizers of the edges of lakes. At the lake margins, sphagnum mosses grow upward to the light, depriving lower layers of moss the available sunlight. The light-starved moss beneath dies and creates peat (a brown layer of partially decayed plant matter). Gradually, the accumulating peat turns the edges of the lake into a spongy bog, which rises higher and begins to dry out as the peat layer grows. Rushes colonize the margins of the lake. Over decades, the sphagnum mosses progressively grow toward the center of the lake, and the area of open water shrinks. Shrubs and trees take root in what was once boggy ground. Eventually, the succession from an aquatic community, through boggy conditions, to dry land penetrates to the center of the former lake. Forest has replaced open water. Similar successions, but involving different types and species of plants, occur in lakes in other climates.

Many factors cause lakes to disappear. Climatic changes can reduce the level of precipitation in a particular region so that lakes and rivers dry up. In limestone regions, prolonged drought starves the ground of water and sinkhole ponds and lakes dry up. Sudden geological events can drain the water from a lake or divert the water flow so that the lake no longer fills. In limestone country, erosion or subsidence can create an outlet that causes a sinkhole lake to drain into an underground cavern within a matter of days or hours. The lake can disappear overnight. An erupting volcano or a rumbling earthquake can alter the contours of the landscape, building a volcanic cone or causing the ground to fracture and sink, so that flowing water takes new paths. Human interference can divert the supply of water that would otherwise fill lakes and rivers, as in the case of the shrinking Aral Sea (see sidebar "The Aral Sea disaster," page 194).

## The creation of rivers

The surface of the land is rarely flat. It invariably has crevices and gullies, and surface water—attracted by the pull of gravity—flows downhill. In so doing, it accumulates in channels where it is unable to escape other than by flowing along the channel. Once running water is confined within a channel, it becomes much more effective at eroding and transporting sediment. In a channel that carries running water, erosion tends to increase the depth and width of the channel, which in turn increases the rate of the erosion, enlarging the channel further. In other words, once a small stream channel forms, it tends to enlarge.

Simply by following the contours of the landscape under the influence of gravity, smaller channels tend to join up with larger channels downstream to create a river system. From its headwaters in uplands to its mouth that discharges into the sea, a typical river has a characteristic profile, or shape. as revealed by a section along its length. Usually, the

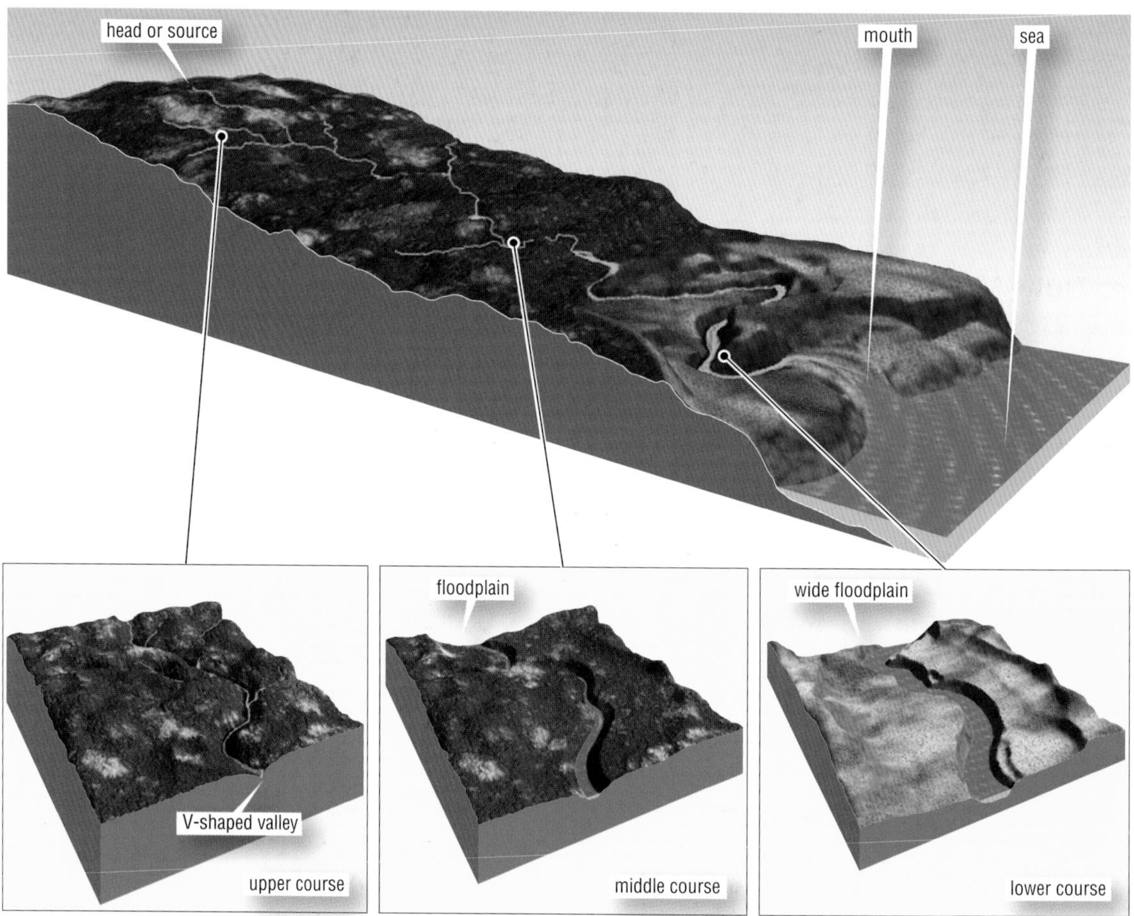


*The long profile of a river system. Details show the profile of the river and its valley at different locations.*

river starts high and descends at a steep slope, then gradually descends to a gentler slope that bottoms out where the river enters the sea.

Understanding the effect of geology on rivers is important because underlying rock and the rock types in the watershed influence the way a river cuts through the landscape and determine the chemistry of the river's water. These factors, in turn, influence the community of microbes, plants, and animals that live in and around the river.

## Drainage patterns

The spatial arrangement of a river system, as viewed from the air, is called its drainage pattern. The most common form of drainage pattern for a river system is *dentritic,* a term derived from the Greek *dendron,* meaning "tree." This pattern resembles the trunk and branches of the tree, with the main river as the trunk and the tributaries as branches. Over time, the branches or tributaries extend as the hill slopes of the drainage divide become eroded.

The dentritic pattern develops where the rock types are fairly uniform and the underlying rock is not strongly folded or faulted (fractured and then displaced). Where there are numerous faults or joints in the rock that intersect at nearly right angles, tributaries flow in parallel. They join each other, and the main river, at nearly right angles. This pattern is called rectangular. Similar to it is the trellis pattern that arises where the landscape is buckled into a series of parallel folds, as in the Ouachita Mountains of Oklahoma and Arkansas.

In 1945, an American engineer, Robert E. Horton (1875–1945), published his system of "stream ordering" for comparing rivers or comparing different sections of the same river. Horton's system has since been modified by a number of geographers, hydrologists, and engineers to form the system in common use today. In a river network, the smallest streams (those that have no tributaries themselves) are called first-order streams. When two first-order streams meet, they form a second-order stream. Where two second-order streams meet, they flow into a third-order stream, and so on. All river systems have these components, and the larger and more

## *Rivers are fractal*

Rivers are fractal, meaning that at different scales of magnitude they have a similar appearance. Study a satellite image of a river system such as that of the Missouri River, and the river and its major tributaries look like the trunk of a tree with branches. Study a photograph taken from an aircraft flying at several thousand feet, and it is clear that minor tributaries join a major tributary in a similar manner. When viewed on a 1:24,000 scale U.S. Geological Survey map, it becomes evident that small streams merge with larger streams in a similar way.

There are many theories as to why the branching of dentritic streams and rivers is fractal in nature. It appears that the branching pattern of such rivers comes about through a combination of random and predictable processes. When a river network is developing, the path a river channel takes is determined, in part, by the flow characteristics of the river at that point and randomness in the way it interacts with the terrain. Whether the river turns to the left or right at a particular junction in the landscape depends on the precise flow conditions at the time. Once the river has made the "decision" which way to flow, erosion ensures that the established channel grows larger. The combination of random and predictable processes, repeated again and again, results in rivers developing a branching network as tributaries join together. These principles of randomness and predictability operate at different scales—from a small stream to a major tributary—and so the network generated has a similar appearance at different scales of magnitude.

complex the stream system, the more orders of stream it has (see sidebar). In very large river systems, the main channel may be a 10th-order stream, as in the case of the Mississippi. The Amazon is usually rated as a 12th- or 13th-order stream.

Using Horton's stream-ordering system, geographers and geologists began to notice patterns in the landscape when they studied maps of river systems. Experts organized these patterns into "laws of drainage basin composition." They are not scientific laws, in the normally accepted sense, but are general rules of thumb based upon observation and common sense. Among them are the following:

- In a given drainage basin there are more first-order streams than all other stream orders combined.

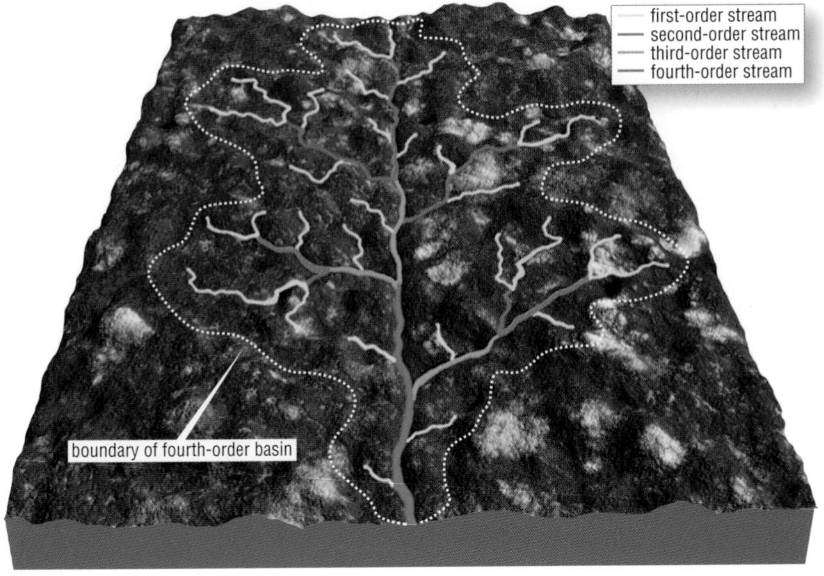


*Stream ordering. Two first-order streams join to form a second-order stream, two second-order streams join to form a third-order stream, and so on.*

- Within a drainage basin, stream length increases with stream order. In other words, a fourth-order stream will be longer than a third-order stream, which in turn will be longer than a second-order stream.
- The size of the drained area increases with increasing stream order.
- With increasing stream order, the average gradient of the slope decreases.
- With increasing stream order, the volume of river discharge increases.

Knowing such rules helps hydrologists, geologists, and engineers interpret how a river system collects and distributes water. It helps them work out, for example, where and under what conditions flooding is most likely and how a river system is likely to evolve in the future.

## Shaping the landscape

Once created, a river of any size has immense power to shape the landscape. In temperate latitudes, rivers are the most important agents of erosion on land. When rivers flow, they erode sediment from the surrounding rock, transport the sediment, and deposit it. The river's velocity (the speed at which water flows in one direction past a given point) is the key to knowing where and when a river erodes, transports, or deposits sediment. The faster a stream flows, the greater its capacity to erode land and to carry sediment and debris. The slower it flows, the greater its ability to deposit sediment. While factors, such as the specific properties of the water and the shape of the stream channel, also come into play, two main factors determine the speed at which water flows in a stream or river: gravity and friction.

Water flows downhill under the pull of gravity. All else being equal, water flows faster down steeper slopes. Mountain streams flowing down gradients of five degrees or more average speeds of some five to 10 mph (8–16 km/h). Lowland rivers in level plains with a gradient of less than .01 degrees usually idle along at less than 0.5 mph (0.8 km/h), unless the river is in a state of flood or is being strongly affected by tides.

Friction between river water and the sides and bottom of the channel tends to reduce water flow. All else being equal, water flows faster the smoother the surface across which it flows. Warm water is runnier (less viscous) than cool water, and so flows more readily. The shape of the river channel also affects river flow by causing more or less turbulence. Turbulence is uneven or haphazard flow, visible as the swirls and eddies that occur in running water.

Water is capable of two very different types of flow, laminar and turbulent. In laminar flow, water flows smoothly so that stream water in one layer does not mix with that in the layer above or below. In nature, laminar flow is rare and only really occurs in slow-running, very shallow water in a smooth channel. Laminar flow has little power to uplift and move particles.

Turbulent flow is the typical flow of streams and rivers. As the water rushes along, swirls and eddies are created that mix water from different levels. Turbulence picks up and carries particles, and the faster the flow, the greater the turbulence and the greater the river's capacity to erode and transport sediment. In mountain streams, white water is evidence of turbulence; in lowland rivers, swirling eddies at the surface are telltale signs of turbulence.

The velocity of a river varies with the season. It is greatest when rates of precipitation are high (the wet season) and the river contains a large volume of water, and it is least during the dry season, when the watercourse contains correspondingly less water.

Velocity typically changes along a river's length. It is often high for first- and second-order streams, because they have steep gradients, and lower for higher-order streams with their gentler gradients. This is a generalization, however, and in reality situations are not as clear-cut. Although tributaries *appear* to flow faster than the lowland rivers into which they feed, this is not always the case. A small stream flowing at five mph (8 km/h) looks livelier than a wide river flowing at the same velocity. The effect of friction upstream can account for the water velocity increasing downstream even though the slope there is gentler. Friction between flowing water and the sides and bottom of the river acts as a brake to water flow. Volume for volume, the water in a mountain stream is in touch with a much larger surface area of sides and bottom than is the case for a swollen lowland river. This effect alone can slow a mountain stream much more than a lowland river. When hydrologists put their current meters in the water to measure water velocity, they sometimes find surprising results. The lower Amazon, for example, flows faster than many of the mountain streams that feed it.

Finally, velocity changes across the stream channel. In a moderately straight section of river, velocities are highest near the surface in the middle of the river. This region is farthest from the effects of friction along the riverbed and sides. In a curved section of the river, friction slows water on the inside of the bend while centripetal force (a force that constrains a body to move along a curved path as it moves around a bend) tends to accelerate the water on the outside of the bend. The outside of the bend tends to erode, while the inside tends to collect sediment.

## Erosion and transport

Stream erosion proceeds in three ways: by hydraulic action, by corrosion, and by abrasion.

*Hydraulic* comes from the Greek words *hydôr,* meaning "water," and *aulos,* meaning "pipe." *Hydraulic action* refers to the movement of liquid; specifically, the action of the stream as it physically uplifts and drags particles from one place to another. Small particles that present a large surface to the river's flow, such as fine sand grains, are those most liable to be eroded in this way. A sand grain the size of the period at the end of this sentence would be eroded by a stream flowing at about 0.75 mph (1.2 km/h). At the other end of the scale, fast-moving water exerts an immense force—comparable to the force exerted by the blast from jet engines—and the blasting effect of water crashing against rock can split bedrock. Strong turbulence can then uplift large chunks of the shattered rock.

*Corrosion,* or chemical weathering, occurs when the river water dissolves substances in the underlying rock or sediment. This can weaken the rock along joints and cracks, making the rock more liable to be eroded in other ways. In rivers flowing through limestone country, corrosion can account for more than half of stream erosion in terms of mass of material removed.

*Abrasion* is the action of moving particles—such as sand, pebbles, or boulders—scraping or chipping at the sides and bottom of the river. On some hard river bottoms, swirling eddies laden with sand or pebbles wear potholes in the bedrock. At low water, these potholes—with telltale abrasive particles at the bottom—are obvious even to the casual observer.

Erosion causes a stream channel to deepen, widen, and lengthen over time. How much hydraulic action, corrosion, or abrasion contribute to erosion depends on a variety of factors, such as the steepness of the gradient, the shape of the channel, and the temperature of the water. The nature of the bedrock is particularly significant. For a river flowing through shale, for example, hydraulic action and abrasion predominate and corrosion is relatively unimportant. This is because shale is structurally weak but contains chemical constituents that are fairly insoluble in water.

*Vertical erosion,* or down-cutting, which erodes the riverbed, initially produces a steep-sided river valley. Although a freshly cut river valley usually begins with steep or near-vertical sides, the valley sides are soon worn back by weathering. The weathered material falls into the river, and the valley sides develop a shallower slope. A gentler V-shaped valley develops. Where the rock is very hard, or where a particularly dry atmosphere slows chemical weathering, the valley sides can remain steep, forming a gorge. The near-vertical sides of the famous Three Gorges section of China's Yangtze River (see "Yangtze River," pages 75–77) is a testament to dry air and hard rock.

The river's ability to deepen its valley depends, in part, on its height relative to the sea. For a river that flows into the sea, assuming the horizontal distance between source and sea remains the same, the higher the upland reach of the river in relation to the sea, the greater the river's potential to erode the riverbed. Relative height can change markedly over time. If the sea level drops—for example, during an ice age, when precipitation stays frozen on land rather than flowing to the sea—or the land rises—for instance, because of uplift caused by two of Earth's plates colliding in the nearby vicinity—then the river's gradient steepens. This increases the river's rate of flow, and the rate of down-cutting increases. The Grand Canyon has been down cut by the Colorado River in this way as the land has become gradually uplifted several times in the last few million years (experts cannot agree on how many times or the exact time period involved).

*Lateral erosion* cuts back the sides of the river channel. This is most pronounced on the outer banks of a curve in the river. In still another type of erosion, headward erosion, smaller streams lengthen the river system by gradually cutting into the hillsides from which the streams originate.

Technical terms describe the particle size (measured in diameter) a section of stream or river can carry and the total amount of sediment that can be carried in a given time. A stream's *competence* is the largest particle size it can carry. Competence grows exponentially with increasing stream velocity. Competence increases by a factor of between the mathematical square and cube of the stream's velocity, depending on the shape and density of the particles concerned. So, a stream that doubles in velocity is able to carry particles with diameters of four times (two squared) to eight times (two cubed) the size of those it could carry before.

A stream's *capacity* is the total amount of sediment it can transport. Slow-flowing rivers tend to carry much more sediment overall than their fast-flowing smaller tributaries. This is so in part because the volume of water in lower sections of the river system is so much greater.

Once running water picks up sediment, it transports it in three ways. The *dissolved* (or *solute*) *load* represents the chemicals that dissolve in river water. This tends to be made up of ions (charged atoms and molecules) that are small and are attracted to water molecules (see "Water's unique properties," pages 9–12). The dissolved load may be exceptionally high—reaching some 30 percent of the total sediment load—in rivers crossing limestone regions.

Typically, more than 50 percent of a river's transported sediment is suspended in the water as small particles, often as silt or clay. This portion is called the *suspended load*. It gives the river water its cloudiness (turbidity). The Mississippi River is coffee-colored in its lower reaches because of its high levels of suspended mud. China's Yellow River is so called because of the yellowish wind-deposited silt (loess) suspended in its waters.

The river's *bed load* includes all those particles that are too large to be suspended in the water but are rolled, slid, or bumped along the riverbed by the moving water. Some of the bed load only moves when the river is in flood conditions

## Sizes of sediment particles

| Sediment class | Diameter (inches) | Diameter (mm) |
|---|---:|---:|
| clay | 0.0008 | 0.02 |
| silt | 0.0008–0.0024 | 0.02–0.06 |
| sand | 0.0024–0.08 | 0.06–2 |
| gravel | 0.08–2.52 | 2–64 |
| cobbles | 2.52–10.1 | 64–256 |
| boulders | >10.1 | >256 |

and stream velocities are highest. The table distinguishes sediment particles by size.

Much of the sediment transported by a river arrives from elsewhere and is not eroded by the river system itself. *Weathering* refers to rock being broken down into fragments or dissolved substances by natural processes—physical, chemical, and biological. Weathered material enters the river system in water flowing off the land.

Material is dumped directly into the watercourse when nearby land collapses. *Mass wasting* is the term for movement down slope of rock, soil, or sediment under the influence of gravity. All slopes experience it. Steep slopes experience dramatic rockfalls and landslides, but even gentle slopes show gradual slippage of material, so all rivers receive at least some material by mass wasting. In some cases mass wasting can dramatically alter the path of a river or block the channel entirely to create a lake (see "The creation of lakes," pages 26–28).

*A glacier-fed stream in Chugach National Forest, Alaska. Notice the river-smoothed cobbles in the foreground and the temporary "islands" of deposited cobbles on the inside bend of the river.* (Carr Clifton/ Minden Pictures)

## Deposition and precipitation

Particles of sediment settle when the stream's velocity slows sufficiently so that the particles are no longer swept along. In a river, two of the most common types of deposition are *lateral accretion* and *over-bank deposition.*

Lateral accretion takes place on the inside of bends in the river channel, where the water flow slackens. This deposition, coupled with erosion on the outer edge of the bend, causes the bend to gradually widen farther into a broad meander, or loop.

Over-bank deposition takes place in the floodplain, the broad flat areas between the river channel and the valley's sides. During a flood, water spills over the banks and spreads onto the floodplain. On the floodplain, over-spilling water first deposits coarse sand and gravel, close to the banks of the original channel. With repeated floods, this material forms natural levees (raised riverbanks). On the floodplain and away from the river channel, the over-spilling water tends to be shallow and slow-flowing and deposits finer particles—silt and mud (see sidebar).

Sediment deposited by a river is termed *alluvium* (from the Latin *lavare,* meaning "to wash"). The alluvial soils on the floodplains of the world's great rivers, such as the Nile and the Ganges, are among the most fertile soils in the world. Alluvium is usually rich in dissolved nutrients. Despite this benefit, alluvial floodplains are, of course, at risk of flooding.

The dissolved load transported by a river does not settle out in slack water, but it can come out of solution (precipitate) under certain conditions. This can happen when dissolved substances become concentrated in situations where rates of evaporation are high. When the Jordan River empties into the Great Salt Lake in Utah, its dissolved load becomes concentrated by evaporation and contributes to the layer of common salt that crystallizes on the salt flats at the margins of the lake.

Chemical transformation that leads to deposition occurs when carbon dioxide diffuses out of solution and into the air from waters rich in carbonates. Calcite, the most common form of crystalline calcium carbonate, then accumulates on the riverbed or sides of the channel or in isolated pools after flooding.

## *Tracing sediment*

In April 1986, when an explosion occurred in Ukraine's Chernobyl nuclear reactor, significant amounts of radioactive material were released into the air and drifted across large areas of the Soviet Union and northern Europe. What proved a catastrophe—with hundreds of people dying in the cleanup operations and potentially thousands having their lives shortened by the long-term effects of radiation poisoning—also provided an opportunity. British scientists traced how radioactive substances from Chernobyl, notably the radioactive isotope (form of an element) cesium-137, became distributed and stored by the Severn River in England and Wales. Their research revealed that about 23 percent of the river's suspended sediment became stored for months within the floodplain, with only 2 percent remaining in the channel.

## From source to sea

Hydrologists and freshwater biologists usually describe a river that originates in uplands as having three more or less distinct sections: the upper reach (or course), the middle reach, and the lower reach.

In the upper reaches of a river system, streams are typically flowing down fairly steep gradients. The water flows rapidly. Although rates of erosion are high, the sediment load is not great because the river system has not yet drained a wide area. The stream is *underloaded,* meaning it has capacity to transport additional sediment. Valleys tend to be V-shaped or form steep gorges because streams are eroding vertically.

The middle reaches of a river system have more moderate slopes than those upstream. Water velocities tend to be slower than those upstream, although they vary considerably with season of the year and precise location in the channel. Erosion and deposition operate in approximate balance, and their combined activities cut and deposit features such as *meanders* (loops) and *braided streams,* in which the river splits into several smaller channels that cross and recross one another.

In the lower reaches of the river system, flow velocity usually, but not always, reduces further. The river water becomes *overloaded*—containing more sediment that it can transport—so deposition predominates. Where the river empties into a lake or the sea, a *delta,* where the river breaks into several channels separated by deposited material, may form.

The river's one-way flow, from upland to the sea, generates a range of environmental conditions as the river water progresses across the landscape. Overall, the river water starts off fast flowing and often slows as it progresses to the sea. At the same time the river channel progressively widens. Moving downstream, the sediment particles on the riverbed become smaller, while the river water itself becomes progressively more sediment-rich. All these factors influence the community of organisms that live in the river and on its banks, so that upper, middle, and lower reaches of the river system have distinctive communities (see "How freshwater communities function," pages 133–139). Not only this, but within a particular reach of the river, different parts of the channel harbor different communities. For example, shallows (riffles) that extend across straight sections of river tend to be fast-flowing at all states of river height. Deep pools, on the other hand, contain fast-flowing water only when the river level is high.

## The landforms of upper reaches

In highland regions recently uplifted by tectonic activity, vertical erosion predominates. This erosion tends to produce steep-sided gorges or V-shaped valleys. These valleys have little, if any, floodplain—the flat area on either side of the river channel where sediment from the main channel is deposited during floods.

Waterfalls and rapids are common features of upland streams and rivers. *Waterfalls* occur where the land level changes abruptly, so that the river water tumbles through the air from the higher level to the lower. In a *cataract,* there is a single long drop. The world's tallest cataract is Angel Falls in Venezuela, where the Rio Churún plunges 3,212 feet (979 m). In *cascades,* the drop proceeds incrementally through several levels, as in the case of several river systems in the Cascade Range of mountains in the U.S. Pacific Northwest.

Waterfalls typically occur where relatively hard rocks (which resist river erosion) overlie soft rocks (which erode readily). The layer of resistant rock forms an abrupt step in the otherwise smooth gradient of the river's course. The soft rock lying beneath the hard layer erodes so that the slope becomes undercut. Waterfalls retreat upstream as erosion progresses. Niagara Falls, on the border between Canada and the United States, is being cut back at the rate of more than three feet (0.9 m) a year. Where the boundary between hard and soft rock runs through the landscape for hundreds of miles, a recognizable "fall line" forms, marked by waterfalls or rapids at the discontinuity (see sidebar).

## The landforms of middle reaches

In the middle reaches of a river system, where erosive processes have been operating for long periods of time, the valley is typically broader than that upstream, the valley sides slope more gently, and a floodplain has developed. The river channel may run straight along certain sections, meander along others, and even split into several channels elsewhere. The channel may occupy almost any part of the floodplain, from the valley middle to its edge.

### *The Fall Line*

Between New Jersey and Alabama, the hard rocks of the Appalachian Mountains meet the softer rocks of the coastal plain. The rocks of the coastal plain have eroded much more rapidly than those associated with the mountains. The result is an abrupt drop in land level from west to east, and rivers that flow across the boundary—known as the "Fall Line"—do so through rapids or waterfalls. The Fall Line marks the boundary between the lowland river with access to the Atlantic Ocean and the upland river cut off from the ocean. Over more than two centuries, many cities—including Philadelphia, Baltimore, Washington, D.C., and Columbia—have grown up alongside the Fall Line. They benefit from river transport links to the coast, while cascading water nearby traditionally drove water wheels to power local industry.

*Meanders*—wide, looping bends—can occur in most parts of a river system but are especially typical of the river's middle reaches. These loops in the river gain their name from the winding course of the fabled Turkish river the Maiandros of ancient times, today called the Menderes.

Meanders form naturally as a result of turbulence in the river's flow. This turbulence causes some sections of the bank to erode rapidly and others to deposit their sediments, so establishing a bend. Similar alternating patterns of erosion and deposition occur on the riverbed, deepening some sections to form pools lined with fine sediment and filling other sections to create gravelly riffles.

Another way a meander forms is by obstruction. Where a mass wasting event or a fallen log temporarily blocks one side of the river channel, increased flow on the opposite side of the channel severely erodes that bank. The bank becomes undercut, and the channel deepens at that point, so that the channel begins to bend away from the obstruction.

Once a bend forms, the fast flow on the outside of the bend and the slower flow on the inside encourage the bend

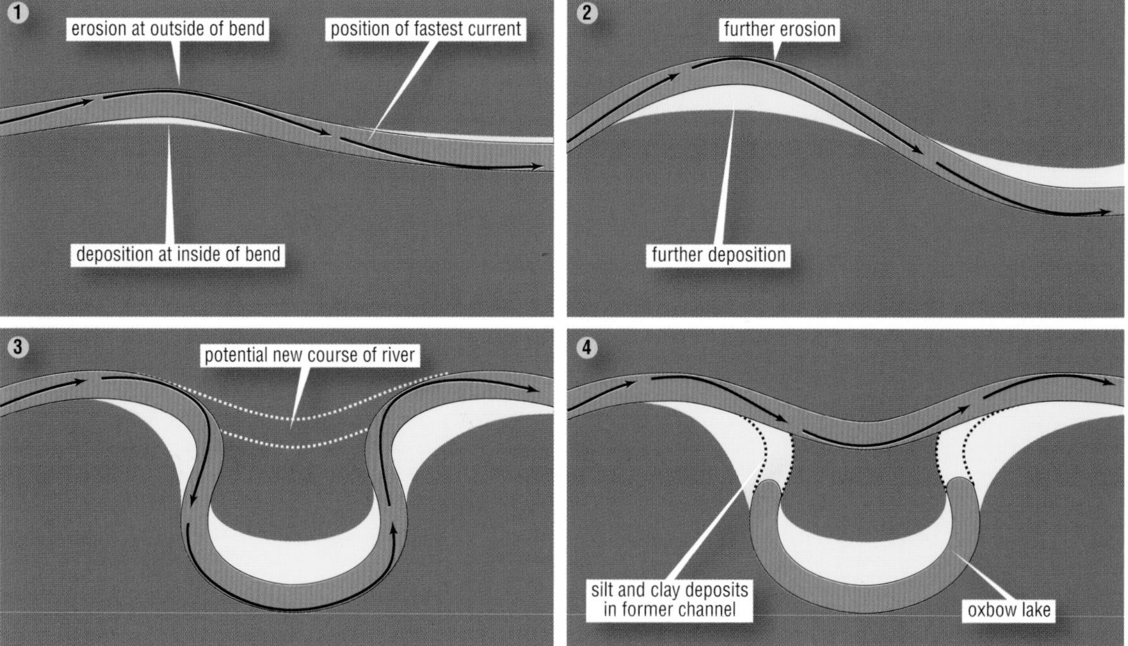


*Stages in the formation of a meander and then, when it is cut off, an oxbow lake*

to shift farther outward, particularly during the seasons of peak water flow. At the same time, the meander moves gradually downstream.

Sometimes a meander loops back on itself to the point that two quite separate parts of the river channel join up. The river then takes the shortest route, and the original meander becomes starved of water. Eventually, the meander becomes cut off from the main river, forming a so-called *oxbow lake* (named after the U-shaped collar that forms part of an ox's harness). The floodplain of an old river is often pockmarked with the silted-up remains of oxbow lakes, marking the position of the river's course hundreds or thousands of years ago.

*Braided streams*—where the river channel splits into several channels that may rejoin and split apart again in an intricate pattern—can occur in the upper and middle reaches of the river system. They develop where the channel is unusually broad and shallow and there are very high sediment loads at certain times of the year. The stream channels become separated from one another by deposited sediment. Depending on the volumes of river water and their sediment loads, braided streams may maintain their arrangement for decade after decade or may rearrange themselves every few months.

## The landforms of lower reaches

In the lower reaches, the floodplain tends to be wide and the river channel bordered by natural levees. On well-established floodplains, cities are sometimes built behind the natural levees at several feet below river level. This is the case at Vicksburg, Mississippi, where the Mississippi River flows nearby at several feet above the height of passersby in nearby streets.

Where natural levees prevent a tributary from reaching the main river, the tributary may flow parallel to the main channel for many miles before a break in the levee system allows the tributary to join the main river. Such tributaries are called *yazoo streams* after the Yazoo River, which runs parallel with the Mississippi River for more than 100 miles (160 km) before joining it at Vicksburg. *Backswamps* are marshes that form in damp depressions behind levees. Oxbow lakes—called bayous

*River channels meandering through the rain forest of the Kikori Delta, Papua New Guinea. Those channels that discharge into the sea are called distributaries.* (Gerry Ellis/Minden Pictures)

in Louisiana and billabongs in Australia—are also common in the lower reaches of river systems.

Sooner or later, most rivers come to an end when they flow into a lake or into the sea. The river loses its forward motion and gradually releases its sediment load. The coarsest sediment—usually sand—is commonly dropped right at the mouth of the river. Finer sand is dropped farther out, followed by silt and finally, farthest out, clay.

The deposited material in and around the river mouth forms a platform called a *delta,* across which the river channel commonly breaks up into several channels called *distributaries.* The name *delta* is credited to the Greek historian Herodotus (fifth century B.C.E.), who noted that Egypt's Nile River irrigates a triangular wedge of land at its mouth. He named this irrigated land the delta after the triangular shape of the Greek letter delta: Δ.

Over hundreds of years, as distributaries deposit their sediment load, the delta gradually extends outward from the

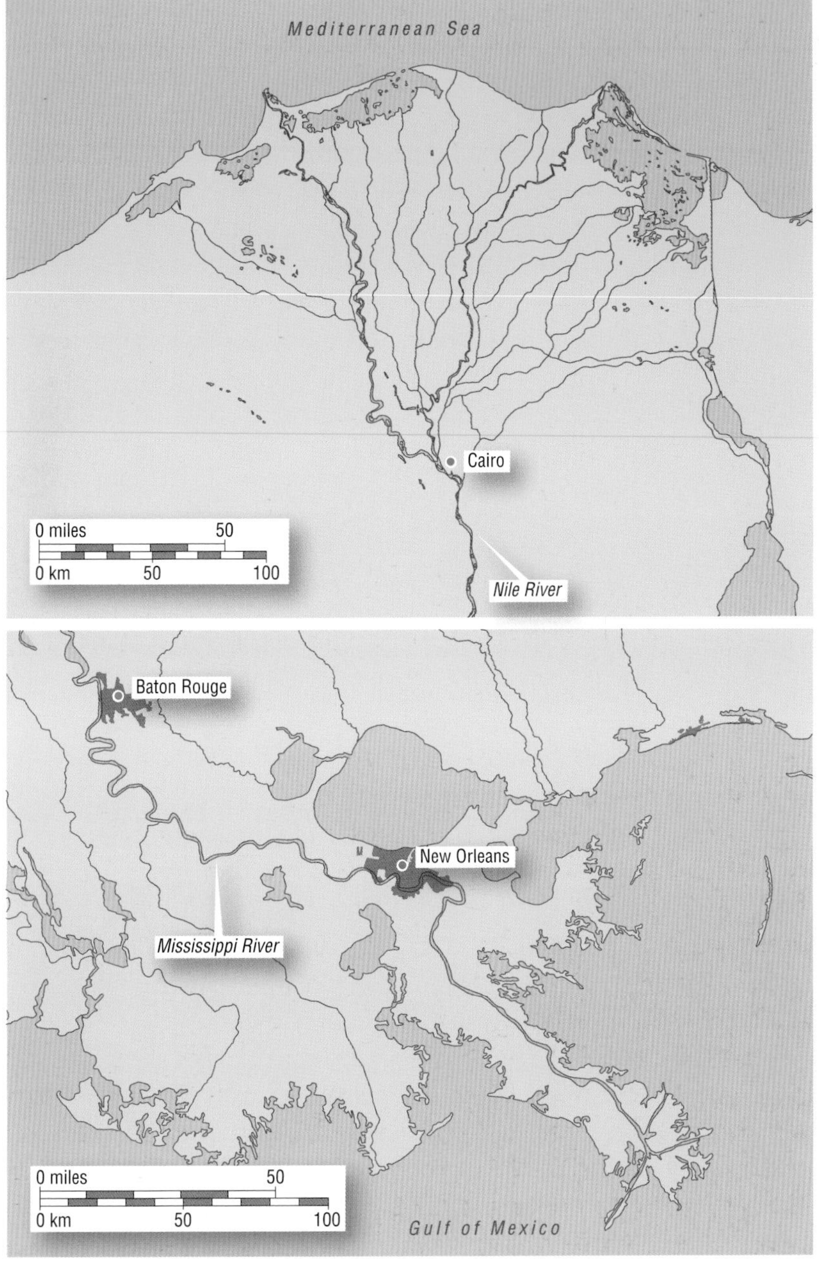


*The classic triangular delta of the Nile River and the unusual bird's-foot delta of the Mississippi River*

mouth of the river. As a delta grows, the major flow of water shifts from one distributary to another, as first one distributary and then another extends and then gradually becomes clogged with sediment. The delta of the Mississippi has grown in this way for about 150 million years. It began life somewhere in the vicinity of the junction of the present-day Ohio and Mississippi Rivers. Since then, it has advanced some 1,000 miles (1,600 km) southward, in the process creating most of the land that now forms the U.S. states of Louisiana and Mississippi. Analysis of sediment deposits shows that the Mississippi delta has shifted position several times in the last 6,000 years, at various times occupying land east and west of its current position.

Not all river mouths deposit deltas. Where waves or currents prevent sediment from settling close to the river mouth, the sediment deposits offshore or elsewhere and a delta does not form. This happens in the case of the Amazon (see "Amazon River," pages 58–60) and Congo (see "Congo [Zaire] River," pages 61–64) Rivers.

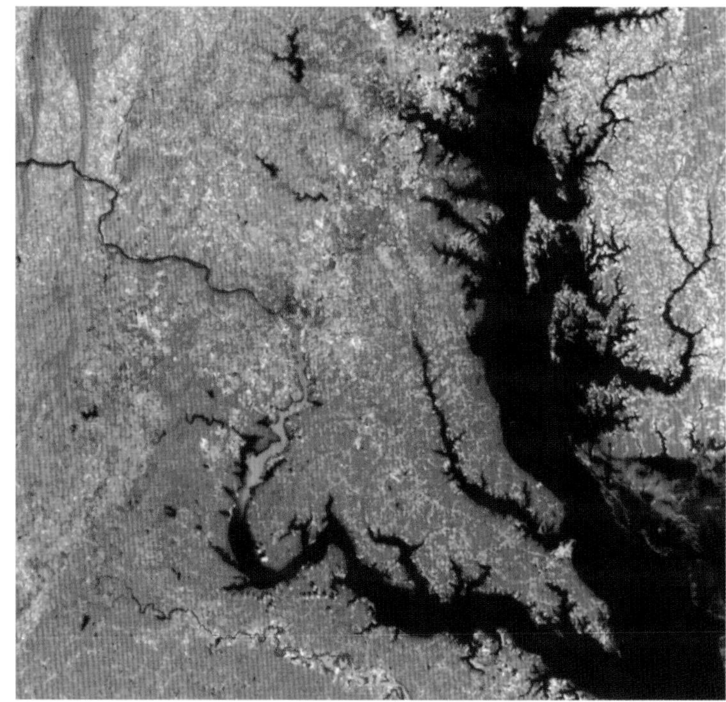

*A satellite image of Upper Chesapeake Bay, in the northeastern United States. This infrared image shows the land as predominantly red and water as various shades of blue. The Potomac River snakes from upper left to bottom right. Chesapeake Bay is the valley of the lower Susquehanna River drowned by rising sea levels since the last Ice Age. Riverborne sediment does not accumulate in the bay to form a delta.* (Courtesy Department of Commerce/National Oceanic and Atmospheric Administration)

The depth of water, the rate of sediment supply, and the relative strengths of river flow and coastal currents affect the form of a coastal delta. The Nile River has a classic fan-shaped (arcuate) delta. The Mississippi, by contrast, has a bird's-foot delta, with distributaries bounded by sediment deposits, but with stretches of clear water between them. This gives the delta the appearance of a bird's foot when viewed from the air. The Mississippi's bird's-foot arrangement establishes itself because the river flow is strong, the channel is kept clear by dredging, the continental shelf is shallow, and waves and currents in the Gulf of Mexico are not strong enough to redistribute the sediment more thoroughly.

## Floods

Technically, a *flood* occurs when part of a river system rises above its banks and the water inundates some of the surrounding land. *Flood stage* is the level at which the river begins to overflow its banks.

The water level in a river system usually varies with season. The water level rises to flood level when the input of water, either from recent precipitation or from stored, frozen water that has thawed, is much greater than the rate at which water is discharged from the river system. There is a temporary major imbalance between input and output. Water that enters the river system cannot escape quickly enough through the mouth of the main channel, so the river level rises.

In many rivers, flooding is a common feature and happens every year or almost every year. In other cases, floods are rare. For a given river system, major floods tend to be rarer than minor floods. By studying historical records—and increasingly, by monitoring precipitation levels and river-height measurements using automatic sensing equipment—hydrologists can estimate the likelihood of flooding by entering the data into their latest computer models. Using radar sensors carried by aircraft, scientists can accurately plot the contours of the land close to the river and calculate which areas will flood under different conditions.

Floods are described in terms of how often they are likely to occur. For example, suppose a hydrologist has 100 years of data for a river and finds that 10 times in that century the river rose three feet (0.9 m) above flood stage. Such a flood is called a 10-year flood because, on average, it is likely to occur once every 10 years. Put another way, such a flood has a one in 10 chance (or 10 percent probability) of happening in a given year. If the river rises five feet (1.5 m) above flood stage twice in the century, it is a 50-year flood, and in a given year it has a one in 50 chance (or 2 percent probability) of happening.

Such flood estimates are not predictions. Rather they are expressions of probability based on previous experience. If climatic or river conditions change, these estimates—based on past experience—become much less reliable. Global warming, for example, is altering patterns of precipitation and is causing sea level to rise, making flooding of lower reaches more likely (see "Climate change," pages 196–199). And the construction of artificial levees is also altering flood patterns. Flood defenses such as levees make small floods less likely but can make the effects of larger floods more catastrophic. Instead of being dissipated gradually over the land as the water rises, the floodwater may breach flood defenses only when the water reaches a high level, resulting in a destructive surge that sweeps across the landscape. Flood defenses may make people assume the land on floodplains is safe because the region experiences floods much less frequently. The reduced occurrence of smaller floods may encourage developers to build upon the floodplain. Such constructions on floodplains may remain as susceptible to large, occasional floods as they were before—perhaps even more so.

The worst U.S. flood (with the exception of coastal flooding associated with Hurricane Katrina in 2005) occurred in 1993 in the middle and lower reaches of the Mississippi River. Prolonged rain over the northern Great Plains caused extensive flooding—a 100-year flood. It killed 487 people and caused in excess of $15 billion of property damage. At St. Louis, Missouri, the river remained above flood stage for 144 of 183 days between April and September. Since the 1993 flood, hydrologists have had to reconsider the extent to which the Mississippi is constrained by artificial levees (see "Mississippi River," pages 69–72). In response to the catastrophic flood, the population of Valmeyer, Illinois, has now relocated most of the town to higher ground near its pre-1993 location.

# CHAPTER 3

# RIVER AND LAKE PORTRAITS

Across the world there are many thousands of rivers and several million lakes. Each river system and major lake has its own hydrology, ecology, and human history. This chapter gives a snapshot of eight of the world's most important rivers and three of its lakes, chosen in part to reflect a representative diversity across the major continents.

The Amazon River is the world's most important, both in terms of size and its biological diversity. Africa's Congo (Zaire) River, like South America's Amazon, is a giant tropical river, but unlike the Amazon its flow is fairly regular, not highly seasonal. The Danube River is a representative example of a major European river with a temperate climatic regime. Like most major European rivers, it has been heavily affected by pollution and by activities such as damming and channel deepening and straightening, which have radically altered the river's flow characteristics. The Ganges River is a tropical Asian river that is a lifeline for some of the world's most densely populated regions. The Ganges is massively affected by water extraction for agriculture and is heavily degraded by pollution from untreated sewage. The Mississippi is in some ways North America's counterpart to Europe's Danube, being a heavily polluted thoroughfare carrying busy boat traffic. Like the Danube, the Mississippi experiences massive fluctuations in river flow and floods severely. The Nile River—the world's longest—straddles tropical and warm temperate climatic regimes. It provides a classic example of the very mixed effects that damming can have on a major river system. China's Yangtze River is, like the Ganges, a provider of irrigation water for some of the world's most important agricultural regions, providing food for many millions of local people. The Yangtze's current dam projects will profoundly affect the river, its wildlife, and its people. Finally, Russia's Yenisey is a river straddling cool temperate to subpolar regions. And like the lakes and other rivers chosen, it has a unique history of interaction with people.

Three lakes—Baikal, Superior, and Victoria—have been chosen as representatives from three different continents: Eurasia, North America, and Africa, respectively. Lakes Baikal and Superior are both cool temperate lakes, but Baikal is deep and Superior relatively shallow. They have very different levels of dissolved plant nutrients (Superior much higher than Baikal). Africa's Lake Victoria, like Lake Baikal, is among the world's most biologically diverse lakes. Lake Victoria provides an example of intensive exploitation of biological resources in an economically impoverished locality. Developing countries that border Lake Victoria have massively exploited its fish resources within the last century and introductions of alien fish species have dramatically altered the structure of the lake's fish community.

## Amazon River

South America's Amazon, measured by the size of its drainage basin and its annual flow, is by far the world's largest river. The Amazon is joined by more than 200 major tributaries that together drain an area more than three-quarters the size of the 50 U.S. states. Averaged across the year, the Amazon empties an astonishing 200 billion U.S. gallons (about 760 billion L) into the South Atlantic every hour. The Amazon delivers more than 20 percent of the freshwater that all the world's rivers empty into the sea each year. At Manaus, the biggest port on the river, the channel is some 10 miles (16 km) wide and yet it still has 1,000 miles (1,600 km) to flow before it reaches the sea. Here, oceangoing vessels import manufactured goods and food produce. They export animal and plant materials—including live specimens—gathered from the prolific rain forest and its rivers.

The Amazon originates as the Apurímac River, a small stream high in the Peruvian Andes lying about 100 miles (160 km) from the Pacific Ocean. The Amazon's upper course, called the Marañón, flows north and then east. The

## Amazon River fact file

**Importance:** The world's second-longest river and by far the largest by volume
**Length:** 4,000 miles (6,437 km)
**Area of basin:** 2,722,000 square miles (about 7,049,980 sq km)
**Vertical drop from source to mouth:** 18,000 feet (5,500 m)

river descends about 16,400 feet (5,000 m) in its first 600 miles (970 km). In this fast-flowing section, rates of erosion are high and the sediment-laden river appears pale yellow.

The Amazon then descends into the Amazon Basin—a vast depression sinking under the weight of material eroded from the surrounding highlands. In the slow-flowing lowland river, rates of erosion are reduced and the river's waters, stained dark by rotting vegetation, are called blackwaters. The Amazon meanders for more than 2,500 miles (4,050 km) across the basin and along the way is joined by massive tributaries

*The Amazon River*

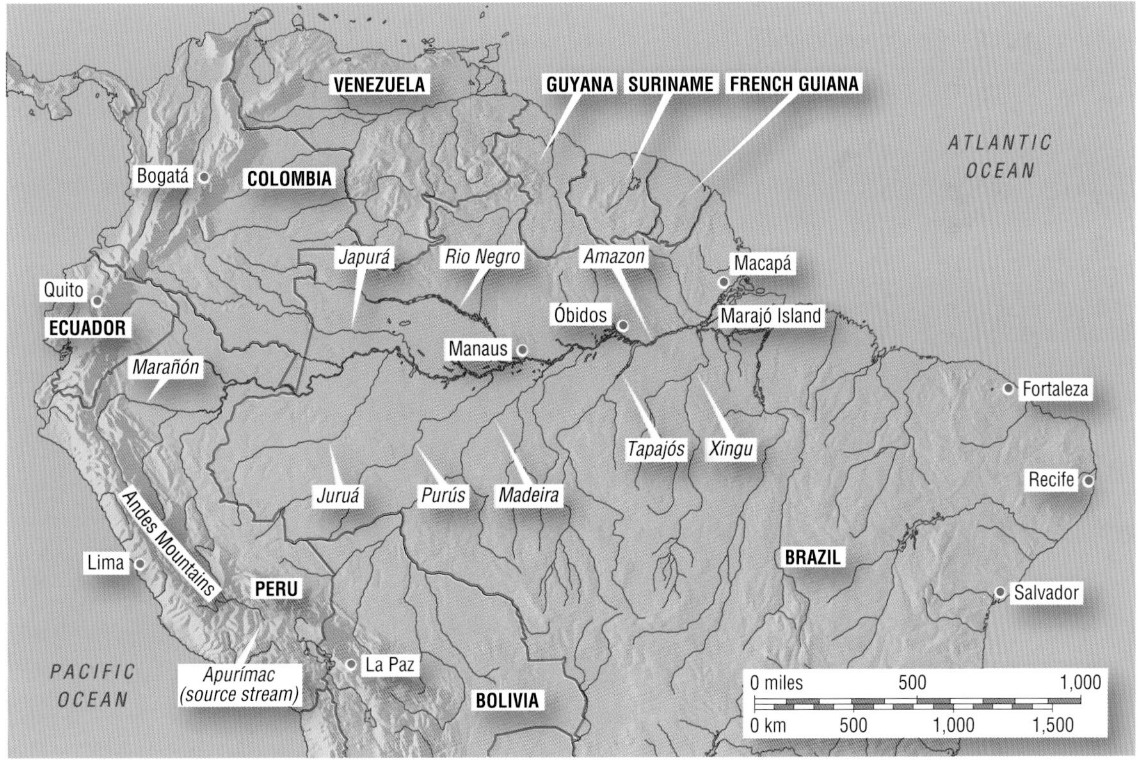

*A view across the Amazon River at sunset. The Amazon is by far the world's largest river in terms of volume of discharge. Here, near the port of Manaus and more than 800 miles (1,290 km) from the sea, the river channel is about 10 miles (16 km) wide.* (Claus Meyer/ Minden Pictures)

—the Japurá and Rio Negro, which drain the Guyana Shield to the north, and the Juruá, Purús, Madeira, Tapajós, and Xingu, flowing from the Brazilian Shield to the south.

The Amazon flows sufficiently fast that it does not lay down a delta at its 50-mile (80-km)-wide, mangrove-fringed mouth. Instead, the river's sediment load settles as a wide submerged fan offshore. Surprisingly, despite its massive size, the Amazon discharges less sediment than the Mississippi, which has about one-tenth the water flow of the Amazon (see "Mississippi River," pages 69–72).

Unlike Africa's major equatorial river, the Congo (see "Congo [Zaire] River," pages 61–64), the Amazon's flow is highly seasonal. During floods between January and May, the river spills onto the floodplain and increases its size by an area twice that of the Netherlands (about 25,000 square miles, 65,000 sq km). The river submerges large tracts of forest in water more than 10 feet (3 m) deep. Many river-dwelling species are well adapted to exploiting the flooded forest. Fish such as the piararucú (*Arapaima gigas*) feast on fruit falling into the water, while arowhana fish (*Osteoglossum bicirrhosum*) leap several feet into the air in precision attacks to grab insects from the leaves above.

The Amazon Basin harbors the world's largest tropical rain forest. It is home to more than 1 million species of animal and plant. The amazing biological diversity of the Amazon region is reflected in the fish in its rivers, which contain at least 1,500 freshwater species—more than 18 percent of the world's total.

The Amazon River system is home to a variety of indigenous species found nowhere else in the world. One example is the giant otter (*Pteroneura brasiliensis*) that reaches more than six feet (1.8 m) in length. Heavily hunted by local people for its luxuriant fur, the otter is now highly endangered.

The rain forest is under threat from both commercial logging and tree clearance for intensive agriculture or subsistence farming. Forestry experts estimate that more than 2,000 square miles (5,250 sq km) of forest are being lost each year. Stripped of vegetation, the soil is susceptible to severe erosion, with its sediment and nutrients being flushed into the Amazon River.

## Congo (Zaire) River

The Congo River (also called the Zaire) is the giant watercourse that drains the western region of central Africa. Its extensive drainage basin, second in size only to that of the Amazon River, produces an annual volume of discharge that is also second to that of the Amazon.

The Congo rises at the meeting point of the Lualaba and Luvua Rivers south of the city of Kabalo in the Democratic Republic of the Congo (DRC). The headwaters of the Congo are fed by tributaries that collect rainwater from the western slopes of the East African Plateau. The fast-flowing upper Congo forms a broken beadwork of lakes, rapids, and waterfalls, interspersed with more continuous sections of river. After Boyoma Falls (formerly called Stanley Falls), a series of seven major cataracts just upstream of Kisangani city, the river becomes the slow-flowing middle Congo. Several

## Congo River fact file

**Importance:** The world's fifth-longest river and the second largest in terms of volume
**Length:** 2,700 miles (4,344 km)
**Area of basin:** 1,425,000 square miles (3,700,000 sq km)
**Vertical drop from source to mouth:** 5,775 feet (1,760 m)

major tributaries—the Aruwimi, Kwa, Lomami, Tshuapa, and Ubangi—flow into the middle Congo, which becomes a wide, slow-flowing river up to eight miles (13 km) across. In many places, islands break the main course into channels.

*The Congo River*

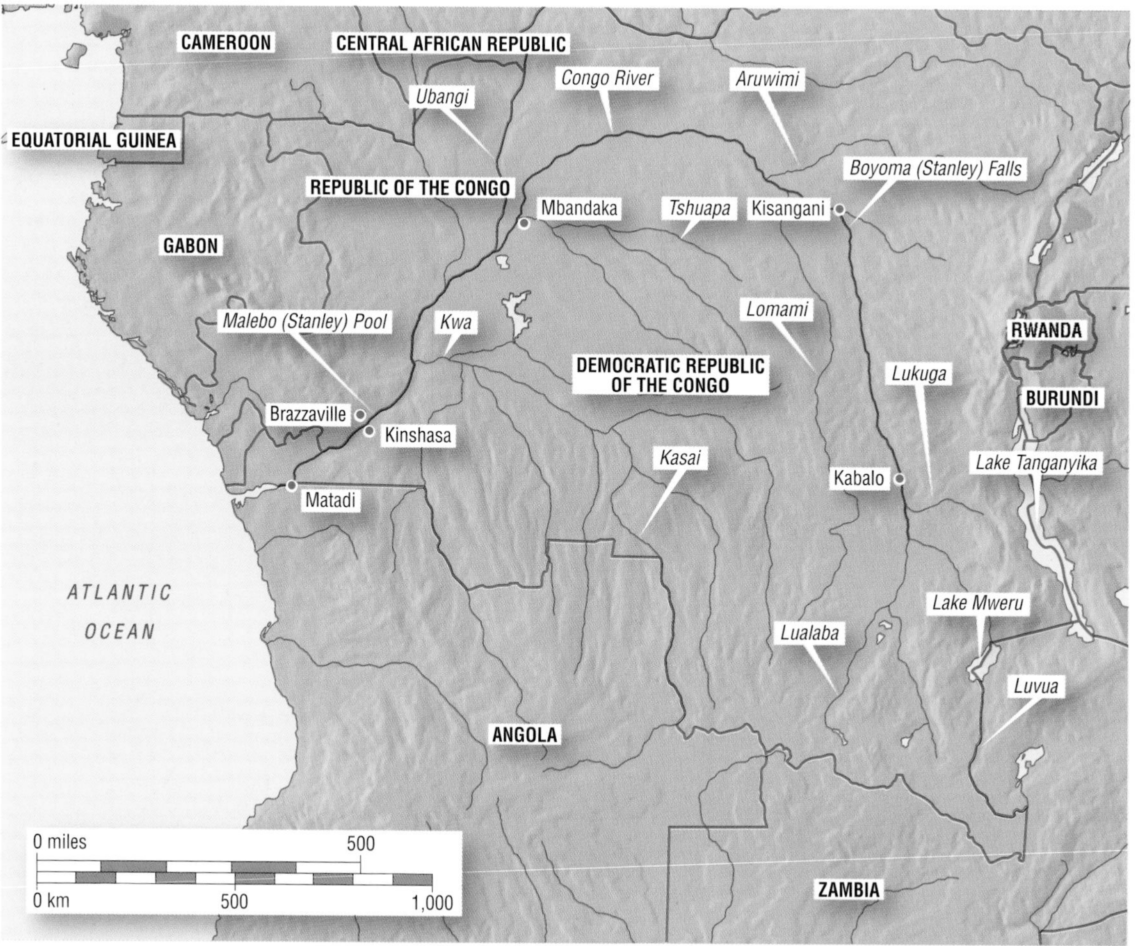

The banks, lined with dense equatorial rain forest, flood at almost any time of the year.

About 500 miles (800 km) southwest of the Boyoma Falls, the Congo becomes the border between the Republic of the Congo and DRC. Near Kinshasa, DRC's capital, the Congo

*The Congo River meandering through tropical rain forest* (Frans Lanting/ Minden Pictures)

expands into the Malebo Pool (formerly called Stanley Pool), which reaches about 17 miles (27 km) across. Approaching the coast, the Congo drops more than 1,000 feet (300 m) in a series of waterfalls and cataracts. The erosional power of the fassavannat-flowing river means that the mangrove-lined Congo River estuary does not have a delta. The sediment in its muddy waters settles as a deep submarine canyon that spills onto the floor of the Atlantic Ocean.

The Congo, together with its extensive system of tributaries, creates a network of navigable waterways more than 10,000 miles (16,000 km) long that fuels the economic development of the Democratic Republic of Congo and neighboring countries. The river itself is navigable by commercial traffic in two main stretches, the first between the Atlantic Ocean and Matadi, and the second between Kinshasa and Kisangani.

Tropical rain forest, interspersed by savanna, tropical grassland with scattered trees and shrubs, occupies much of the land of the Congo River Basin. The Congo Basin has fairly uniform rainfall throughout the year, so the river flow is unusually regular. The large yet fairly consistent volume of water flowing down a series of rapids and waterfalls gives the Congo great potential to generate hydroelectricity—a potential that has yet to be exploited.

## Danube River

The Danube flows roughly west to east across central Europe and either passes through or borders a total of 10 European countries. Three national capitals are situated along its course: Vienna, Austria; Budapest, Hungary; and Bratislava, Slovakia. The Danube is Europe's second-longest river (after the Volga of northeastern Europe), but in terms of the volume of water it discharges it reigns supreme among European rivers. Its volume varies greatly, and at times of extreme flood the Danube discharges 10 times more water than during droughts. In 2002 unusually heavy summer rains in central Europe caused the Danube to burst its banks in many places, flooding parts of many historic towns and cities. That year in Austria, the Danube reached the highest flood levels on record.

## Danube River fact file

**Importance:** Europe's second-longest river and Europe's largest by volume
**Length:** 1,771 miles (2,850 km)
**Area of basin:** 315,444 square miles (817,000 sq km)
**Vertical drop from source to mouth:** 2,174 feet (662 m)

The Danube rises at the confluence of two small rivers, the Brigach and Breg, in Germany's Black Forest. It flows through Austria before descending through Hungary and then cutting the deepest gorge in Europe, the Iron Gate, with 2,600-foot (800-m)-high walls. The Danube eventually

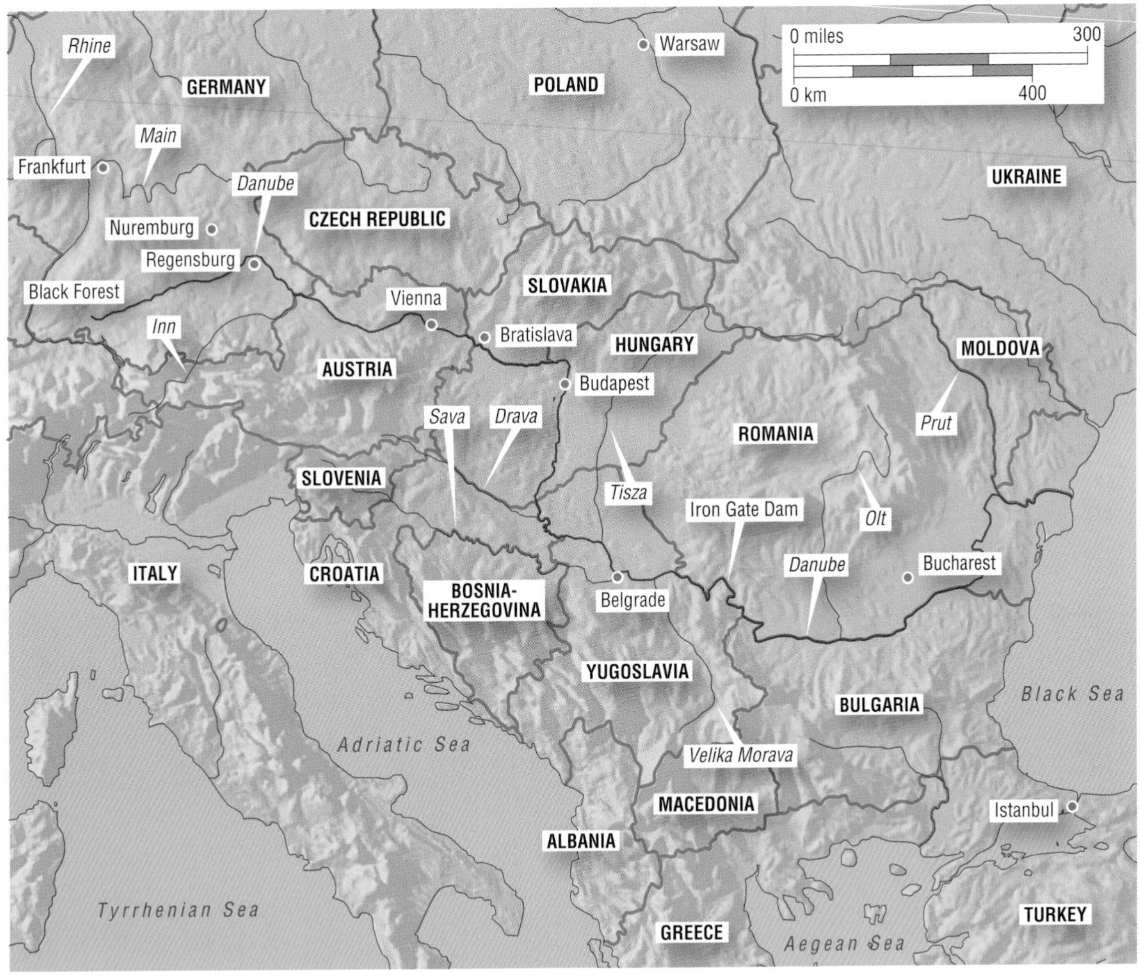


*The Danube River*

empties into the Black Sea through three distributaries in a triangular delta that straddles the border of Romania and Ukraine.

The nature of the Danube changes markedly from one stretch to another. The river's upper reaches, in Germany and Austria, are popular for swimming and boating. Water pollution, dam-building, river-straightening schemes, and, in the 1990s, war damage have greatly changed the character of parts of the river's middle section. Bridges were bombed during the Yugoslavian-Croatian conflict of the early 1990s, and collapsed bridges still impeded boat traffic in the early 2000s. The wartime destruction and burning of an oil refinery and petrochemical works led to atmospheric fallout that heavily polluted the Danube. The river's delta, the second largest in Europe, is popular for commercial and sport fishing and wildlife watching.

The Danube forms part of a major transportation corridor that connects the North Sea with the Black Sea through the Main-Danube Canal, which was completed in 1992. About 35 major ports are dotted along the Danube, and between them ships and barges carry a wide range of freight, from agricultural produce to mineral ores and steel.

The largest dam on the Danube is the Iron Gate Dam, which generates hydroelectricity for Yugoslavia and Romania. Like the river's other dams, the Iron Gate blocks the natural migration of valuable sturgeon. Farther downstream, Bulgarian and Romanian environmental organizations are seeking to recreate wetlands that were previously drained for growing crops.

The lakes, marshes, forests, dunes, and waterways of the Danube Delta are home to more than 300 bird species. Within the 1.7-million-acre (679,000-ha) Danube Delta Biosphere Reserve, established in 1992, previously unsuccessful fields and fishponds are being returned to their former state as lush wetlands.

## Ganges River

The Ganges River, the great river of India's northern plains, arises at the confluence of the Alaknanda and Bhagirathi

Rivers in the southern Himalayas, where it is fed by glacial meltwater. The fast-flowing upper Ganges flows first southward and then southeastward before descending onto the north Indian plain about 70 miles (110 km) east of Delhi. From here, as the river's middle course, the Ganges meanders across a wide floodplain before reaching the Bengal lowlands. Here it divides into a network of thousands of distributaries that discharge into the Bay of Bengal. The distributaries combine with those of the Brahmaputra River to form the 250-mile (400-km)-wide Ganges-Brahmaputra delta, which straddles the borders of India and Bangladesh. The main western distributary of the Ganges is the Hooghly, and on its banks lies the populous city of Calcutta.

The Ganges floodplain, irrigated by silt-rich water from the Ganges and its tributaries, is one of the most fertile regions of the world. The intensively cultivated land—where the subsistence crop of rice is grown, as well as cash crops of wheat, sugarcane, cotton, and oilseed—supports an astonishingly large population of about 500 million people. The Ganges is sacred to the Hindu religion. Its waters are said to cleanse and purify believers. According to those of Hindu faith, the bodies of the dead that are cast into the Ganges are carried to Paradise.

The greatest pollution problem in the Ganges comes from human waste (sewage), not industrial discharges. Heavy metals and other noxious chemicals enter the river system as waste products of the local leather industry. The last 1,000 miles (1,600 km) of the Ganges flows sluggishly from a height of only 600 feet (180 m) above sea level. The river is therefore flushed only slowly and flooding is a hazard.

## Ganges River fact file

**Importance:** Discharges more sediment into the sea than any other river system

**Length:** 1,557 miles (2,506 km)

**Area of basin:** 625,000 square miles (about 1,600,000 sq km)

**Vertical drop from source to mouth:** 10,300 feet (3,139 m)

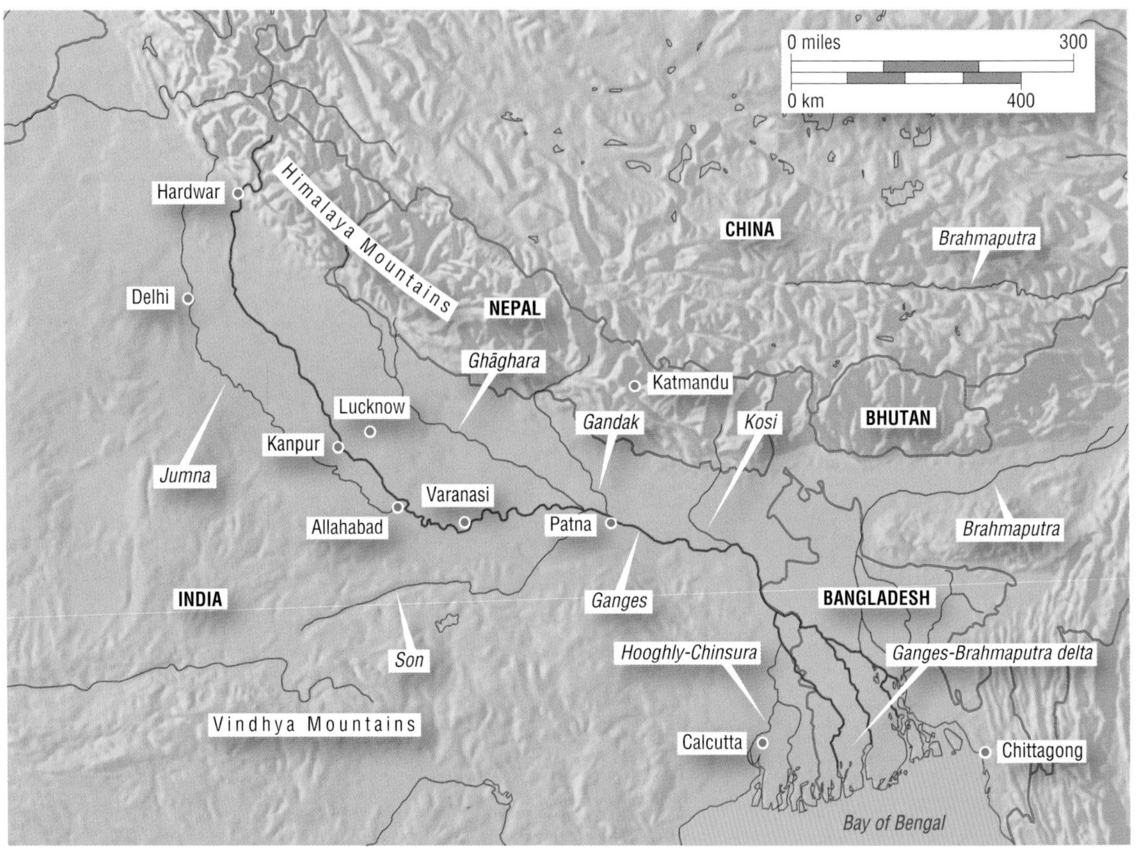


*The Ganges River*

The Ganges floods in late summer and early fall. The extra water comes from combination of Himalayan snow melting in the heat of summer and rising warm air in India and Bangladesh drawing in moisture-rich air from above the Indian Ocean, which falls as monsoon rains. However, tropical cyclones (Indian Ocean hurricanes) that sweep northward into the Bay of Bengal pose an even greater flood threat. The bulge of water (storm surge) that accompanies a cyclone can raise seawater levels, causing the river flow to reverse and flood vast areas of low-lying land. In October 1998 such a storm surge affected about 30 million people in Bangladesh. They were displaced from their homes and workplaces, while floodwaters destroyed their crops and cattle and swept away roads and bridges.

The Ganges-Brahmaputra delta discharges an estimated 2.2 billion U.S. tons (2 billion metric tons) of silt into the Indian Ocean's Bay of Bengal each year, making this river system a greater contributor of suspended material to the world's oceans than any other river.

## Mississippi River

The Mississippi River, its name derived from the Algonquian for "Father of Waters," is, in terms of volume, the biggest river in North America. Together with its major tributaries it drains an area that extends across all or part of 31 U.S. states and two Canadian provinces, from the Rocky Mountains in the west to the Appalachians in the east. This drainage basin includes the most productive cereal-growing regions of the United States.

The Mississippi rises as a 10-foot (3-m)-wide clear stream that gushes out of Lake Itasca in northwestern Minnesota. It flows southward in a series of bends to the Gulf of Mexico, collecting water from two massive tributaries, the Missouri and the Ohio, about halfway along its length.

From its source, the upper river flows southeastward through marshland and skirts high ground to the west of Lake Superior. The upper Mississippi retains its relatively clear waters until it reaches St. Paul, Minnesota. Just south of Minneapolis the Minnesota River joins the Mississippi and the main river retains its middle-course nature until just upstream of St. Louis, Missouri, where the Missouri and Illinois Rivers join. Their silt-laden waters turn the Mississippi muddy—the color the river retains for the rest of its length.

The Ohio River flows into the Mississippi at Cairo, Illinois, doubling the Mississippi's volume of water. This marks the

### Mississippi River fact file

**Importance:** In terms of volume, the largest river in North America
**Length:** 2,357 miles (3,792 km)
**Area of basin:** 1,235,000 square miles (3,198,650 sq km)
**Vertical drop from source to mouth:** 1,475 feet (450 m)

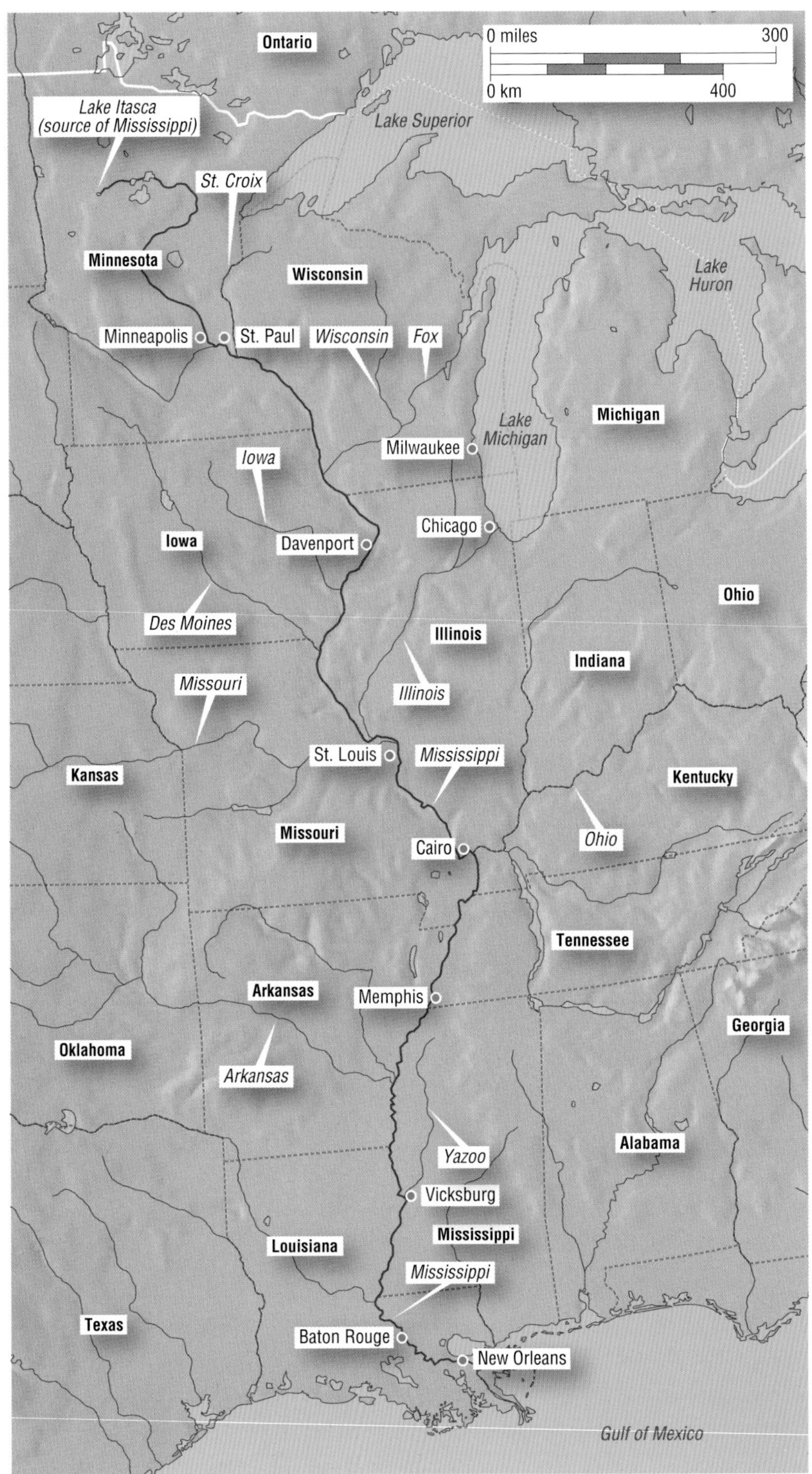


*The Mississippi River*

position of the original Mississippi delta, which formed some 150 million years ago. Since then, the delta has been inching southward. Within the last 2 million years the Mississippi has cut a broad valley through alluvial deposits south of Cairo. Here, the Mississippi reaches its full grandeur. The valley is more than 50 miles (80 km) wide in places through which the river meanders in wide loops that occasionally pinch off into oxbow lakes. The lower Mississippi, aptly nicknamed "Ol' Man River," is often 1.5 miles (2.4 km) wide.

South of New Orleans, Louisiana, the river has created the present delta, extending into a bird's-foot arrangement that projects into the Gulf of Mexico. Several distributaries discharge into the ocean, and the waters offshore are so high in dissolved nutrients and suspended solids that an oxygen-depleted "dead zone" extends from the delta into the Gulf of Mexico every summer. In some years, the zone covers an area of about the size of New Jersey, where very few organisms can survive.

The Mississippi and its major tributaries form the system of waterways that distribute freight far and wide across the central United States. More than 460 million U.S. tons (about 420 million metric tons) of freight are transported on the Mississippi each year. In terms of bulk, the major southbound cargoes downstream of Cairo include petroleum and coal products, iron and steel, aggregates such as sand and gravel, and agricultural produce such as wheat, soybean, and corn. Coal and steel from the Ohio River system are transported north up the Mississippi.

A complex flood-control system operates on the Mississippi River system. The main river is dammed north of St. Louis, and a series of dams on the Missouri and Ohio Rivers controls water entering the Mississippi. Many parts of the lower Mississippi are constrained within levees, with floodways for draining off excess water onto low-lying land. The river channel is continuously dredged to maintain high levels of flow and ensure navigability. But even these precautions are insufficient to cope with very high levels of rainfall combined with melting snow that raises the river's level exceptionally high, as has happened five times in the 50-year period 1950–2000. High levels of rainfall over the upper

Mississippi River basin between summer 1992 and summer 1993 raised the water table to unprecedented heights. By early summer 1993, the lower Mississippi was bursting or overflowing numerous levees. Many tributaries temporarily reversed their flow because the Mississippi could not accommodate their water. The extensive flooding—unprecedented in the United States—inundated nearly 14 million acres (about 5.5 million ha) of land, displaced at least 50,000 people, and caused about 50 deaths (see "Floods," pages 55–56)

Bass (*Micropterus* species), sunfish (*Lepomis cyanellus*), and trout (*Oncorhynchus, Salmo,* and *Salvelinus* species) are among the fish that thrive in the clear waters of the upper Mississippi, while carp (*Cyprinus carpio*), catfish (*Ictalurus* species), and buffalo fish (*Ictiobus* and *Bubalichthys*) are abundant in the lower Mississippi. The swamps and marshland of the delta are home to large rodents called nutria (*Myocastor coypus*). Thousands of migratory birds, including ducks and geese (order Anseriformes), nest in the delta, and egrets and herons (order Ciconiiformes) and pelicans (order Pelecaniformes) inhabit the estuary throughout the year.

## Nile River

The Nile, the world's longest river, flows northward from East Africa and empties into the Mediterranean Sea. In its upper course, the river has two main branches. The watercourse that becomes the White Nile (a loose reference to the river's pale green color in the middle Sudan) emerges from the northern end of Lake Victoria as the Victoria Nile. This arm of the Nile can be traced upriver as far as the Luvironza River in Burundi, south of Lake Victoria. The Victoria Nile spills

### Nile River fact file

**Importance:** The world's longest river
**Length:** 4,160 miles (6,695 km)
**Area of basin:** 1,100,000 square miles (about 2,800,000 sq km)
**Vertical drop from source to mouth:** 3,725 feet (1,135 m)

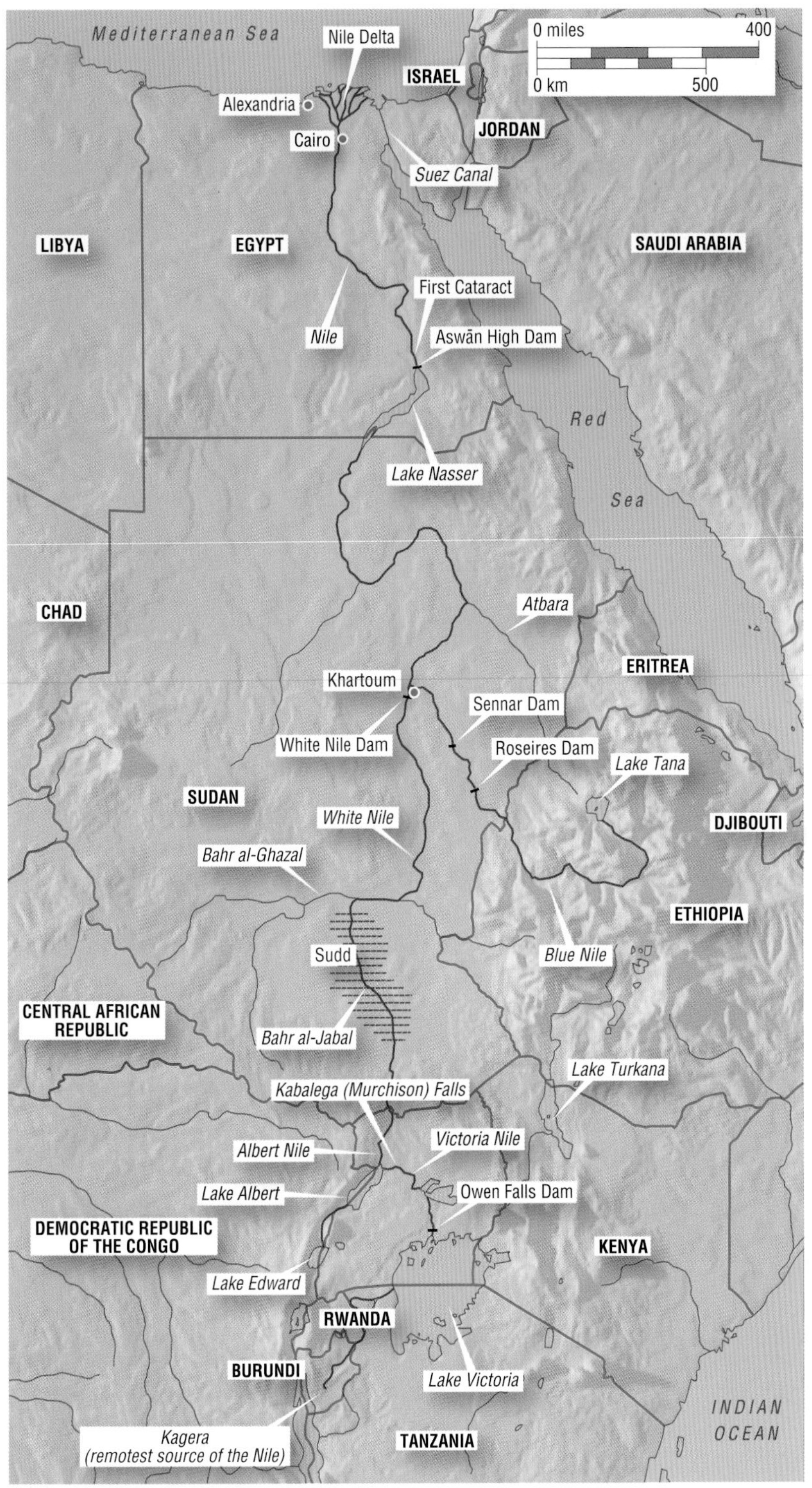


*The Nile River*

over the Kabalega (Murchison) Falls into the northern part of East Africa's Great Rift Valley, where it flows into the northern end of Lake Albert, exiting as the Albert Nile. The river descends through several gorges to feed southern Sudan's flat, marshy, plain—the Sudd—where high temperatures cause about half the river's water to evaporate. The river that emerges is the White Nile.

At Khartoum the White Nile is joined by the Blue Nile (with its darker, blue-tinged water) to form the Nile proper. From there, the Nile flows north through Sudan, descending through six so-called cataracts, which are, in fact, rapids. The final cataract, in southern Egypt, is the site of the Aswān High Dam, completed in 1970. This holds back the Nile's water to create a massive reservoir, Lake Nasser, which extends into Sudan. Prior to the late 1960s, the Nile north of Aswān flooded seasonally in late summer and early fall, depositing silt that fertilized the flooded land. The dam now prevents flooding but also holds back the silt, so that the land has to be fertilized by other means—usually artificial fertilizer that farmers add to the soil. The dam has been a mixed blessing. On the one hand, the dam controls floods, provides hydroelectric power, and stores drinking and irrigation water. On the other, it now starves the delta lands and the Mediterranean Sea of nutrients; it is causing erosion of the delta; and it has increased the incidence of waterborne diseases in Egypt, such as bilharzia (see "Rivers, lakes, and human health," pages 152–157).

Downstream of Aswān the Nile flows roughly northward, reaching the populous city of Cairo after some 500 miles (800 km). Cairo marks the southern end of the Nile delta, where the Nile breaks into several distributaries. Irrigated by Nile water, the land of Egypt's delta ranks among the most productive in the world, with crops being grown year-round. Most of Egypt is desert. The Nile-irrigated land of the delta and the narrow green band of vegetation flanking the Nile south of the delta occupy only 3 percent of Egypt's land area. This land provides almost all of Egypt's food crops together with cotton, one of Egypt's major exports.

The Nile's annual flood, now tamed by the Aswān High Dam, is caused by heavy rainfall on the Ethiopian Plateau in late winter and early spring with runoff into the Blue Nile and Atbara Rivers. The flow of the White Nile is fairly steady throughout the year, fed by rainfall on the East African Lake Plateau.

Among the fish of the Nile, several small, perchlike species of tilapia (*Oreochromis* and *Tilapia* species) are important food sources for local people. Larger food fish include several species of catfish (*Clarias* and *Synodontis* species) and the Nile perch (*Lates nilotica*), which, in Lake Nasser, reaches weights of 300 pounds (140 kg). The 20-foot (6-m)-long Nile crocodile (*Crocodylus niloticus*) is rare north of Aswān but remains quite common in the river's upper reaches.

## Yangtze River

The Yangtze River (also known as Chang Jiang, or "long river") rises on the Tibetan Plateau and flows roughly southeastward for its first 1,000 miles (1,600 km) or so, rushing through steep-sided gorges. The river then turns northeastward across Sichuan Province before flowing through the famous "three gorges" where, along a 56-mile (90-km) stretch, the sides tower 1,200–2,000 feet (350–600 m) above the river. Along this length, the river reaches depths of 500 feet (150 m)—the deepest of any river in the world. After a journey of nearly 3,000 miles (4,830 km) the Yangtze descends to the North China Plain on its final passage to the East China Sea of the Pacific Ocean. The river forms a delta with several distributaries, with the populous city of Shanghai lying between them in the south.

Along parts of the lower course, the river flows several feet above the surrounding plain and is held back by partly

### Yangtze River fact file

**Importance:** Asia's longest river, the third longest in the world, and the fourth largest by volume

**Length:** 3,434 miles (5,525 km)

**Area of basin:** 760,000 square miles (about 2,000,000 sq km)

**Vertical drop from source to mouth:** 18,000 feet (5,480 m)

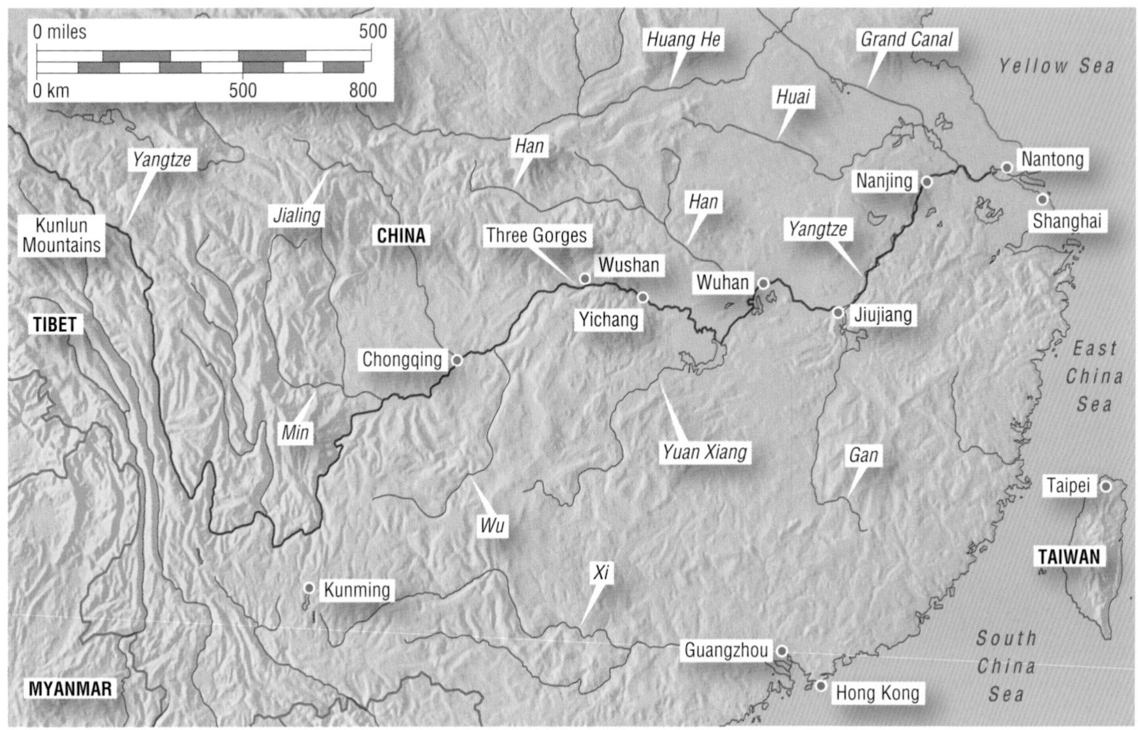


*The Yangtze River*

natural and partly artificial levees. The surrounding plain—a densely populated, rice-growing area—is irrigated by the Yangtze's waters. The Yangtze Basin, often called the "granary of China," contributes nearly half of China's food produce by volume. Maize, wheat, and barley rank high among the other crops grown there. Fishing and fish farming are major commercial and subsistence activities in the region.

During the summer months, monsoon rains swell the river, and if the Yangtze's major tributaries rise at the same time, the onrush of water into the lower Yangtze can cause catastrophic floods. Historical records reveal that this has happened at least 100 times in the last 2,000 years. In 1954 the Yangtze inundated the cities of Nanjing and Wuhan, killing about 30,000 people and making millions homeless.

The Yangtze is China's most commercially important river and is part of a network of inland waterways that connect inland ports and seaports, as well as the major cities associated with them. The Yangtze is linked to the Yellow River and Beijing to the north by the 1,000-mile (1,600-km)-long Grand Canal. Ocean steamers ply Yangtze's waters as far as Wuhan, 680 miles (1,090 km) inland from the coast. Thousands of large traditional Chinese sailing craft, called junks, regularly travel 1,000 miles (1,600 km) farther inland from Wuhan.

Construction of the world's largest dam, the Yangtze's controversial Three Gorges Dam, began in 1994. Planned for completion in about 2010, the 610-foot (186-m) high and 1.3-mile (2-km)-wide dam will create a deep reservoir that extends for 360 miles (580 km) east of Chongqing.

The rare Yangtze River dolphin or *baij* (*Lipotes vexillifer*) is confined to the lower Yangtze. Though river dolphins are legally protected, their numbers have declined to probably fewer than 100 due to decades of pollution, dam construction, hunting, and depletion of their food supplies by people fishing. Dams now prevent dolphins migrating to and from former feeding and breeding grounds.

## Yenisey River

The Yenisey rises in the Sayan Mountains of southern Siberia at the confluence of the Bol'shoy (Great) Yenisey and Malyy (Little) Yenisey Rivers. It flows westward and then northward, winding along the eastern edge of the West Siberian Plain at the base of the Central Siberian Plateau, before emptying into the icy waters of the Kara Sea in the Arctic Ocean.

The Yenisey's upper course is fast-flowing and turbulent and provides hydroelectric power, with major power stations at Sayan and Krasnoyarsk. The climate of the lower Yenisey is subarctic, with the river frozen to a deep level between

### Yenisey River fact file

**Importance:** Russia's biggest river by volume
**Length:** 2,566 miles (4,129 km)
**Area of basin:** 1,003,474 square miles (2,598,998 sq km)
**Vertical drop from source to mouth:** About 3,280 feet (1,000 m)

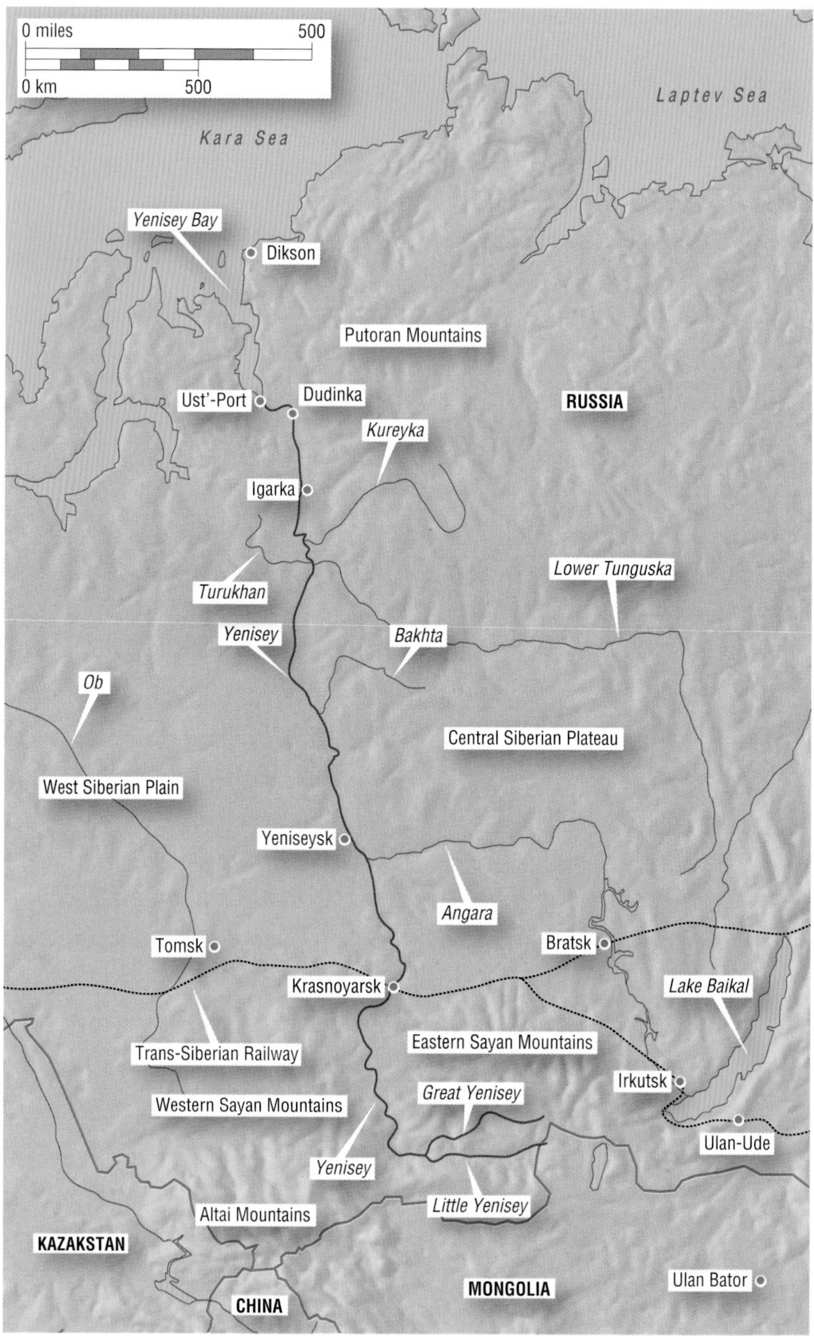


*The Yenisey River*

November and March. As far south as Krasnoyarsk, the river is ice-free and readily navigable only between May and November.

The Yenisey's major tributary is the Angara, which joins the main river about 150 miles (240 km) north of Krasnoyarsk. About half of Yenisey's water is supplied by thawing snow, and most of the remainder by rainwater runoff. The two sources combine to raise the level in spring, regularly causing violent floods, particularly where meltwater is held back behind unthawed ice in the lower and middle courses of the river.

During the warmer months, the middle and lower courses are navigable by steamers, with lumber and grain being the major exports. Igarka, lying about 400 miles (640 km) from the river's mouth, is the region's chief lumber port and receives oceangoing steamers. Salmon and sturgeon fishing are important local industries on the river's lower reaches. Downstream of Krasnoyarsk, coal, copper, and nickel are mined near the eastern riverbank, and various products are transported from Krasnoyarsk, where the Trans-Siberian railway crosses the Yenisey.

Contamination of the Yenisey River by radionuclides (products of nuclear fission) such as plutonium-239, cesium-137, and strontium-90 raises health and safety concerns. These substances may originate from a factory, now closed, located 37 miles (60 km) downstream of Krasnoyarsk that made plutonium for nuclear weapons. Large amounts of nuclear waste are stored in deep caverns close to this site. It is feared that radionuclides might be leaking from the caverns and entering the Yenisey. High levels of radionuclides may also have been discharged directly into the Yenisey while the factory was in use. International teams are currently surveying the Yenisey for radioactive hotspots. There is evidence that some cancer rates in Yenisey communities downstream of the factory are higher than elsewhere in the region.

## Lake Baikal

Lake Baikal, in Russia's southeastern Siberia, is ringed by mountains and lies about 1,200 miles (1,930 km) from the nearest ocean. Baikal is the deepest lake in the world and probably the oldest. Part of Baikal formed in a rift valley some 25 million years ago as two continental plates moved apart and the crust in between subsided. Since then, as the

## Lake Baikal fact file

**Importance:** The world's deepest lake and the biggest by volume
**Area:** 12,160 square miles (31,520 sq km)
**Maximum depth:** 5,712 feet (1,740 m)
**Height above sea level:** 1,497 feet (456 m)

plates continue to move apart, the rift continues to deepen and other basins have flooded and become connected to the lake. Lake Baikal—unlike almost all other lakes—has retained its depth as deepening of the rift has kept pace with sediment accumulation on the lake floor. In places, Baikal's floor overlies sediment that is more than two miles (3.2 km) deep.

Lake Baikal measures about 395 miles (636 km) long and averages 35 miles (56 km) wide and has a surface area considerably less than that of North America's Lake Superior. Because of Lake Baikal's great depth, however, it has the highest volume of any lake and contains about 20 percent of the

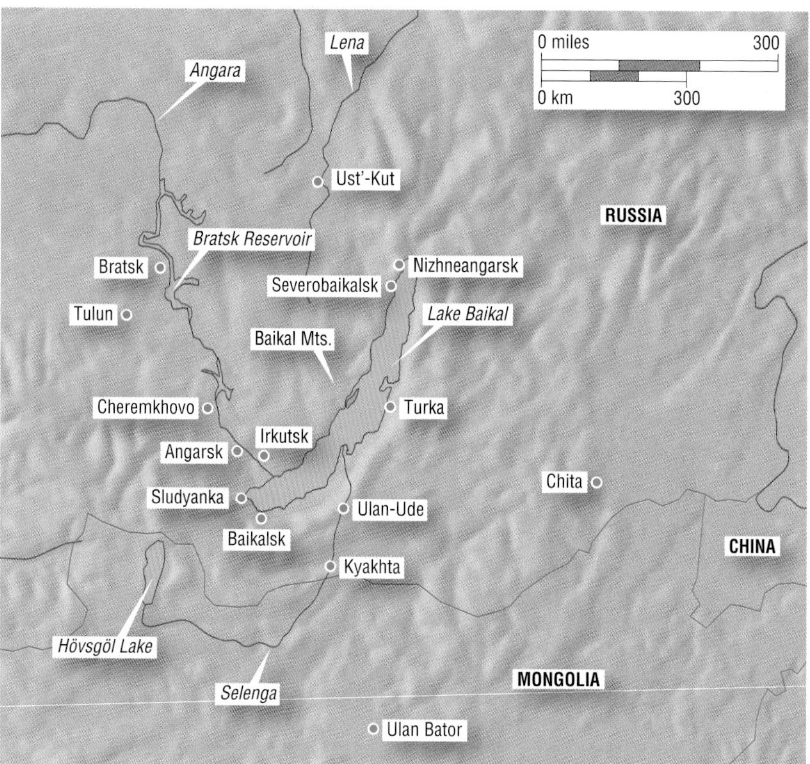


*Lake Baikal*

liquid freshwater on Earth's surface. North America's five Great Lakes together contain less water than Lake Baikal.

A Russian legend tells of God creating Siberia and dropping one of his gems—a pearl of great beauty—that became Lake Baikal, the blue pearl of Siberia. Lake Baikal has among the clearest water of any lake due, in part, to its great depth and the lack of loose debris in the lake's rocky surroundings. Other factors include the relatively low mineral content of the water that flows into the lake and the abundance of *Epischura,* one of Baikal's unique miniature crustaceans (joint-limbed animals belonging to the superclass Crustacea that includes members such as shrimps and crabs). *Epischura* consumes the countless millions of phytoplankton (microscopic algae) that would otherwise cloud the water.

Unlike the waters of some other deep lakes, which become stratified (layered) with the bottom layer starved of oxygen, Baikal's cold waters maintain a circulation so that oxygen supports a fish population at all depths. The lake's surface is almost entirely covered in ice from January through April, reaching a thickness of about three feet (1 m).

More than 300 rivers flow into the lake, but only one, the Angara, leaves it. At its present flow, it would take Angara more than 300 years to drain the lake if all input stopped.

Baikal is a biological wonder. Because of the lake's giant size and the length of time it has remained intact and isolated despite dramatic climatic changes, populations of many Baikal species have been able to evolve separately from populations elsewhere. Baikal is the most biodiverse lake in the world. Of its 1,500 known animal species and 700 recognized plant species, more than two-thirds are found nowhere else. Its unique fish species includes the golomyanka (*Comephorus baicalensis*), a scaleless, nearly transparent fish that is so different from other fishes that it belongs in its own classification family. Baikal also harbors a population of about 25,000 nerpa (*Phoca sibirica*), the world's only freshwater seal.

In the past two centuries Lake Baikal has been threatened with overexploitation of its natural resources and severe pollution. In the early 1900s, for example, the Baikal sturgeon (*Acipenser baerii baicalensis*) were overfished and fast became

*The blue waters of Lake Baikal, the world's largest lake by volume. The rocky shoreline of Barakchin Island lies in the foreground.* (Konrad Wothe/ Minden Pictures)

scarce. This massive fish used to grow to 500 pounds (230 kg) in weight and seven feet (2.1 m) in length but rarely reaches this size today before it is caught. Nowadays, specialized hatcheries release Baikal sturgeon into the lake and stock other lakes and reservoirs in Siberia. The adult fish provide valuable flesh, and the eggs of females are a delicacy called black caviar.

Altogether, more than 100 factories on Baikal's shores and estuaries release pollutants that find their way into the lake. Poorly treated sewage from nearby towns and cities empties into Baikal, and its nutrient load threatens to trigger phytoplankton blooms that would overwhelm the Baikal crustaceans' ability to graze them. In 1987, thousands of nerpa (Baikal seals) died in a disease epidemic. The weakening of the seals' immune systems by the buildup of pollutants, especially dioxins and PCBs (see "Freshwater pollution," pages 205–207), was blamed.

Since 1967 Lake Baikal and its surroundings has received various degrees of protection as a national park, and in 1996 the area was awarded the status of a UNESCO World Heritage site. A site has to meet only one of four criteria to qualify for this status. Baikal meets all four: geological significance, biological-evolutionary importance, natural beauty, and outstanding importance for conservation. Public support for the protection of Baikal remains strong among many Russian people. Since the 1990s many of the most heavily polluting factories—including the pulp and paper mill at Baikalsky—have been renovated for cleaner operation. However, the felling of conifer trees, particularly around the northern end of the lake, is introducing sediment that threatens the crystal clarity of Baikal's waters. The introduction of alien species, such as Canadian pondweed (*Elodea canadensis*), continues to pose a threat. Conserving Lake Baikal will require cooperation between many agencies and government sectors within Russia, with support from the international community.

*Fingerlike growths of the sponge* Lubomirskia baicalensis, *one of about 1,000 identified freshwater animal species unique to the Lake Baikal region* (Konrad Wothe/ Minden Pictures)

## Lake Superior

Straddling the U.S.-Canadian border, Lake Superior is the largest of North America's five Great Lakes. At about 350 miles (257 km) long from east to west and 160 miles (257 km) wide from north to south, Superior has the greatest surface area of any freshwater lake in the world. With its characteristic "wolf's head" outline, Superior is roughly the same shape as South Carolina but slightly larger. The waters of Lake Superior could fill the basins of the four other Great Lakes—Erie, Huron, Michigan, and Ontario—with plenty of water to spare.

Lake Superior gained its name from French fur traders, who named it Lac Supérieur ("Upper Lake") because it is the farthest north of the Great Lakes. Lake Superior's basin is of ancient granite laid down some 3 billion years ago and eroded by ice sheets within the past 65,000 years. Between 15,000 and 10,000 years ago—after the peak of the last glaciation—a giant lake called Algonquin began to fragment, forming Lakes Superior, Michigan, and Huron. The present shorelines of the five Great Lakes stabilized about 3,000 years ago. Today Superior's western and northern shores remain rocky, while the eastern and southern shores are covered in glacial deposits.

Superior is connected to Lake Huron by St. Mary's River, which contains St. Mary's Rapids, where the river drops about 20 feet (6 m) in half a mile (800 m). Canals dug since the mid-19th century bypass these rapids and now carry boat traffic through five locks. More tonnage of cargo passes through these locks than through any others on Earth.

Water flows from Superior, through Huron, and then into Erie and Ontario, before emptying into the St. Lawrence River, which finally discharges into the Atlantic Ocean some 1,000 miles (1,600 km) distant.

### Lake Superior fact file

**Importance:** The world's largest freshwater lake in terms of surface area
**Surface area:** 31,800 square miles (82,362 sq km)
**Maximum depth:** 1,333 feet (406 m)
**Height above sea level:** 601 feet (183 m)

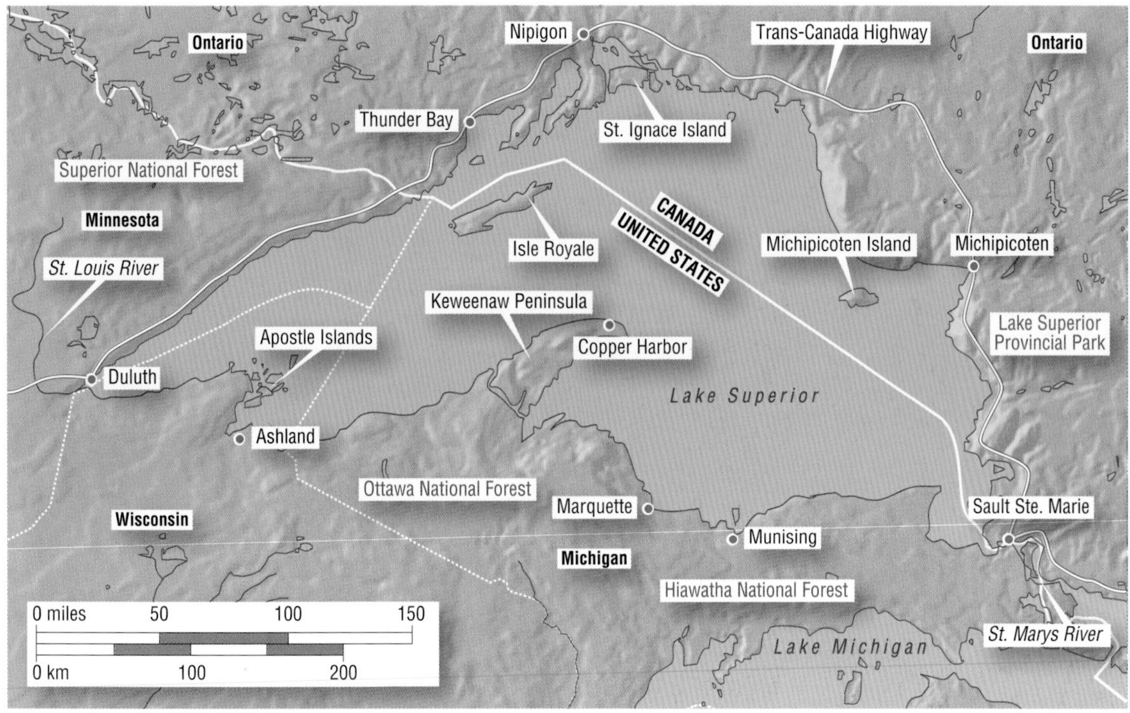


The craggy, forested coastline of Superior is the least developed of the Great Lakes, and Superior is the least polluted of the five lakes. In the 1970s Superior was in danger of becoming eutrophic (overenriched with nutrients) because of inputs of poorly treated sewage. But water treatment facilities have since been upgraded, and the lake is now cleaner and clearer. Most of Superior's contamination arrives by air in the form of atmospheric pollution from cities lying to the southwest, such as Chicago and Detroit.

*Lake Superior*

Lake Superior is popular for fishing and other recreational activities, and the region is a favorite for hikers. The sport and commercial fishery of Lake Superior generates an annual income in the region of U.S.$1 billion. Most of the land around its shores is privately owned.

Perhaps the greatest threat to Superior's current biological community is the arrival of exotic species. By the late 1950s sea lampreys (*Petromyzon marinus*) had traveled from Lake Ontario and the St. Lawrence River system to invade all of the Great Lakes. There these parasitic fish devastated local

*A view of Split Rock Lighthouse overlooking Lake Superior. The lighthouse highlights the vast size of this North American lake and its importance for inland shipping.* (Jim Brandenburg/ Minden Pictures)

populations of lake trout (*Salvelinus namaycush*) and whitefish (*Coregonus clupeiformis*). Fisheries scientists took action by selectively killing lamprey larvae in Great Lake tributaries using chemicals. These and other control measures have been in use since the 1950s and, beginning in the 1960s, the lake has been restocked with trout and other local fish. Exotic species remain a threat, with zebra mussels (*Dreissena polymorpha*) from Russia spreading through the Great Lakes during the late 1980s and 1990s (see "Alien invasions," pages 199–205). This fast-growing mollusk clogs water filtration equipment and encrusts the hulls of ships and the piles of docks, and it has altered the composition of Superior's biological community by grazing plankton, providing additional food supplies for some fish, and competing with other mollusks.

Today other exotic threats remain, such as the threatened arrival of species ranging from larger zooplankton (*Bythotrephes* and *Cercopagis* species) that consume the food of fish larvae, to large species of carp that would compete with existing fish species.

## Lake Victoria

Lying on the equator in east central Africa, the lake straddles the countries of Kenya, Tanzania, and Uganda. Lake Victoria, through its single outlet to the north, the Victoria Nile, is the chief source of the Nile River. The Owen Falls Dam, completed in 1954, has raised the level of Victoria by some three feet (0.9 m) and increased its surface area in the process. Lake Victoria has no major input river but maintains its level from local rainfall and runoff.

Lake Victoria first formed about 2 million years ago when the plateau between the eastern and western arms of Africa's Great Rift Valley tilted, creating a shallow depression that filled with surface water. Recent geological studies of sediment deposits in the vicinity suggest that Lake Victoria dried out completely about 15,000 years ago. Water filled the Lake Victoria basin from nearby ancient lakes and rivers.

In terms of its biology and its importance to people, Victoria has some remarkable claims to fame. Before the 1970s Lake Victoria harbored more than 350 species of tropical fish belonging to the cichlid (Cichlidae) family, more than 90 percent of which were local and found nowhere else. These fishes appear to have evolved from stock within the past 100,000 years, with many species adapting to the wide range of conditions within Lake Victoria in the past 15,000 years. The introduction of Nile perch (*Lates niloticus*) and Nile tilapia (*Oreochromis niloticus*), both valuable food fish, has helped trigger a catastrophic decline in biodiversity in the last 30 years (see "Alien invasions," pages 199–205). At least

### Lake Victoria fact file

**Importance:** Africa's largest lake and the world's second-largest freshwater lake in terms of surface area

**Surface area:** 26,828 square miles (69,485 sq km)

**Maximum depth:** 265 feet (81 m)

**Height above sea level:** 3,720 feet (1,134 m)

200 fish species have been driven to extinction or near extinction since 1960, in many cases because they have been consumed by the voracious Nile perch or have lost out in competition with introduced tilapia.

Fishers used to air-dry their catch of cichlids to preserve them, but Nile perch require smoking over a fire, which has encouraged fishers to cut down trees for firewood. The resulting forest clearance has increased runoff into the lake, and as a result the lake is becoming silted and nutrient-rich.

The excess nutrients have caused problems. Since the early 1990s Lake Victoria's people have been struggling with a proliferation of water hyacinth (*Eichhornia crassipes*)—a floating freshwater weed that grows so thickly it prevents the passage of boats and blocks sunlight from reaching the water beneath. Stagnation makes the waters at the edges of the lake a breeding ground for malaria-spreading mosquitoes and bilharzia-transmitting snails, which spread life-threatening diseases among the local human population (see "Rivers, lakes, and human health," pages 152–157). Various methods

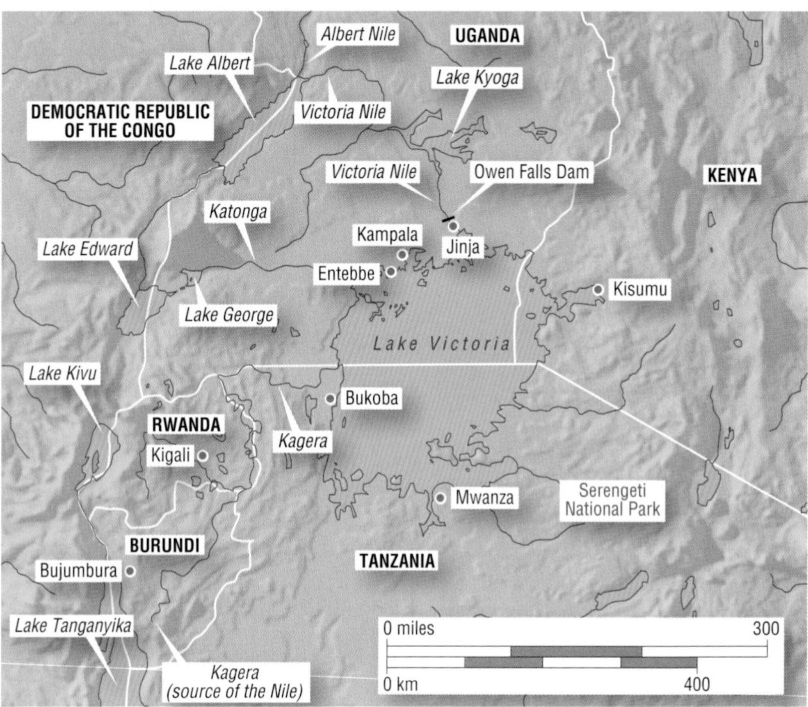


Lake Victoria

have been used to combat the problem of water hyacinth overgrowth, including introducing weed-consuming weevils, removing the weed using mechanical harvesters, and poisoning the weed with herbicides. Despite these measures, water hyacinth still remains a major problem in parts of the lake. Attention is now turning to planting trees in nearby land areas that have been previously deforested. Trees take up nutrients that might otherwise enter the lake and encourage the growth of water hyacinth.

Lake Victoria is probably the most productive freshwater fishery in the world, yielding at least 550,000 U.S. tons (500,000 metric tons) annually. By 2000 Lake Victoria's fishery was bringing in as much as U.S.$400 million in export income from predominantly three fish species: Nile perch, Nile tilapia, and the sardine-like dagaa (*Rastrineobola argentea*). But only a few people among the 10 million who live near the lake actually benefit from the high-value Nile perch fishery. Most local villagers use the lake as their drinking water supply and their source of irrigation, but many people remain malnourished. International agencies such as the United Nations Development Program (UNDP) and United Nations Environment Program (UNEP), along with nongovernmental organizations such as World Resources Institute (WRI), are pressing for Lake Victoria to be managed in a sustainable manner as an ecosystem that benefits more local people than at present.

# CHAPTER 4

# BIOLOGY OF LAKES AND RIVERS

Scientists argue about where life-forms originally evolved on Earth more than 3.5 billion years ago. The "traditional" view, from the mid-20th century, is that bacteria-like forms evolved in tide pools at the edges of ancient oceans. Since the 1970s, however, archaebacteria ("ancient bacteria") have been discovered in extreme environments. These environments include hot-water vents in the deep ocean, sulfur springs on land, and rocks more than 3,300 feet (1,000 m) beneath Earth's surface. Such extreme environments are now additional candidates for where early life might have evolved. Whatever the origins of earliest life, fossil records reveal that multicellular (many-celled) life-forms evolved in the sea some 600 million years ago. Some of their descendants then colonized the land and freshwaters within the past 500 million years. By this time, oxygen levels in the atmosphere were sufficiently elevated to block high levels of ultraviolet light that would endanger life on land or in shallow water. The multicellular organisms found in freshwater today evolved from ancestors that colonized this environment directly from the sea or via the land.

## Colonizing freshwater

For organisms invading freshwater from the sea, the biggest challenge lies in the marked difference in salt concentration between the two environments. Living organisms contain high concentrations of salts and other solutes, giving an overall concentration of dissolved substances roughly similar to that of seawater. When organisms enter freshwater from the sea, they encounter an environment where levels of dissolved substances are, in many cases, tens or hundreds of times lower than those in the sea and in their own body fluids (see "Freshwater's chemical composition," pages 18–21). This poses several problems. First, salts will be lost across the body surface due to a steep diffusion gradient between the inside and outside of the organism. In the case of animals, salts will also be lost when the creature expels solid or liquid wastes. Meanwhile, water will tend to diffuse into the organism from the surroundings in the process of osmosis (see sidebar).

To colonize freshwater, organisms overcome the problems of maintaining the salt and water balance of their bodies in one or more of three ways. First, they do so by sealing their tissues and body fluids from the water outside, or by developing an efficient mechanism for removing excess water by excretion (waste removal). Second, they actively pump salts from their surroundings into the body. For some freshwater animals, such as the freshwater shrimp *Gammarus,* more than 10 percent of its body's energy consumption is used in

## Diffusion and osmosis

Diffusion is the overall random movement of tiny particles—notably atoms, ions, and molecules—from one place to another down a concentration gradient. Diffusion is a natural physical feature of freely moving small particles. It continues until the particles are evenly spread throughout the region that encloses them.

A concentration (or diffusion) gradient is the difference in concentration of particles between two regions. Where the difference is great (and/or the distance between regions small), the concentration gradient is steep and diffusion is rapid. Where the difference is small (and/or the distance great), the concentration gradient is shallow and diffusion less rapid.

Osmosis is a specific type of diffusion. It refers to the diffusion of water molecules through a selectively permeable membrane (the kind that encloses animal and plant cells). Other factors aside, there is an overall movement of water molecules by osmosis from the side of the membrane where water molecules are most concentrated to the side where they are less concentrated. In the case of freshwater organisms, there tends to be an overall movement of water molecules from the surroundings and into the organism by osmosis.

gaining salts this way. The third option is to reduce salt concentrations within the body. However, because high salt concentrations are necessary for normal metabolism (the sum total of chemical reactions inside the body), very few organisms have adopted the last option.

The difficulty of maintaining salt concentrations in freshwater helps explain why of 33 major groups (phyla) of animals, 30 occur in the sea but only 14 in freshwater.

Most lakes and rivers contain several biological communities that inhabit different parts of the water body, including the boundary between air and water at the water's surface; the thin boundary layer that covers stationary objects in the water; the water column that extends from the surface to the bottom; and the river or lake bottom itself.

## Boundary layers

At the water surface—the boundary between air and water—the surface film is a trap for chemicals. Biological substances, especially those that contain fats and proteins, collect in the surface layer where they provide a rich food supply for microscopic bacteria, fungi, and protists (single-celled animal- and plantlike organisms with complex cell structure). The surface film of water, with its high surface tension, is also a trap for creatures. Tiny animals that fall onto the surface layer cannot escape its grip. In temperate regions they become food for animals such as water strider insects (genus *Gerris*) that are adapted to running about on the surface film. Diving beetles also rise from the depths to snatch miniature creatures trapped in the surface film.

Plants, too, inhabit the surface layer. Duckweed (genus *Lemna*) and water hyacinth (*Eichhornia crassipes*) float on the surface, gaining their nutrients from the water below while their leaves are bathed in sunlight and are exposed to the air. The surface community of microbes, plants, and animals is called, collectively, the *neuston* (from the Greek *neustos*, "swimming").

Boundary layers, between water and its surroundings, also exist at the bottom and sides of the river or lake, but these boundaries are more complex. Coating almost everything—

including stones, sediment particles, plant leaves, and debris—is a living biofilm of microbes (bacteria, fungi, and protists) and miniature plants and animals. The biofilm community plays an important role in recycling biological substances that are dissolved or suspended in freshwater (see "Freshwater's chemical composition," pages 18–21).

Aquatic plants of various kinds and sizes grow on the bottom and sides of lakes and rivers. With their roots anchored in mud, sand, or gravel and their stem and leaves rising through the water column, they gain their nutrients from the substrate (the loose material making up the riverbed or lakebed) and make their food by trapping sunlight that filters down through the water column. Relatively few animals feed upon large aquatic plants directly. However, those that do can be locally very important in shaping the structure of the biological community (see "On two or four legs," pages 117–127, and "Alien invasions," pages 199–205). Such key species include ducks and geese in temperate waters, manatees in some brackish tropical waters, and tilapia and other cichlid fishes found in warm temperate and tropical waters. In general, aquatic plants become a more important food source when they die back and their remains are recycled by bottom-living organisms. While they are alive, however, aquatic plants play a vital role in providing shade and shelter for aquatic animals and extracting carbon dioxide and adding oxygen when they photosynthesize. The stem and leaves offer a large surface area on which biofilm organisms can thrive.

Living in and on the bottom sediment of lakes and rivers is a community of animals that are larger than microscopic. Called the *benthos* or *benthic community* (from the Greek *benthos* for "depth" or "bottom"), it includes bottom-living insects, water mites, crustaceans such as freshwater shrimp, various worms, and mollusks such as clams and snails. Some, such as the larvae (immature forms) of caseless caddis flies (genus *Polycentropus*), feed by straining food particles from the water using nets. Others use fringes of hairs that act like combs, as in the case of blackfly (genus *Simulium*) and many caddis fly larvae (order Trichoptera), or microscopic hairlike structures called cilia, as in the case of most clams.

Some bottom feeders, such as snails and freshwater shrimp, graze on the inhabitants of the biofilm. Among those that feed on particles in or on the sediment are oligochaete worms (genus *Lumbriculus*), which resemble miniature earthworms, and the water louse (genus *Asellus*), a type of isopod crustacean (similar to a pill bug). Some members of the benthos, such as the voracious dragonfly larvae (genus *Aeshna*), are active hunters. Fishes, diving birds, and aquatic mammals are often important predators of bottom-living animals.

## The water column

Between the lake or river surface and its bottom lies the water column. The animals that move about in this open water form the *pelagic community* (from the Greek *pelagos,* "the open sea") as distinct from the benthic community. The pelagic community, in turn, has two components: the *plankton* or drifting organisms (from the Greek *planktos* for "wandering") and the nekton or swimming organisms.

Plankton are those organisms—mostly microscopic or slightly larger—that float in the water and are at the mercy of water currents. If they swim at all, they swim weakly and cannot battle against even slowly moving water. The plankton include bacteria, protists, and invertebrates such as rotifers and small crustaceans, especially copepods and water fleas. Only lakes and slow-flowing rivers contain large resident populations of plankton. In swift-flowing waters, any plankton that enter from lakes or slow-flowing tributaries are soon washed downstream.

In most freshwaters, the dominant components of the nekton are fishes, although various kinds of insect larvae are important predators and grazers of the plankton. Most lakes and rivers contain a resident population of a handful to several dozen types of fishes. In lakes, the assemblage of different fishes exploits a variety of foods. Some fishes are bottom feeders; others consume plankton; many are opportunistic, consuming a wide range of food types; and a few species restrict themselves to eating mainly other fishes. A similar situation usually exists in rivers, but the species involved commonly differ, at least in part, from those found in nearby still waters.

## Adaptations for life in running water

At its simplest, the difference between a lake and a river is the presence or absence of running water. In a river, water is normally flowing and this movement brings with it both benefits and challenges for organisms.

Among the benefits is the arrival of fresh supplies of oxygen (needed by microbes, animals, and plants for respiration), food (consumed by animals), and nutrients (required by plants to manufacture their own food). At the same time, the moving water flushes away waste substances released by organisms, such as carbon dioxide (a product of respiration) and nitrogenous (nitrogen-containing) wastes such as ammonia that aquatic animals release. Moving water may reduce the energy required for obtaining food or nutrients because these are delivered by the water flow. Offset against this, however, is the additional energy required by organisms to maintain their station in running water.

Many river animals have a combination of behavioral and structural adaptations that enable them to avoid the full force of the current that could sweep them away. Bottom-living insect larvae, such as those of mayflies (order Ephemeroptera) and caddis flies, and crustaceans such as crayfish (genus *Austropotamobius*), automatically move away from higher light intensities. This behavior means these animals gravitate to locations under stones, behind boulders, in crevices on the riverbed, and in dense beds of aquatic plants, where the water flow is reduced. Most of these bottom-living animals are also flattened, elongated, and small. These features enable them to remain concealed from predators while remaining in the bottom-hugging flow of water that presses them against the river bottom rather than lifting them off.

Most fishes in the fast-flowing waters of upper reaches have one of two body shapes. Strong swimmers, such as trout and salmon, that can maintain their station in a strong current have bodies that are typically round or oval in cross section and torpedo-shaped (fusiform) overall. This shape minimizes frictional resistance. Water tends to flow around the fish rather than press against it and push it downstream. Such fish swim continuously, even when asleep.

Bottom-dwelling fishes, such as sculpins (genus *Cottus*), have adaptations that tend to press the animal against the stream bottom. The head and trunk and the paired pectoral (shoulder) fins have flattened lower surfaces and curved upper faces. When the fish is facing upstream, these shapes act as reverse hydrofoils, pressing the fish against the river bottom. The swim bladders of bottom-dwelling fish are often reduced in size to lessen their buoyancy (see "Freshwater's physical properties," pages 13–18).

## On the surface

Those organisms that live on the upper side of the surface film of water are collectively called the *epineuston* (from the Greek *epi* for "on"). They include several types of water bug (members of the order Hemiptera) such as water measurers (genus *Hydrometra*), back-swimmers (genus *Notonecta*), and water striders. All water bugs possess a beak or rostrum that they stab into their victims to suck out body fluids.

Surface-dwelling water bugs are able to walk about on the surface film partly because they are so light and partly because they have hairs on their body and legs that are water-repellent. The whirligig beetle (genus *Gyrinus*) differs from many other surface dwellers in being able to dive beneath the surface when threatened. Its eyes are modified, with the upper half adapted for viewing above the water surface, and the lower half below. The whirligig gains its name from the strange rotating movement, like a circular dance, that it performs at the water surface. When forced to dive, the whirligig takes a bubble of water down with it as its temporary air supply. Bubble-carrying is a feature of many aquatic insects that visit the surface film but spend most of their time in the water column below.

The *hyponeuston* (from the Greek *hypo* for "below") is the community of organisms that live hanging beneath the surface layer. The larvae (young, feeding forms) or pupae (the nonfeeding stage between larva and adult) of several types of flying insect fall into this category.

For small, air-breathing animals living underwater, the surface film acts as a miniature barrier that must be punctured if the creature is to obtain its air supply. Various freshwater mites and spiders (class Arachnida) break through the surface film with their mouthparts to obtain the air they need. Some trap air in bubbles on parts of their bodies. They take an air supply with them down beneath the surface and return when it is exhausted.

The larvae and pupae of mosquitoes and midges hang down from the surface layer. They have breathing tubes at the hind end of their bodies that puncture the surface film and are guarded by water-repellent hairs. The larva feeds with its head end hanging down and filtering the water for small food particles. The larvae of disease-spreading insects can be killed by spraying oil on the surface film to block their breathing tubes (see "Rivers, lakes, and human health," pages 152–157).

Among the hyponeuston organisms are visitors that spend part of their time on the underside of the surface layer but also move beneath the water surface, often traveling down the leaves and stems of underwater plants. The amoeba-like protist *Arcella* is a microscopic animal-like creature with a dome-shaped shell. From below this it extends feeding extensions called pseudopodia that it uses to engulf small particles trapped in the surface film. Snails and flatworms glide along on the underside of the surface film and consume small particles and organisms trapped in the layer.

## Plants adrift

Drifting in the water of most lakes and slow-moving rivers are thriving populations of microscopic plankton. They include plant forms (phytoplankton), animal forms (zooplankton), fungi, and smaller bacterial forms, the bacterioplankton. Some freshwater biologists group photosynthetic bacterioplankton with phytoplankton. A tablespoonful of freshwater typically contains millions of bacterioplankton, thousands of phytoplankton, and hundreds of zooplankton.

The bacterioplankton are tiny single cells (less than 10 microns, or 0.01 millimeters long) that have a simple cell structure. They include forms, such as cyanobacteria (previously called blue-green algae), that photosynthesize. Cyanobacteria are unusual in that they can trap nitrogen gas, the major gas in air and readily soluble in water, and incorporate the nitrogen in food substances that they manufacture from photosynthesis. Most photosynthetic organisms, including phytoplankton, cannot do this, and they must absorb nitrogen in some other form, usually as nitrate. Nitrates are often in short supply, and cyanobacteria are at a competitive advantage in such circumstances.

Most freshwater biologists regard phytoplankton as single-celled, plantlike forms that are larger than bacterioplankton and have a more complex cell structure. In temperate waters, phytoplankton are most abundant in spring and early summer. In nutrient-rich lakes and slow-moving rivers the rising temperatures and increasing daylight hours enable phytoplankton to photosynthesize more readily. The phytoplankton grow quickly, divide into two, then grow and divide again, so that soon the water becomes colored by a soup of miniature plants. These "blooms" can transform the color of a lake within a matter of days, turning clear water a murky green or brown. During a bloom, the phytoplankton population is growing so fast that their numbers are replaced faster than zooplankton and other organisms graze them. Dense blooms do not normally last more than a week or two. The phytoplankton eventually become starved of nutrients, or some combination of inhibiting factors—such as the buildup of wastes, growth in populations of grazers, or changing weather conditions—causes the bloom to subside.

There are thousands of freshwater phytoplankton species, and their classification into groups is complicated and confusing. Some species, such as the flagellate *Euglena,* have animal-like features (they absorb ready-made, carbon-rich food from their surroundings) as well as plantlike features (they photosynthesize), and animal biologists and plant biologists have traditionally placed the same organisms in different groups. However, most freshwater phytoplankton belong to two groups: the dinoflagellates and diatoms.

Dinoflagellates such as *Ceratium* possess two whiplike structures called flagella that they use to propel themselves through the water and keep themselves in the upper parts of the water column where they are bathed in solar radiation. Diatoms have an outer glassy skeleton (exoskeleton) made of

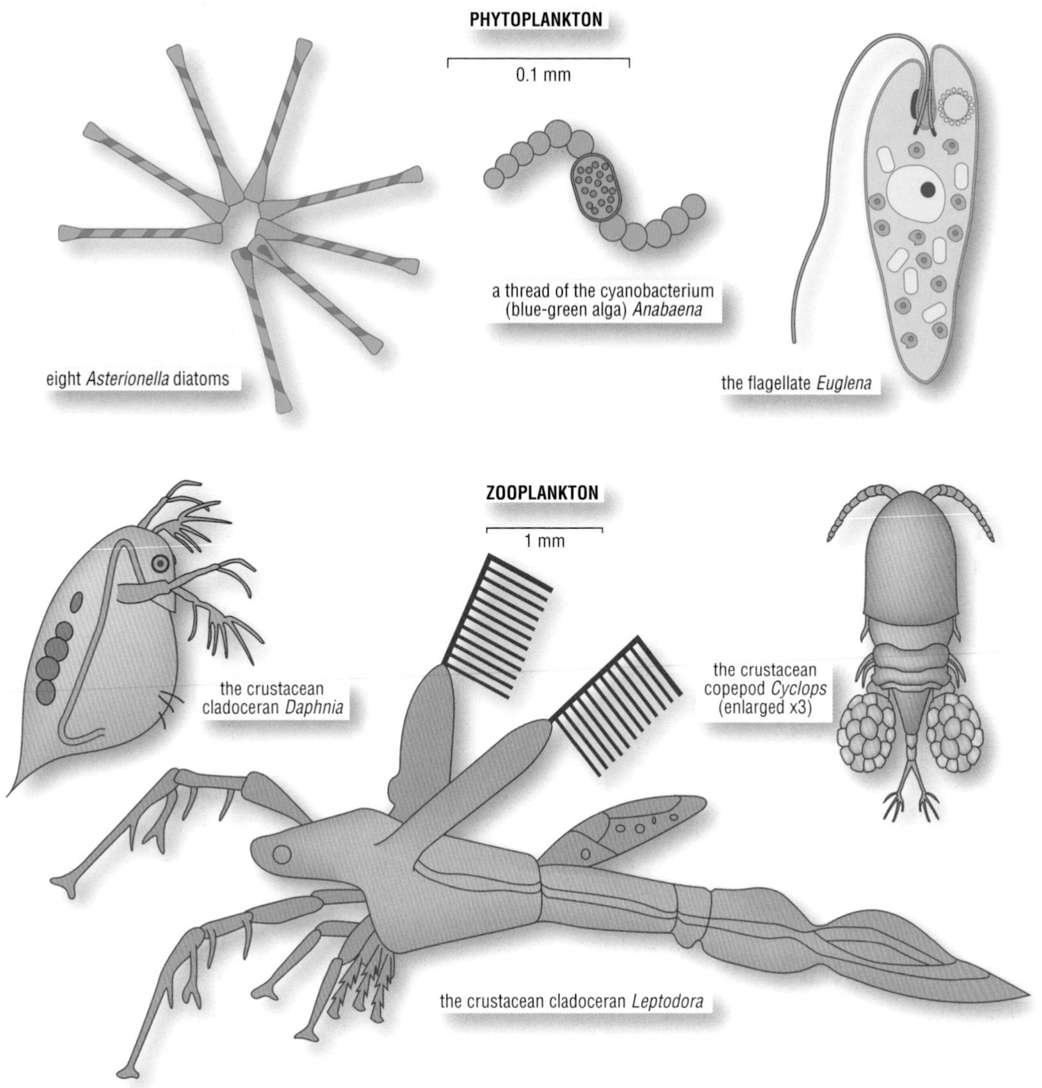


*Some members of the freshwater plankton community of temperate waters*

silica ($SiO_2$) called a frustule. It has two halves that fit closely together, hence the name *diatom* (from the Greek for "cut in half"). Diatoms often have flattened shapes and spiny outgrowths that together increase friction with the surrounding water and slow the organism's descent.

Overcoming the tendency to sink is a problem that all plankton must overcome at some time or another. Some diatoms and larger kinds of green algae come together with individuals of the same species to form a loose assemblage of cells, as in the diatom *Asterionella,* or an even more highly organized arrangement called a colony, as in the green alga *Volvox. Asterionella* cells form star-shaped arrangements of six to nine individuals, creating a shape that sinks lazily through the water in a slow spiral. *Volvox* cells form a ball-shaped colony about 0.02 inch (0.5 mm) across and just visible to the naked eye. It consists of hundreds of individuals that arrange themselves with their flagella to the outside, beating together in a coordinated way to keep the colony near the water's surface. The colony's relatively large size probably enables it to avoid being consumed by all but the largest filter-feeding zooplankton.

Many phytoplankton employ other strategies to maintain buoyancy. Some harbor oil droplets and others maintain tiny gas-filled spaces, called vacuoles, to reduce their density. All these techniques help phytoplankton maintain the exposure to sunlight that is essential to their survival.

## Animals adrift

Freshwater zooplankton, or animal plankton, include mainly animal-like protists (single-celled organisms with complex cell structure), rotifers (phylum Rotifera), and various types of crustaceans (superclass Crustacea), especially shrimplike copepods (order Copepoda) and cladocerans (suborder Cladocera).

Unlike protists, rotifers are multicellular (many-celled). Called "wheel animalcules" by early naturalists, rotifers gain their name from the circle of hairlike structures (cilia) around the mouth. As the cilia beat, they rotate the animal and propel it forward. Rotifers also use their cilia to gather small food items, such as bacteria, that drift in the water.

Rotifers rarely grow larger than 0.1 inch (2.5 mm) in length, and many are much smaller, with males smaller than females. Some rotifers begin life swimming in the open water, but as they mature they settle. In later life they remain attached and form part of the biofilm covering the surface of plants and objects on the pond or lake bottom.

The crustaceans of the zooplankton community tend to be larger than rotifers. Cladocerans are small crustaceans, typically less than 0.25 inch (6 mm) long, except for some predatory forms, such as *Leptodora,* that exceed this size. One of the most common cladocerans in temperate waters is the water flea (genus *Daphnia*). It gains its name from its body shape, which resembles that of parasitic fleas, although the water flea is only distantly related to them.

Water fleas swim by flicking their long, branched antennae. These structures also stir up a water current toward the mouth, where comblike structures filter phytoplankton and small zooplankton from the water. Water fleas have a single eye that they use to orient themselves toward the water surface to which they swim. Female water fleas normally produce two types of eggs. In summer, when food is abundant, they produce eggs without the help of males. These eggs are like clones of the female and enable her to produce many offspring, all female, in a short time. In winter, she produces far fewer eggs and males fertilize these. The fertilized winter eggs are the resistant, dispersal stage in the life cycle. The eggs develop a tough outer coating and float up to the surface. They can travel long distances when blown along the surface by the wind or when carried from one place to another attached to the legs or plumage of birds.

Some cladocerans are carnivorous. *Leptodora,* resembling a miniature praying mantis ready to pounce, reaches a length of more than 0.5 inch (1.25 cm). Like the water flea, it uses antennae for swimming but also to grasp prey, such as smaller crustaceans.

Copepod crustaceans tend to be less than 0.25 inch (6 mm) long, of similar size to water fleas but smaller than the carnivorous *Leptodora*. Many, including *Diaptomus,* are filter feeders that strain the water for phytoplankton and small zooplankton. *Cyclops*—so named because it has one eye, like Cyclops of Greek mythology—is a predatory copepod only about 0.03 inch (1 mm) long. Together with water fleas, copepods are dominant zooplankton in many still water or slow-flowing freshwater communities.

Zooplankton are important links in food webs (see "Energy flow, food chains, and food webs," pages 128–133). They transfer energy from phytoplankton to larger animals, including young fishes.

## Freshwater plants

Almost all but the smallest or fastest-flowing stretches of freshwater have visible plants growing in them or on their margins. Many ponds and lakes in North America and Europe have duckweed (genus *Lemna*) floating on the surface. Strands of waterweed (in Europe, called Canadian pondweed, *Elodea canadensis*) commonly float in the water column. On the water surface, water lilies (genus *Nymphaea*) spread their broad leaves while their roots are anchored in the substrate on the lake bottom. Reeds of various kinds (such as genera *Phragmites* and *Sparganium*) grow in shallow water at the edge of the lake, with their stalks and leaves raised high above the water surface.

All these leafy freshwater plants are seed-bearing plants that belong to the class Angiospermae ("cased seeds"), the

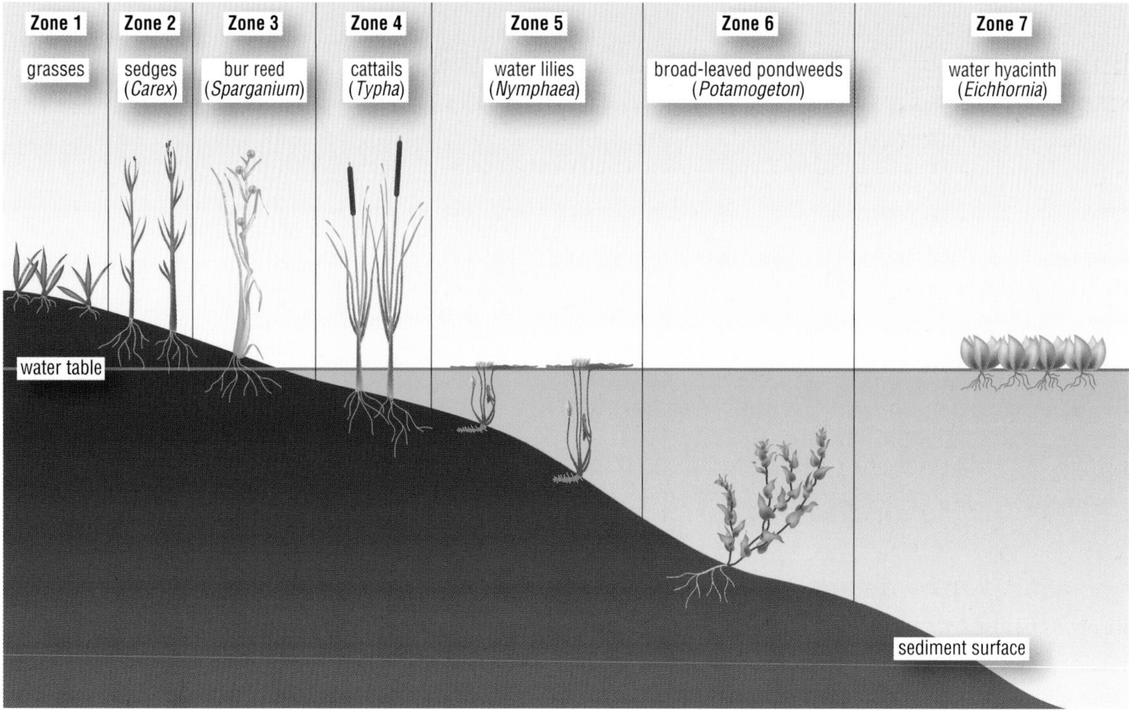


*Larger freshwater plants. Moving from dry land toward the center of a lake there is a gradation in environmental conditions from comparatively dry soil to deep water overlying water-saturated sediment. Different species of plants favor the conditions in a particular zone. One representative type of plant is shown for each zone.*

flowering plants or angiosperms. The ancestors of these plants evolved on land. Flowers, for example, are organs of sexual reproduction that are adapted to life on land. They evolved as a means of ensuring that male and female sex cells meet by transfer of pollen (enclosed male sex cells) in a water-scarce environment.

Many other angiosperm features are also adaptations for life on land, where water may be scarce and the air provides little physical support. Flowering plants have root systems for absorbing water from the soil and an internal system of tubing—the vascular system—for conveying water around the plant. Associated with the vascular system are strengthened cell walls that provide an internal skeleton to support the plant's stem and leaves in air. Angiosperms that have adapted to life in freshwater have lost or modified some of their former adaptations to life on land.

Freshwater is about 700 times denser than air at normal temperatures and pressures. Plants that need considerable support in the form of an internal strengthening tissue when growing in air need very little when supported by water. Except for those aquatic plants, such as reeds and rushes, that rise well above the water surface, most aquatic plants have little strengthening tissue. When taken out of water, their stems and leaves are limp.

Instead of strength and support, these plants need buoyancy. To provide it, the stems and leaves of most freshwater plants contain numerous air spaces. The spaces make the plant float up from the bottom, toward the surface and the light. The air spaces also serve as a source of carbon dioxide for photosynthesis.

Two factors limit the depth to which freshwater plants grow: pressure and light intensity. Pressure increases by 1 atmosphere for each 33 feet (10 m) of depth, and about 33 feet is the greatest depth to which freshwater angiosperms can grow. At depths beyond this, high pressure prevents the formation of internal air spaces and the growth of roots.

Light intensity decreases rapidly with depth because water filters out solar radiation. Anything suspended in the water—whether living phytoplankton or nonliving particles—also blocks sunlight penetration. Poor light penetration in cloudy

*Water lilies (genus* Nymphaea) *seen from underwater with their leaves floating on the water surface to catch sunlight. The lilies' roots are anchored in the lakebed, where they obtain nutrients from the substrate. Air spaces within the plants' tissues make the leaves and stems float up in the water.* (Frans Lanting/ Minden Pictures)

(turbid) water can prevent angiosperms from growing leaves at depths of three feet (about 1 m) or even less.

Despite these constraints, rooted aquatic plants are at an advantage compared with their land-living relatives. Not only do they have access to a supply of nutrients in the bottom sediment of the lake or river, but they can also absorb nutrients from the water. Phosphates and nitrates are the nutrients most likely to be in short supply. In temperate waters, the levels of these substances in both freshwater and bottom sediment vary considerably with time of year. Overall, levels of nutrients dissolved in the water tend to be highest in late winter, when plants have died back and decomposed and their nutrients have been released. Nutrient levels in water tend to be lowest in mid- to late summer, when plant and phytoplankton growth has been rapid and nutrients have been absorbed and incorporated in living tissues.

Plants need carbon dioxide gas as one of the two raw materials for photosynthesis (the other being water). Carbon dioxide dissolves readily in water. Levels of the gas in freshwater are usually higher than in air, so submerged plants normally have plentiful supplies.

Lack of water and nutrients are the two major factors that usually limit the growth of land plants. The supply of these for aquatic plants is not as problematic. Those plants that live with their roots in water and their stems and leaves in the air can have the best of both worlds. Their leaves are bathed in sunlight while their roots have access to water and nutrients. These so-called emergent plants, such as reeds and rushes, are among the most productive plant communities in the world. Their productivity—that is, the amount of living tissue they can lay down in a given area in a year—ranks with that of tropical rain forests.

Freshwater angiosperms produce flowers that require pollination, like those of their land-living relatives. In aquatic plants, as in land-living ones, flying insects usually carry pollen from the male parts of one flower to the female parts of another. For this to happen, flowers must lie on or above the water surface, and this is another factor limiting the depths to which aquatic plants can grow. Most submerged plants must raise their flowers to the surface if they wish to reproduce sexually.

Most aquatic plants reproduce asexually (without transferring genetic material) as well as sexually. Commonly, the plant dies back in winter and an overwintering dormant form, such as a tuber—a horizontal stem in the bottom sediment—survives to grow into new plants the following season.

Aquatic angiosperms, along with phytoplankton, release oxygen as a product of photosynthesis. The gas dissolves in the water and supplies most aquatic organisms—animals, plants, and microbes—with the oxygen they need for respiration. In summer, oxygen levels in the water rise during the day, when plants and phytoplankton photosynthesize, and fall during the night, when photosynthesis ceases.

Plants also provide a vital platform to which microbes and tiny plants and animals can attach (see sidebar on page 106). The network of stems and leaves provides many hiding places from which organisms can avoid grazers or predators. Many aquatic insects lay their eggs on submerged vegetation. The eggs hatch underwater, and after feeding and growing the aquatic larvae pupate, they enter a dormant, nonfeeding stage prior to emerging as an adult. As adults, dragonflies, mayflies, caddis flies, stoneflies, and alderflies emerge from their aquatic pupae. They use the emergent leaves of aquatic plants as launch pads on which to dry their wings before making their first flights.

At the edge of lakes and rivers, rather than in open water, are found marginal plants. They are particularly associated with the silting up of a lake or pond as a transitional stage in the succession from open water to wetland and then dry land. (see "Lakes through time," pages 31–35). In running water, the growth of marginal plants can slow bank erosion at that point. In swift currents, clumps of marginal plants may break away and then settle downstream in gently flowing shallow water. These reestablishing clumps divert the

## Attached algae

A variety of small plantlike forms—simpler in structure than flowering plants but more complex than many of the microbes found in phytoplankton—grow as a film or strands on almost any sunlit surface beneath the water. These are attached freshwater algae, ranging from microscopic diatoms to green or red algae that grow in thin strands up to three feet (about 1 m) long in running water. Microscopic attached algae form part of the biofilm (a living layer made up of small organisms that establishes itself on almost any stationary object in freshwater).

Many types of attached algae—including the large green algae *Cladophora* and *Ulothrix*—grow in both still and running water. However, some species favor only swiftly running water, probably because they require well-oxygenated conditions and the rapid removal of wastes. These species—such as the large algae *Chaetophora* and *Draparnaldia*—have strong holdfasts (rootlike anchoring structures) attached to large stones and other objects that prevent them being swept away by the current.

Attached algae are the principal food of many grazing animals, including some caddis fly larvae and mollusks such as freshwater snails and limpets.

water flow so that sediment settles downstream of the clump where further plants can establish. In this way, an island can develop in midstream. Marginal plants therefore play an active role in reshaping the form of the river.

After death, decaying plants in lakes and rivers offer a rich food source to a legion of decomposers, ranging from bacteria and fungi to detritus-feeding insects, worms, and crustaceans. By the activities of these decomposers, the nutrients locked up in vegetation are recycled and returned to the water and sediment, where they can fuel future plant or phytoplankton growth.

## Larger invertebrates

Invertebrate animals are those without backbones. In freshwater, as on land, the most abundant larger invertebrates—those longer than 0.2 inch (5 mm)—are insects. Many orders of insects have members that are land-living (terrestrial) and able to fly as adults but live in freshwater at earlier stages in their life cycles. Among these are Diptera (true flies), Ephemeroptera (mayflies), Odonata (dragonflies), Plecoptera (stoneflies), and Trichoptera (caddisflies). Insects that have adult freshwater stages include beetles (Coleoptera), such as the whirligig beetle and diving (dytiscid) beetles, and members of the order Hemiptera (true bugs), such as water striders (see "On the surface," pages 96–97).

In running water, most larvae of dipterans, caddis flies, mayflies, stoneflies, and beetles are omnivores—they eat plant and animal material. Some species scrape biofilm from underwater surfaces, while others filter fine particles from water or consume decaying organic material such as rotting leaves. Some larvae—especially those of caddis flies—construct a case around themselves of sediment particles or detritus cemented together. Some of the larger invertebrate larvae are voracious predators, and in still waters damselfly and dragonfly nymphs will take tadpoles and even small fishes.

Crustaceans—animals with jointed limbs and an outer skeleton made of calcium carbonate—are second to insects in their obvious presence among larger freshwater invertebrates.

In still and flowing waters, small amphipod (order Amphipoda) and isopod (order Isopoda) crustaceans, and larger shrimps and crayfish, are omnivores consuming large amounts of detritus. Mysid shrimps (family Mysidae) are swimming predators found is still waters or slow-flowing rivers.

Important members of the bottom-living community in most still and slow-flowing waters include mollusks (phylum Molluska), such as snails and clams, and tiny oligochaete worms (segmented worms of the class Oligochaeta). Snails graze algae, while clams filter the water for zooplankton or particles of detritus. Freshwater oligochaetes consume attached algae, detritus, and sediment particles that are covered in biofilm organisms. Along with various mud-dwelling midge larvae that are rich in the red, oxygen-carrying pigment hemoglobin, some oligochaetes are described as "bloodworms."

As a general rule, freshwater invertebrates are able to withstand more demanding environmental conditions than vertebrates such as fish. Being smaller than vertebrates—and in many cases having a flying stage in their life cycle or other means of dispersal in air—some invertebrates will colonize even the remotest mountainous lakes and streams, as well as temporary ponds and puddles that dry out seasonally, where fishes are absent.

## Fishes

In terms of abundance and variety, fishes are the most successful vertebrates (animals with backbones). The 25,000 or so living species of fish make up about half of all vertebrate species. The plural form *fishes* is used here to describe fish of more than one species; *fish* is the singular form, or the plural form where only one species is involved.

All fishes have a backbone or a similar structure made of bone or cartilage. They all have fins, and nearly all have gills for extracting oxygen from water. A few—such as lungfish, which live in muddy, oxygen-depleted freshwater—have more or less abandoned gills in favor of lungs for breathing air.

Today, freshwater fishes are major predators and grazers in most lakes and rivers. More than 10,000 species, or about 40 percent of all fish species, live in freshwater for all or part of their lives. Yet lakes and rivers cover only 1 percent of Earth's surface, while salt waters cover 71 percent. The rich diversity of fish life in freshwaters is largely a function of two factors. The first is the wide variety of freshwater habitats. They range from tiny hot springs, where water temperatures reach well above 104°F (40°C), to the 5,712-foot (1,740-m)-deep Lake Baikal, with clear, chilly waters that hover close to 32°F (0°C) for about half the year. Freshwater habitats range from warm, nutrient-rich tropical lakes to clear, swift-flowing mountain streams where currents reach speeds of more than 20 mph (32 km/h). Even within the same stretch of a river or the margins of a lake, there can be several different habitats between the surface and the bottom (see "Boundary layers," pages 92–94, and "The water column," page 94).

The other factor accounting for freshwater fish diversity is the presence of natural boundaries between one river or lake system and another. Stretches of freshwater can be cut off from nearby expanses for thousands of years, during which time the isolated populations adapt to the changing conditions and new species evolve.

The earliest fishes evolved in the sea some 500 million years ago. They lacked the jaws and paired fins found in almost all fishes today. Among freshwater fishes, the eel-like lampreys (class Cephalaspidomorphi) lack these features and are most closely related to the earliest fishes. Instead of jaws to chew, lampreys have a roughened or toothed tongue that rasps at a victim's flesh.

Although some species of lamprey spend their entire lives in the sea, others hatch from eggs in freshwater, migrate to the sea to mature, and then return to rivers and streams to spawn. A few species, including landlocked forms of the marine lamprey (*Petromyzon marinus*) in the United States, spend their entire lives in freshwater.

The adults of most lamprey species are parasites. They have a large sucker surrounding the mouth that they anchor to their fish hosts. Then lampreys use their toothed tongue to rasp away flesh. This draws blood and damages tissues that they consume as a nutritious soup. The lamprey releases chemicals called anticoagulants into the wound, which stops the victim's blood from clotting. When lampreys have taken their fill, they release their quarry. Often the damage inflicted is enough to kill the victim (see "Alien invasions," pages 199–205).

Almost all freshwater fishes today are jawed fishes. They have true jaws supported by bone or cartilage that enable them to bite and chew. Most jawed fishes also have paired fins as well as a dorsal (back) fin and a tail (caudal) fin. The tail fin, when moved side to side, propels the fish forward. The dorsal fin helps in steering and prevents rolling. Two pairs of fins—pectoral fins, at the shoulder, and pelvic fins, farther back on the underside—offer improved control in swimming. With paired fins, fish can more easily hunt their prey and better escape their predators.

A handful of cartilaginous fish species live in rivers; cartilaginous fishes are those with skeletons of cartilage rather than bone. Most enter from the sea and cross brackish water to reach freshwater. The majority of cartilaginous fishes are sharks, skates, or rays (class Chondrichthyes). Skates and rays are essentially flattened versions of sharks that have adapted to life on or near the seabed.

Cartilaginous fishes have a skeleton made entirely of cartilage—familiar to people as the hard, shiny gristle normally found at the joint at the end of a bone. The gristly skeleton may be a way of lightening the load because cartilaginous fishes do not have an air-filled swim bladder to help maintain buoyancy, as bony fishes do (see "Freshwater's physical properties," pages 13–18). Sharks and their relatives store oil in the liver to make them more buoyant. Their paired fins are airfoil-shaped, like the wings of an aircraft. When a shark swims forward, the paired fins generate lift. Key differences between bony and cartilaginous fishes are summarized in the following table.

The bull shark (*Carcharhinus leucas*), a known human-eater, enters some tropical rivers in Asia and Africa. In the Amazon Basin, the freshwater stingray (*Potamotrygon motoro*) is abundant and well adapted for river life. Overall, however, cartilaginous fishes play a much more important role in the sea

## Major differences between cartilaginous and bony fishes

| | Cartilaginous fish such as a shark or ray | Advanced bony fish (teleost) such as a trout or perch |
|---|---|---|
| Skeleton | Made of cartilage | Made of bone and cartilage |
| Fins | Paired fins have limited range of movement. The upper part (lobe) of the tail fin is usually larger than the lower, to drive the head upward | Paired fins are highly maneuverable. The upper and lower lobes of the tail fin are usually the same size |
| Gills | Usually five pairs of gill slits | Usually a single pair of gill flaps |
| Buoyancy | Swim bladder absent. A fat-filled liver creates buoyancy. Fins generate lift | Swim bladder usually present |
| Skin | Covering of toothlike placoid scales | Covering typically of bony scales |
| Reproduction | Produce live young or lay a few large eggs, which are fertilized internally | Most lay many eggs, which are fertilized externally |

than in freshwater. In the freshwater environment they appear to have lost out in competition with bony fishes. Poorer ability to cope with low levels of dissolved salts is probably part of the explanation.

Nowadays, more than 95 percent of freshwater fishes are bony fishes. They have a skeleton made of bone. Most bony fishes are teleosts (from the Greek *teleios* for "perfect" and *osteon* for "bone"). These fishes have fins supported by thin bony rays and a body covering of lightweight, flexible scales. Most of the familiar food fishes from freshwater—such as trout, salmon, pike, perch, and carp, for example—are teleosts.

The flexible fins of teleost fishes are a major contributor to their success. Their paired fins can rotate, enabling the fish to almost turn on a dime, hover in the water, or even swim backward. This maneuverability is enhanced in most bony

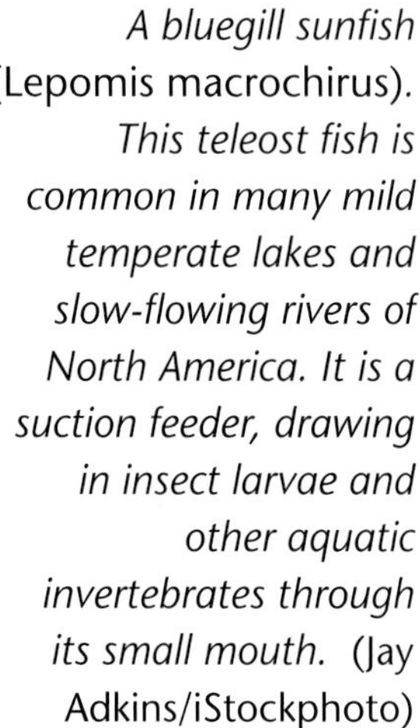

*A bluegill sunfish* (Lepomis macrochirus). *This teleost fish is common in many mild temperate lakes and slow-flowing rivers of North America. It is a suction feeder, drawing in insect larvae and other aquatic invertebrates through its small mouth.* (Jay Adkins/iStockphoto)

fishes by a swim bladder—an air-filled sac. By altering the amount of air in the sac, those bony fishes that possess a swim bladder can control their buoyancy so they do not rise or sink in the water. They can stop swimming and still float, thus saving energy. The gills of teleosts are particularly efficient at extracting oxygen from water that is needed to supply plentiful energy to muscles for swimming.

Different species of bony fish employ various kinds of teeth (in the mouth or in the throat) and gill devices to capture and process their food. Such adaptability is another key to their success. Many freshwater fishes—such as members of the carp family (Cyprinidae)—are suction feeders. They remain almost stationary in front of the item they wish to consume, and then expand the mouth cavity and gill chamber so that water rushes into the open mouth. Prey are swept into the mouth with the inrush of water. The archerfish (*Toxotes chatareus*) of Southeast Asia and Northern Australia effectively reverses the process. It spits out jets of water through its mouth by compressing the mouth cavity and gill chamber. Its precisely targeted droplets knock prey insects from overhanging trees and into the water. Pike (genus *Esox*), on the other hand, are ram feeders. They swim onto their prey with their mouth open and use a mouth well armed with sharp teeth to grasp their victims. Most ram feeders have long, slender bodies with fins located toward the tail, which transfers power for rapid acceleration when ambushing prey. Freshwater herrings (such as genus *Pristigaster*), like most of their marine counterparts, strain water for zooplankton using gill rakers—a comblike array extending from the bones that support the gills.

## Fish senses

Vision is important in most fishes, but with water visibility restricted to three feet (1 m) or less at certain times, other senses, such as smell, hearing, and touch, are highly developed in most fishes. Nevertheless, in the murky world of freshwater, many fishes can see images at light levels that would be perceived as darkness by humans.

Fishes have nostrils and a highly developed sense of smell. The fish's sense of taste (detecting chemicals by direct contact with items) is spread around the head region, both inside and outside the mouth. Some fishes, such as catfish, have whiskerlike projections that are heavily armed with chemoreceptors for "tasting" items in the vicinity.

Both cartilaginous and bony fishes possess a sensory system that is absent in land-living vertebrates. A series of pores running along the flanks reveals the presence of the lateral line system—sense organs that detect movements and vibrations in the water. Typically, each sensory organ, called a neuromast, comprises a jelly-filled chamber that opens in a pore on the flank of the fish. The neuromast is lined at the base by sensory cells with hairlike extensions attached to a jelly-like structure called the cupula. Vibrations in the water cause the cupula to move, pulling on the hairlike structures and triggering nerve impulses in the neuromasts. The impulses travel as messages to the central nervous system where they are interpreted. The position, sequence, strength, and speed in which neuromasts are stimulated gives the fish precise information about the source of vibrations and movement in its surroundings. The lateral line system effectively works as a "touch at a distance" sense.

Many bony fishes have ears, although these structures are not obvious and have no opening to the outside. Several groups of freshwater fishes, including carp, catfish, and minnows, have inner ear mechanisms connected by a series of small bones to the swim bladder. Gas-filled spaces are highly sensitive to vibrations, and this arrangement gives these fishes extremely sensitive hearing. Fishes that hear this way are better able to discriminate different pitches of sound that are signs of approaching predators or potential prey. Some freshwater catfish also grunt and click to communicate with each other using sound.

Cartilaginous fishes possess an additional sensory system in the head region that, like the lateral line system, opens onto the skin through pores. The system detects weak electrical fields produced by the normal muscular activity of living creatures. At close range, sharks and rays can use this electrodetection system to find prey that are not in view, such as fishes hiding in the bottom sediment or behind obstacles.

Some bony fishes, on the other hand, generate their own electrical field for both sensory and communication purposes. The elephantfishes (Mormyroidei) of Africa—so called because they have a trunklike extension of the lower jaw—have organs in the tail region that generate an electric field. The field is detected by electroreceptors in the head region. These fishes live in murky freshwaters and often hunt at night when vision is of little use. An elephantfish detects any creatures entering its electric field, gaining advance warning of approaching predators or prey. The pulses of electricity also act as a communication system that enables individuals to recognize others of the same species. The electric knifefishes (Gymnotoidei) of South and Central America have evolved a similar sensory and communication system.

Some freshwater fish species generate strong electrical discharges for stunning prey and deterring predators. The electric eel (*Electrophorus electricus*) delivers 550 volts at 1 amp—sufficient to give humans a nasty shock. The electric catfish (*Malapterurus electricus*) produces slightly less powerful shocks. Both fishes use arrays of specialized muscles, arranged in series like batteries, to generate the electrical discharges.

## Fish habitats

The headwaters of river systems tend to be cool, fast-flowing, and highly oxygenated. Cool water retains more dissolved oxygen than warm, and turbulent water, with its bubbles and ripples, has a larger surface area in contact with air across which fresh supplies of oxygen can dissolve. These fast-flowing waters lack plankton and large aquatic plants, and most of the fish inhabitants are carnivorous (eat other animals) or omnivorous (eating a mixed diet of animals and plants). Typical inhabitants are one or more members of the family Salmonidae, the group that includes trout and salmon. These predators have keen eyesight and require plentiful oxygen supplies to support their fast-swimming lifestyle.

In the lower reaches of river systems, temperatures are higher, oxygen levels lower, plankton are abundant, and the water tends to be rich in sediment. Such waters support a very different fish community from those of upland streams and rivers. Members of the carp family (Cyprinidae) are common in these waters, and they include a range of species that are quite generalist feeders. Various carp family members, such as European roach (*Rutilus rutilus*) and common bream (*Abramis brama*), consume larger plankton, attached algae, small bottom-living animals, and the carpet of detritus that settles on the riverbed.

In many tropical rivers, such as those of the Amazon Basin, seasonal rainfall causes the main channel to rise and spill onto the floodplain. Many fish species time their reproduction to occur just prior to the floods so that their offspring can spread out into flooded rain forest, which forms their nursery. Many fish species, as young and as adults, consume the leaves, fruits, and seeds of trees in the flooded forest.

About 200 fish species, most of economic importance, migrate between freshwater and seawater. When fish migrate between the two environments they have to make major adjustments to body function because their surroundings change so markedly in salt concentration (see sidebar).

*Anadromous fishes* (from the Greek *anadromos,* "running upward") are those that spawn in freshwater but migrate to the sea to grow and mature before returning to freshwater to reproduce. They include a variety of salmon (genera *Salmo* and *Onchorhynchus*) and sturgeon (family Acipenseridae) species. Freshwater eels (family Anguillidae) are among the few species that adopt the reverse strategy, spawning in the sea and maturing in freshwater. They are *catadromous fishes* (catadromous means "running down"). Fish that migrate between seawater and freshwater tend to be of commercial importance because during migration they congregate in great numbers and become easier to catch.

Compared with rivers, most lakes are short-lived. Lakes usually contain fish species similar or identical to those found in nearby sluggish rivers. However, a few lakes have existed in one form or another for more than 500,000 years, during which time a wide range of local fish species has been able to evolve. The two most striking examples of this phe-

## From saltwater to fresh

The body tissues of bony fishes that live in the sea have a salt concentration less than that of the surrounding seawater. There is an overall tendency for salts to move into fish from the surroundings by diffusion (see sidebar "Diffusion and osmosis," page 91) and for water to move in the opposite direction. This movement occurs at partially permeable barriers on the body surface such as the gills, where gas exchange takes place (in which oxygen is absorbed and carbon dioxide expelled). Ocean-dwelling fishes are equipped to eliminate excess salts. As fast as salts diffuse into a marine fish, it pumps them out using specialized cells in the gills. But when salmon and eels enter freshwater, the salt/water balance problem is reversed. The body tissues now have a salt concentration much higher than the fish's surroundings; water tends to enter the body and salts leave. How do these fishes cope? The salt-pumping cells change their direction of action, pumping salts in rather than out. This remarkable adjustment takes place in a matter of hours, when eels and salmon remain almost immobile in brackish water before continuing their migration.

### Cave fishes

Several dozen species of fish, belonging to 10 families, have adapted to the conditions inside caves. Unrelated species have adapted to the lightless conditions in similar ways. Most species are blind, lack skin pigment (and are therefore pink, from the blood showing through pale skin), and have developed additional touch-sensitive organs on their skin, such as ridges or raised mounds with hairlike structures called papillae. Such fishes have a heightened sensitivity to vibrations in the water. In some forms, the loss of skin pigment and lack of vision is reversible. If juveniles are raised from young in illuminated conditions, they develop the eyes and skin coloration of their non-cave-dwelling ancestors.

nomenon are Lake Baikal in Siberia (see "Lake Baikal," pages 78–83) and Lakes Malawi, Tanganyika, and Victoria (see "Lake Victoria," pages 87–89)—the Great Lakes of Africa.

At least 20 million years old, Lake Baikal is the world's oldest lake. It is also the deepest. It contains more than 50 species of fish found nowhere else, including two unique families (Comephoridae and Abyssocottidae) related to sculpins.

The African Great Lakes have existed in one form or another for at least 500,000 years. During that time more than 1,500 local species of cichlid (family Cichlidae) have evolved there to take advantage of the diverse range of habitats in these giant still waters.

Such is the flexibility of fish design that various species across the world have evolved to live under normal light conditions as well as in the pitch dark of caves. Depending on the light conditions in which they grow, they can develop fully functional eyes or not (see sidebar).

## On two or four legs

There are 10,000 species of freshwater fishes, but fewer than 5,000 species of amphibians and just a few hundred types of reptiles, mammals, and birds spend all or most of their lives in freshwater. However, because of their relatively large sizes and high levels of food consumption, some of these limbed vertebrates play a disproportionately important role in freshwater ecosystems.

The first amphibians appear in the fossil record about 370 million years ago, when swamps were extensive on land and freshwater pools commonly dried out or became congested with vegetation. Amphibians were descended from fleshy-finned bony fishes rather than those with thin, flexible fins supported by rays. The early amphibians had fishlike features such as mucus-covered scaly skin and finned tails. They also breathed with lungs like their fish ancestors. However, amphibians evolved to have jointed limbs for walking—pentadactyl limbs based on an arrangement that included five or four digits (toes). The limbs enabled amphibians to walk on land. Amphibians also developed eyelids (allowing them to keep their eyes moist in air), an ability to smell in air using nostrils, and a tongue that moistened food prior to swallowing. Unlike reptiles, which were to evolve later, amphibians were still tied to freshwater, or damp conditions at least, for the survival of their unshelled eggs. The skin of amphibians was naked, moist, and smooth. Amphibians exchanged gases through their skin as well as their lungs. The skin was permeable to water and, to prevent drying out, adult amphibians had to remain in damp conditions.

Today most amphibians (class Amphibia), including newts and salamanders (order Caudata), caecilians (order Gymnophiona), and frogs and toads (order Anura), remain tied to freshwater for at least part of their life cycle. The 470 or so species of newts and salamanders—with their slender bodies, long tails, and typically four legs of similar size—are superficially similar in appearance to early amphibians. There is no strict scientific distinction between newts and salamanders. Newts tend to live in damp places on land, returning to water to breed. Salamanders either live in water throughout their lives or are wholly land-living.

Most newts and salamanders have larvae with large, feathery gills for exchanging gases (oxygen and carbon dioxide) and an elongated, finlike tail for swimming. In amphibious forms—those with part of the life cycle in water, part on land—the aquatic larva metamorphoses into an adult that lacks gills and exchanges gases through lungs and skin. The adult returns temporarily to freshwater to breed. In most species, males fertilize the female's eggs internally. Both larvae and adults are carnivorous, eating a wide range of small animals.

In most of the 4,000-plus species of frogs and toads, males shed sperm onto the eggs as the female lays them. The eggs hatch into larvae with gills, called tadpoles, which undergo a dramatic change in form (metamorphosis) to become a four-legged adult, with lungs and without a tail. Tadpoles typically feed on vegetable matter; adults are carnivorous, seizing a wide range of prey, including fishes and aquatic insects as well as small land-living snakes, birds, and mammals.

The first reptiles (members of the class Reptilia) evolved from early amphibians some 340 million years ago. Reptiles had major advantages over amphibians that no longer tied them to an aquatic habitat: They have a hard scaly skin that protects them against drying out, and they lay eggs that have chalky or leathery shells in which the embryo develops in a water-filled sac called the amnion. These features enabled reptiles to free themselves of their amphibian ancestors' reliance on freshwater, and reptiles could move away from the margins of lakes and rivers. However, some reptiles returned to the freshwater habitat of their ancestors, where they could take rich pickings from the abundant aquatic life. Prominent among these returners are freshwater turtles (order Chelonia), crocodilians (crocodiles, alligators, and their relatives), and some species of snakes (order Squamata).

Across the world there are several hundred species of freshwater turtle, including more than 45 species in Canada and mainland United States. Freshwater turtles hatch from eggs laid on land, and the young turtles typically feed on aquatic insects, with adults eating a more mixed diet of animal life plus some aquatic vegetation. Some turtle species—including the common snapping turtle (*Chelydra serpentina*) and alligator snapping turtle (*Macroclemys temminckii*) of North America—are ambush predators, lying in wait to capture passing animals, from fishes and crustaceans to small birds and mammals. The alligator snapping turtle even sports a wormlike lure on the floor of its mouth, which it wriggles to entice victims to their doom.

The crocodilians (order Crocodilia) include crocodiles, alligators, caimans, and the gharial. All but one of the 23 species live in freshwater, with the remaining species, the estuarine or saltwater crocodile (*Crocodylus porosus*), favoring brackish or full-strength seawater. Little changed since the age of dinosaurs, more than 65 million years ago, crocodilians have several highly successful adaptations for life in freshwater. Their eyes and nostrils are set on top of the head so they can see above water and breathe air while the body is almost totally submerged. The crocodilian's throat contains a valve that closes off the entrance to the windpipe. This enables the animal to swallow prey underwater without letting water enter the lungs. Other valves close the animal's ears and nostrils when it is diving. Pits in the crocodilian's scales, particularly in the head region, are believed to act as pressure receptors, enabling the animal to sense the size and direction of a disturbance in the water, which the animal then investigates.

Crocodilian swimming is accomplished by sinusoidal (S-shaped) movements of the body and particularly the tail, which is flattened in the vertical plane. The legs are used in steering at slow speed and are folded against the body for streamlining at high speed. The webbed feet are splayed out and help reduce the tendency to sink when the animal is floating on or just below the surface.

Crocodilians are top predators (they occupy the highest trophic level in food chains) in many tropical and subtropical freshwater environments. They consume fish and other vertebrates. In the case of the Nile crocodile (*Crocodylus niloticus*) and the saltwater crocodile, prey include large mammals such as antelope, buffalo, and even people who venture on or near the river.

Many land-living snakes enter freshwater to hunt fishes and other aquatic wildlife. The anaconda (*Eunectes murinus*)—the world's largest snake at up to 33 feet (10 m) long—is an excellent swimmer and lies in wait in the shallows with little other than its nostrils and eyes above the water. It ambushes creatures that come to the water to drink. Deer and capybaras (giant rodents) are regular victims, and even caimans succumb to the anaconda. The snake coils its body around the prey, gradually tightening its grip each time the animal exhales so that the animal becomes asphyxiated. The anaconda then swallows the victim headfirst.

Relatively few bird species spend their entire lives in and around freshwater habitats. Among those that do are kingfishers, herons, ibises, grebes, cranes, and fish eagles. Many more, including ducks and geese, visit freshwater habitats and estuaries but also feed on seashores and in wetland habitats.

Some birds play an important role as top predators in freshwater habitats, taking fish and small birds and mammals. Different species use a wide range of feeding strategies so they do not compete too intensively with one another for the same food resource.

Birds that fly long distances on migration are important in dispersing small aquatic organisms that do not have other means of dispersal. It is amazing how quickly virgin bodies of freshwater become colonized by plankton and even larger organisms, including fishes. Many of these will have been transferred on the feet or feathers of birds and often, as in the case of fishes, as eggs attached to weed.

Across the world, more than 20 species of divers (family Gaviidae) and grebes (Podicipedidae) dive underwater for up to several minutes to take freshwater fishes and small invertebrates. Of the 60 or so species of pelicans and their relatives (order Pelecaniformes), many are exclusively marine, but darters, cormorants, and pelicans can be found on inland waters. Cormorants (genus *Phalacrocorax*) dive and pursue their prey underwater. Darters (genus *Anhinga*) use their long beaks to spear fish from on or above the water surface. Pelicans (genus *Pelecanus*) dive or use their large bill to scoop up fish.

The 100 or so species of herons and their relatives (order Ciconiiformes) are important long-legged waders inhabiting freshwater environments. Most herons (family Ardeidae), ibises (Threskiornithidae), and storks (Ciconiidae) hunt singly and move slowly through shallow water on their stilt-like legs to strike at prey with lightning speed. Small flocks of spoonbills (genus *Platalea*) working in a row use their spoon-shaped, touch-sensitive bills to probe the water for fishes and crustaceans.

Cranes and their relatives (order Gruiformes) favor freshwater environments. Apart from long-legged cranes (family Gruidae) the group includes rails (family Rallidae), such as coots and moorhens, which have lobed (broad-ended) toes to assist in swimming, and limpkins (family Aramidae), which have slender toes for walking on floating aquatic vegetation.

The five species of flamingo (order Phoenicopteriformes) are restricted to saltwater, brackish water, or alkaline lakes (see "Freshwater's chemical composition," pages 18–21, and sidebar "Saline lakes," page 29), where they assemble in flocks of many thousands. They use their bills, which have a comblike filtering device, to strain organisms from the water. Larger species tend to feed on zooplankton and bottom-living animals, and smaller species on phytoplankton and attached algae.

The nearly 150 species of waterfowl (also called wildfowl; order Anseriformes) include ducks, geese, and swans. Waterfowl are strong flyers and swimmers, with most species found in freshwater rather than marine environments. Duck species dive or upend to feed on aquatic vegetation and small invertebrates, while some species of geese and swans graze on land rather than in water but spend much of their time in the water where they are comparatively safe from land predators. Migrating hundreds or thousands of miles, waterfowl play a major role in dispersing small aquatic organisms attached to their feet or plumage.

A few birds of prey (order Falconiformes), notably the osprey and fish eagles, hunt almost exclusively in freshwater. Osprey (genus *Pandion*) pluck fish from the water following a spectacular feet-first dive during which they often submerge themselves. Fish eagles (such as *Haliaeetus vocifer*), on the other hand, swoop down onto the water surface and grasp their fish prey with a backward sweep of their talons. The bald eagle (*Haliaeetus leucocephalus*), the national bird of the United States, occasionally hunts for fish, snatching them from the surface with its claws.

*A black-necked stilt* (Himantopus mexicanus) *wading through a North American reed bed. Its long beak is well adapted for taking bottom-living invertebrates from shallow water.* (Tim Fitzharris/ Minden Pictures)

Kingfishers (order Coraciiformes) are also adept fish hunters. A kingfisher (family Alcedinidae) will wait on a perch near the water looking for signs of movement before swooping down to pluck fish from the water with its beak. It returns to the perch and repeatedly beats the prey's head against a hard surface to stun it before swallowing.

Members of the order Charadriiformes (waders, gulls, and auks) are predominantly marine, but some species of waders—particularly stilts, avocets, curlews, snipe, plovers, and oystercatchers—hunt for small fish and invertebrates in freshwater shallows and wetlands. Gulls and terns dive for fish and are frequently found in inland as well as coastal waters.

Among the passerines, or perching birds (order Passeriformes), many species—including flycatchers, swallows, and some warblers—take flying insects that congregate above the water surface, while others—wagtails and pipits among them—forage along the banks of lakes and rivers. Only a few passerines actually hunt in freshwater. The dippers of fast-flowing streams have waterproof feathers and walk underwater to find insect larvae, snails, and fish eggs.

Among mammals, a variety of rodents are adapted for spending some of their lives in freshwater. They include the muskrat (*Ondatra zibethicus*), the European water vole (*Apodemus flavicollis*), the South American capybara (*Hydrochaerus hydrochaeris;* the world's largest rodent), and beavers (genus *Castor*). The two species of semiaquatic beaver—the North American and European—are widely distributed, and in some wooded areas they have a major impact on inland waterways.

The North American beaver (*Castor canadensis*) weighs up to about 65 pounds (30 kg) and grows to about 48 inches (120 cm) long. With its dense waterproof fur, paddle-like tail and webbed feet, the beaver is an excellent diver and swimmer and can stay submerged for up to 20 minutes at a time.

Beavers live in and around lakes and slow-flowing rivers in extended family groups of four to six animals. They fell trees and build dams, transforming their local environment on a scale out of all proportion to their small size. They gnaw through tree trunks to fell trees, to reach the bark and shoots, and to provide logs and branches to build their dams and their home (called a lodge). Dam building is crucial to creating a secure home. By regulating a river's water level, beavers can ensure the entrances to their lodges are kept below water level, making it difficult for land predators to gain access. By building dams in small to medium-size watercourses (especially second- to third-order streams), beavers create ponds that fill with sediment. Such beaver activity encourages water plant growth and succession to dry land in diverted sections of the river. It also creates a greater diversity of freshwater habitats and may well increase overall biological diversity (see "Biodiversity," pages 187–190).

Otters are members of the family Mustelidae, carnivorous mammals that include weasels, skunks, and badgers. Of the 13 species of otter (subfamily Lutrinae), 12 live in freshwater. Otters have tightly packed underfur and long guard hairs that together trap air and repel water. The body is long and sinuous, with a broad tail that tapers to a point. The animal swims by the undulating movements of body and tail.

Otters close their nostrils and ears when diving and rely on eyesight and their sense of touch when hunting underwater for crustacean or fish prey. Otters have long tactile (touch-sensitive) whiskers around the nose and snout that sense water turbulence and detect disturbances caused by prey items. Most species of freshwater otters have clawed fore-limbs and grab their prey with their mouths, but the Oriental smooth-coated otter (*Lutrogale perspicillata*) and the two species of African clawless otters (genus *Aonyx*) grasp their prey with forepaws. Otters usually bring their prey to the riverbank and manipulate the food item between their fore-limbs while gradually chewing off chunks.

Otters are opportunistic feeders. They tend to take fish that are slow swimmers or those that seek to escape by hiding, such as eels, lampreys, and perch. Trout and other fast-swimming game fish are less favored. With the changing seasons, otters will take whatever food becomes readily available, from crayfish and frogs to ducklings. Being small, active hunters, they have a high energy demand, and an otter weighing 20 pounds (9 kg) can readily consume two pounds (about 1 kg) of fish each day. In so doing, otters control the size of fish populations in small rivers.

Herbivorous (plant-eating) as well as carnivorous mammals affect the rest of the biological community of rivers, and perhaps none more so than hippopotamuses. There are two hippo species. The larger, common species (*Hippopotamus amphibus*) is widespread across central Africa, while the much scarcer pygmy hippopotamus (*Hexaprotodon liberiensis*) is restricted to swampy forests in western Africa.

The common hippopotamus has a major impact on the rivers and surrounding riparian zones where it lives. Adults weigh up to 1.5 U.S. tons (about 1.4 metric tons). They feed at night on grasses growing near the river, often consuming about 90 pounds (40 kg) of vegetation in one night. They spend the day submerged in water away from the heat of the sun. As they walk between their daytime resting areas and nighttime feeding grounds, they carve deep ruts in the river-banks and surrounding countryside. These form drainage channels that are large enough to be visible in satellite imagery. In the river, hippos stir up mud, increasing turbidity

## *River dolphins*

A few large river systems, including the Amazon and La Plata in South America, and the Indus, Yangtze, and Ganges in Asia, contain local species of river dolphin. Researchers currently recognize five species, although one species, the Franciscana (*Pontoporia blainvillei*) of South America, lives in coastal waters rather than rivers. All river dolphin species are quite similar in appearance, but only two, the Indus and Ganges dolphins (genus *Platanista*), belong in the same family.

River dolphins differ from their marine counterparts in being comparatively slow swimmers and having a pronounced bulbous head above a narrow beak and tiny eyes. In the murky waters where these dolphins live, visibility is limited, and the dolphins rely on their acute echolocation ability, "seeing" their surroundings with sound. Their echolocation involves sending a beam of sound from nasal passages below the blowhole, focusing the beam using a fat-filled structure called the melon in the dolphin's forehead, and then channeling the returning echoes through the lower jaw to the inner ear. By interpreting the time delay and qualities of returning echoes, the dolphins can determine the distance, position, movement, size, and even the internal structure of their prey.

River dolphins are vulnerable to, and endangered by, a wide variety of human environmental impacts. These threats include hunting, entanglement in fishing nets, and freshwater pollution. Dams, by forming boundaries across rivers, split up breeding populations of river dolphins and block their migration between feeding and breeding areas. The small, isolated populations then become much more vulnerable to extinction.

and reducing sunlight penetration. This impedes the growth of phytoplankton and attached plants but encourages the development of detritus-feeding communities and decomposers generally. When hippos defecate in the water, they effectively transfer nutrients from the surrounding land to the river.

The hippo's adaptations for a semiaquatic life include webbed toes; the ability to close nostrils underwater; and nostrils, eyes, and ears positioned on the top of the head, which protrude above the water surface when the animal is almost entirely submerged. This way it can still breathe easily and remain receptive to its surroundings. The hippo's body is slightly denser than water. With lungs filled with air, a hippo can float with little effort. With lungs partially deflated, it can walk lightly along the riverbed. By remaining submerged during the day, the hippo massively cuts down on the energy it would otherwise consume in heat regulation and in supporting its heavy body on land.

Sirenians or sea cows (order Sirenia; manatees and the dugong) look superficially like a cross between a walrus and a small whale, but they are not closely related to either. Sirenians, together with cetaceans (whales, dolphins, and porpoises), are the only aquatic mammals adapted to a life entirely in water, including giving birth underwater. Of the four species of sirenians, the three manatees (West Indian, West African, and Amazonian; genus *Trichechus*) commonly enter large river systems and freshwater lagoons. Unusually among large aquatic mammals, they graze on underwater plants. Manatees have flippers with rudimentary nails, which they use to dig up and grasp plants for eating.

# CHAPTER 5

# ECOLOGY OF LAKES AND RIVERS

When biologists study the environment (the living and nonliving surroundings) they often choose an area with recognizable boundaries and analyze biological relationships and processes within that locality. They define this area as an ecosystem. It consists of a *community* of organisms (microbes, fungi, plants, and animals) together with the locality, or *habitat,* in which they live. Ecologists are biologists who study the populations of organisms within an ecosystem.

A puddle, a pond, and a section of river are all examples of freshwater ecosystems. The great Amazon River system can be regarded as an ecosystem, but so can a farm pond that dries out each summer. Ecologists decide the size of the ecosystem based on the processes and interactions they wish to study.

An ecosystem must be definable, but its edges may not be distinct. A mature pond, with sides heavily overgrown with vegetation, does not necessarily have a clear dividing line between the wetland edges at its borders and the open water of the lake. In winter, marginal vegetation may die back and water levels rise, so the area of open water may enlarge appreciably. The edges of the lake, grading between open water and wetlands, are examples of ecotones—regions where one biome grades into another.

## Energy flow, food chains, and food webs

Directly or indirectly, sunlight is the source of energy that sustains almost all freshwater ecosystems. Sunlight energy enters the biological community when it is trapped by photosynthetic freshwater organisms—phytoplankton, filamentous algae, and attached plants. These organisms store the trapped energy as chemical energy in food substances. When animals consume plants (or later, when animals consume other animals), the energy is passed on. Ultimately, the energy leaves living organisms and enters the environment as heat energy. This is released during the process of respiration, when organisms break down food substances to provide energy for body functions.

Photosynthetic organisms also absorb useful chemical elements, such as nitrogen (N) and phosphorus (P), from freshwater and from the lakebed or riverbed. These elements, combined with others such as carbon (C) and hydrogen (H), are then passed on to animals when they consume microbes, plants, and other organisms. The constituent elements are recycled when animals release wastes or when they die and decay. By contrast with energy, which enters, flows through, and leaves an ecosystem, most nutrients are recycled within the ecosystem.

To understand how ecosystems function, ecologists commonly start by examining feeding relationships: Who eats what? They gather this information in many ways, such as observing feeding behavior, studying the gut contents of animals, or using radioactive tracers to track substances as they pass from one organism to another. At its simplest, this information is summarized in a *food chain.*

A food chain is a flow chart with arrows pointing from the organism that is eaten to the organism that eats it. Plants are often the first step, or link, in the chain, because they make their own food and other creatures depend upon plants—directly or indirectly—for their food supplies. Because plants manufacture food, ecologists call them *producers.* In freshwater ecosystems, phytoplankton, attached algae, and aquatic flowering plants are producers.

Each link or level in a food chain is called a *trophic* (feeding) *level,* from the Greek *trophos,* meaning "nourishment." Producers form the first trophic level. Animals that eat producers form the second link in a food chain. Ecologists call them *primary consumers.* In a freshwater pond, snails are among the few animals that consume both filamentous algae and the leaves of large pond plants. Copepods, water fleas, and zebra mussels are among those animals that consume phytoplankton.

Larger animals, classified as *secondary consumers,* eat primary consumers. In ponds they include voracious dragonfly nymphs and carnivorous water beetles such as diving beetles (genus *Dytiscus*) and the water boatman (genus *Notonecta*).

At the fourth trophic level, larger predators eat secondary consumers; notable among these *tertiary consumers* are small- to medium-size fishes, such as sticklebacks (family Gasterosteidae) and perch (genus *Perca*). Top consumers—water birds such as herons (family Ardeidae) and larger fishes such as pike (genus *Esox*)—occupy the fifth and typically final trophic level of a temperate North American or European pond.

The number of trophic levels in a food chain is rarely greater than five. Only a small proportion of the energy at one trophic level is passed on to the next. Phytoplankton, filamentous algae, and flowering plants, for example, use up some of their food supply in respiration, and so this energy is unavailable to consumers. And not all the chemical components in an organism are readily digestible. Flowering plants, for example, typically contain supporting tissues that incorporate the chemical lignin as strengthening material. Lignin is relatively indigestible. Respiration and indigestibility apply to all trophic levels with the result that only about 10 percent of the energy in one trophic level is passed on to the next. This limits the number of trophic levels that an ecosystem can sustain.

Food chains are great simplifications of the real situation in nature. When drawing a food chain, an ecologist often uses a single species to represent many at each trophic level. At higher trophic levels, many species consume organisms from more than one of the lower levels. So, for example, a water bird such as a duck might eat tertiary, secondary, and primary consumers, and producers, such as filamentous algae and smaller macrophytes. Ducks are primary consumers as well as being secondary, tertiary, and top consumers.

To show feeding relationships more realistically, biologists draw complex flow charts called *food webs* that incorporate many food chains. Even these are a simplification. They show only a few dozen of the hundreds of species involved, and it is difficult to incorporate the dynamics of a living

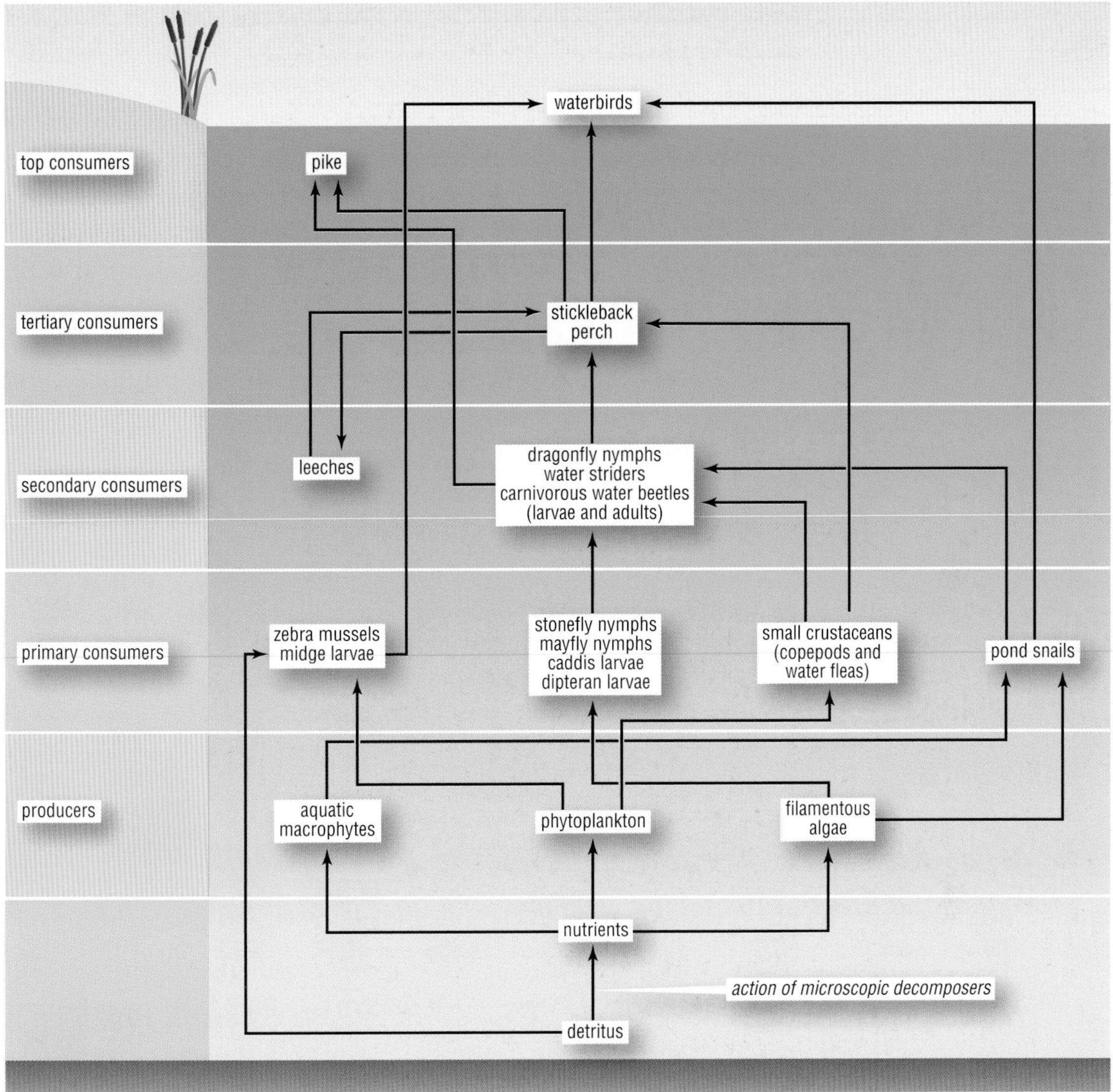


*Part of a generalized food web for a shallow, mild temperate, European pond*

ecosystem, with diets changing according to season of the year and age of the animal.

To quantify the flow of energy through an ecosystem, ecologists today often seek to estimate the energy flow (measured in kilojoules per square meter of water surface per year; kJ/sq m/year) through specific pathways in food webs or food chains. Gathering such data is time consuming and labor intensive but yields extremely useful information. Scientists use light meters to measure the amount of sunlight that plants are exposed to during the year. They take tissue samples from local plants and animals, dry them out, and burn them in sensitive devices called calorimeters that measure the amount of energy released. This gives the scientists values for the amount of chemical energy stored temporarily at different trophic levels. They note how the populations of plants and animals grow and decline with season, and from year to year. They also analyze the stomach contents of animals and trace how much dead material a weed bed produces each year, how much waste matter animals produce, and

## *Niches and competition*

A niche is an organism's functional role in the community. It encompasses where the organism chooses to live within a habitat, what it eats, how it deals with its enemies, and so on at all stages in its life cycle. As a general rule, two species cannot occupy exactly the same niche because one will be slightly better fitted to the niche—it can gain its food more effectively, defend its living space better, and so on—and will outcompete the other. However, differences between the niches occupied by different species can be quite subtle. And because environmental conditions change over short time scales, particularly in rivers, two species can appear to coexist in the same niche, when further study reveals that they do not. For example, net-spinning caddis fly larvae of the family Hydropsychidae gain their food by trapping plankton and debris in their miniature nets. In parts of the Usk River in Wales and the Lower Rhône in France, the two species *Hydropsyche siltalai* and *H. pellucidula* coexist. However, close study reveals that they occupy slightly different niches. *H. siltalai* favors faster-flowing water and more turbulent conditions than *H. pellucidula.* Both can coexist within a few inches of each other because obstacles in the river generate complex flow patterns. Rainfall can dramatically alter the river's flow, making both species shift position to avoid being swept away.

Studying the niches of organisms, not just what they eat but other aspects of their lifestyle, is not purely of academic interest. It provides scientists with more insight into how they can manage freshwater ecosystems, natural and artificial, so that disruption to biological communities is minimized. Or, if disturbance cannot be minimized, its likely impact can at least be better predicted and the environmental alteration steered in a planned direction (see, for example, "Managing freshwater fisheries," pages 225–229).

how decomposers process the dead or waste matter. In this way, scientists gradually piece together the patterns of energy flow through the ecosystem.

Such detailed analyses provide biologists with the data they need to manage ecosystems and to work out the impacts of environmental changes, both natural and human-induced. They can estimate the effect that removing a predator might have on the rest of the biological community or the impact of pollution that kills certain members of the community but not others (see sidebar).

## How freshwater communities function

The all-important feature that distinguishes a river system from a lake is the appreciable one-way flow of water under gravity across the landscape. In a given section of the river, the interaction between flowing water and the bottom (bed) and the sides (banks) generates a wide variety of habitats. At its simplest, a stretch of flowing water has three major zones: riffles (shallows), pools (deeps), and channel margins (sides). When the water level in a river is low and the stream is flowing comparatively slowly, riffles experience faster rates of water flow than pools and margins. The organisms living in riffles, or just downstream of them, are subjected to moderately fast water currents and turbulence that tend to dislodge them and push them downstream. On the other hand, these organisms benefit from plentiful fresh supplies of moving water, which bring nutrients and oxygen and flush away wastes. Organisms living in pools and at the river margins are less likely to be swept away, but they exist in less favorable conditions for the delivery of oxygen supplies and removal of wastes. The situation changes when the river is in flood and water levels are high. At such times, riffles, pools, and margins have much more similar stream velocities. This reveals an important feature of most rivers: stream conditions change at all time scales, from days to weeks, months, and more, and these changes alter the nature of river habitats and disrupt the communities of organisms that live in them.

Although ponds and smaller lakes can undergo dramatic seasonal alterations, even drying up entirely at certain times of the year, larger lakes tend to show less dramatic habitat alteration over short time scales than rivers do.

River and lake ecosystems are fueled by mineral elements, such as nitrogen (N) and phosphorus (P), which photosynthesizers absorb in dissolved inorganic form, such as nitrate ($NO_3^-$) and phosphate ($PO_4^{3-}$). Photosynthesizers incorporate the nitrogen and phosphorus into their cells in organic forms (combined with carbon and hydrogen). These organic forms then become available to other organisms when consumed. Nitrogen and phosphorus are components of vital biochemical compounds, such as proteins, nucleic acids, and other metabolically active substances such as coenzymes, which work with protein catalysts (enzymes) to speed up biochemical reactions.

However, many nutrients enter lakes and rivers not in an inorganic form but already in an organic form. They are byproducts from organisms that live on the water surface or on land adjacent to the river. These organic inputs include leaf litter, microbe-rich soil particles, and the dead remains and excreted wastes of plants and animals. When consumed or decomposed by organisms living in the river, the organic nutrients are eventually recycled and made available once more in inorganic forms, which plants can then absorb. In this way, nutrients are cycled.

In lakes and most ecosystems on land, nutrient cycling takes place within the same geographical area. In rivers, however, chemical elements are continually transported downstream, either dissolved in river water as sediment or detritus or incorporated within living organisms (such as phytoplankton and insect larvae). Nutrients, instead of cycling repeatedly in one locality, "spiral" downstream, shifting from dissolved inorganic forms to incorporated organic forms and back again. The loops of the spiral are closer together where nutrients are rapidly recycled in comparison to the rate at which they are carried downstream.

As already observed in chapter 2 (see "From source to sea," pages 47–48), the physical and chemical conditions in rivers change in a systematic manner from source to sink. These changes foster a corresponding shift in the nature of the biological community and its ecological processes.

In upper reaches of a river system (typically, stream orders 1–3), the stream tends to be shallow and narrow and the slope steep. Water flow is fast in relation to channel size, and sediment particles on the stream's bottom tend to be large, ranging from gravel through cobbles to boulders. The water tends to be cool and well oxygenated. Along with these physical and chemical features, vegetation growing on the riverbanks often plays a significant role by shading the water. This, coupled with the high rates of water flow, tends to severely limit the growth of phytoplankton, attached algae, and macrophytes in the upper reaches of a river. Rather than depending on live plants for their food, animals instead rely more on detritus as their primary source of energy. Leaf litter from trees, decomposed by bacteria and fungi in the river, often forms the main source of energy input under these circumstances. The activities of microscopic decomposers make the leaves more palatable to "shredders"—large-particle detritus feeders with powerful jaws, such as some caddis fly larvae (such as *Agarodes* and *Hydatophylax*) and some stonefly nymphs (including *Capnia* and *Nemoura*). Shredders convert the leaf litter into finer organic particles that are fed upon by "collectors"—fine-particle detritus feeders. Among these are filter feeders, such as some bivalve mollusks (the zebra mussel, *Dreissena,* is an example), or streambed gatherers, such as midge larvae (for instance, *Chironomus*), some mayfly nymphs (*Baetis, Ephemerella*), and some caddis fly larvae (*Lype*). Shredders and collectors are the dominant bottom feeders in most headwaters.

In the middle reaches of a river (typically, stream orders 4–6), flow rates tend to be moderate and there is comparatively less shading by bankside vegetation, so more sunlight is available to photosynthetic aquatic plants. As a result, living phytoplankton and attached algae become a significant source of energy input. Particle sizes in the sediment range from small to medium in the slower parts of the stream, and this provides the opportunity for larger plants to attach. Most submerged surfaces become covered in a biofilm rich in attached algae. Shredders (the large-particle detritus feeders) become a less significant part of the community than they were in the headwaters. Conversely, grazers—animals such as the North American caddis larva (*Leucotrichia*) and the

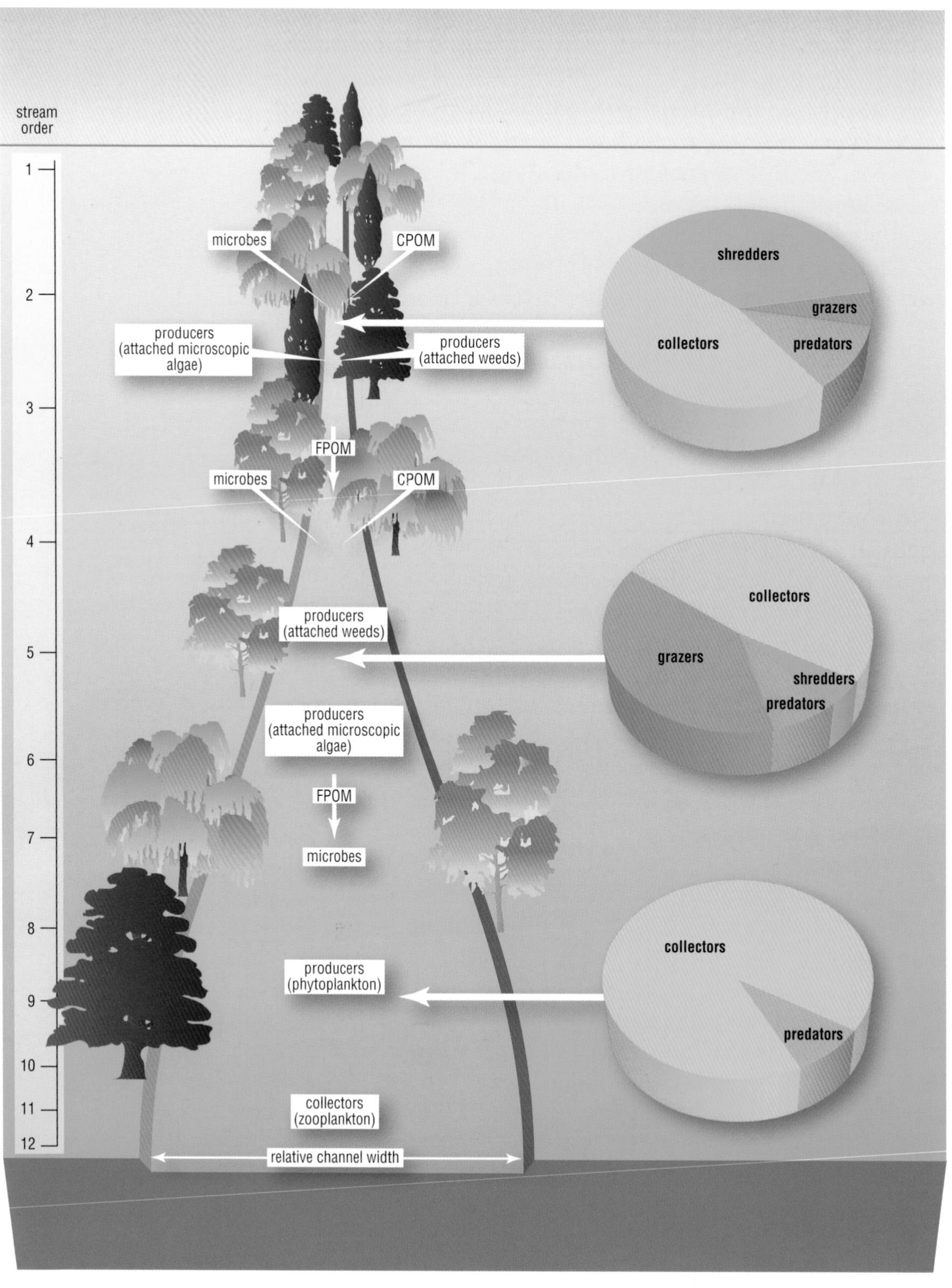
stream order
1
2
3
4
5
6
7
8
9
10
11
12
microbes
CPOM
producers (attached microscopic algae)
producers (attached weeds)
FPOM
microbes
CPOM
producers (attached weeds)
producers (attached microscopic algae)
FPOM
microbes
producers (phytoplankton)
collectors (zooplankton)
relative channel width
shredders
grazers
collectors
predators
collectors
grazers
shredders
predators
collectors
predators

freshwater snail (*Limnaea*)—become more important. Collectors remain abundant because fine particles of detritus accumulate in the slack water of middle reaches.

In the river's lower reaches (commonly, stream orders greater than six), detritus dominates as the source of energy input, as it did in the headwaters. The reason, however, is quite different. In the lower reaches, high levels of suspended sediment block the sunlight penetration needed to support photosynthesis by plankton and attached plants. In the lower reaches, the river system is benefiting from the input of detritus acquired from the upper and middle reaches. Collectors (the fine-particle detritus feeders) dominate the community of bottom animals, and shredders and grazers are less common.

Freshwater biologists have encapsulated this gradual shift in community structure and ecosystem processes, from source to sink, in a model called the *river continuum concept,* or RCC. It was first put forward by a group of North American scientists in 1980. RCC proposes that the nature of energy inputs changes from source to sink according to channel size, light penetration, degree of shading, and other physical factors, and that the nature of the dominant feeding groups (whether shredders, collectors, or grazers) reflects this.

The RCC enables biologists to make predictions. For example, if a dam is sited in the upper reaches of a river, it is likely to have little effect on the clarity of the already clear waters of the river. Shredders and collectors are still likely to dominate in the waters just downstream of the dam. However, a dam placed across the lower reaches of a turbid (cloudy) river would probably have a marked effect on water clarity. The dam would hold back sediment, making the water downstream likely to become clearer. Conditions downstream are

(opposite page) *This illustration summarizes key features of the river continuum concept. According to this model the nature of a river's biological community changes from source to sink because of the nature of energy inputs and changes in physical conditions. The pie charts show the relative abundance of animals with different kinds of feeding strategies. Grazers eat phytoplankton and attached algae. Shredders eat coarse particulate organic matter, while collectors consume fine particulate organic matter.*

thus liable to shift from those more associated with lower reaches to those linked with middle reaches. The increased sunlight penetration that results is likely to encourage the growth of biofilm and larger plants, and grazers are likely to become more common. Their existence in turn influences the nature of the rest of the invertebrate community, such as the types of predators. So this hypothetical dam might bring about middle-reach conditions, which are more likely to encourage a greater diversity of invertebrate organisms than upper-reach or lower-reach environments, assuming the dam provided sufficient water flow (see "Altering the flow," pages 190–193).

The river continuum concept is certainly a simplification, however. Many rivers do not entirely conform to the stereotypical RCC version of a river. For example, trees may not overhang the river in its upper reaches, in which case leaf fall may be of little significance as a source of energy. Natural discontinuities such as local changes in gradient and geology also interrupt the continuum. The overall RCC model is subject to many adjustments that must take into account the fact that rivers become disturbed by human activities such as local pollution, dam building, and changes to local land-use management, such as nearby deforestation. In any case, as already seen, a river system fluctuates markedly over even short periods of time due to changes in water flow, which can impose massive alterations in the physical conditions in different parts of the river system.

One example of how the river continuum concept has been modified and extended is in the application of the *flood pulse concept,* or FPC. North American freshwater biologists developed this model in the mid- to late 1980s to account for large tropical river systems, such as the Amazon of South America and the Niger of Africa, that were not well conceptualized by the RCC. The RCC, as originally conceived, viewed flood conditions as an exception to the normal functioning of a river. However, in many tropical river systems floods are predictable seasonal events. They have a major influence on the nature of the biological community and ecological processes in lower reaches of the river, and the FPC takes this into account.

In such rivers, inputs of nutrients arrive not only from upstream, runoff, or falling leaf litter, but also from the flooded land, which becomes a direct source of nutrients available to the river's inhabitants. Blooms of phytoplankton burst into life on the floodplains as nutrients in the soil are released into the floodwaters. In flood conditions, many of the river's larger inhabitants—notably fishes and other large vertebrates, such as crocodiles—migrate onto the floodplain and obtain their food there before returning to the main channel when the flood subsides. Flooded forest provides fruits and plant litter that fall into the water, along with insects and other land creatures. Many tropical fish species time their spawning to coincide with the flood season, and their young hatch on the slow-flowing waters of the inundated floodplain, gradually growing in size and following the retreating floodwaters to the main river channel. At the height of the flood, ponds, lakes, and creeks within the floodplain become inundated, and their inhabitants can disperse out into the river, while river inhabitants can enter stillwaters. The flood pulse concept is one of a number of modifications to the RCC that apply in specific situations.

## Drift and migration

Placed in the flow of a river at night, a small-meshed net is likely to catch a variety of invertebrates normally found clambering on the riverbed. These invertebrates are part of the "drift"—bottom-living species that are temporarily suspended in the water column and are being carried downstream with the current. They join the drift either as a behavioral tactic, to seek more favorable conditions, or when accidentally dislodged. Either cause is more likely to happen by night, because under cover of darkness bottom-living invertebrates are more active, seeking to move and find food at a time when their predators find it difficult to see potential prey. However, once small invertebrate animals join the drift they are at the mercy of water currents and have little control over how far they will be carried or where they will be deposited. Once animals have joined the drift, their likelihood of falling prey to predators—such as salmonid fish and net-spinning caddis fly larvae—is greatly increased.

Human-induced or natural changes to river systems can dramatically alter the proportion of bottom-living invertebrates that are dislodged and form part of the drift. In one experiment carried out in a New Hampshire stream, the investigators added specific amounts of acid to a stretch of river and noted the effect. The number of invertebrates that entered the drift and were caught in sampling nets massively increased over the few days following the application of the acid. Such experiments show that pollutants do not have to kill invertebrates outright to seriously alter the nature of a stream community. Simply changing the behavior of the animal, such as by causing it to dislodge itself in circumstances when it would not otherwise, can have long-term effects on the local community. In the New Hampshire study, acidification was continued for several months, and the number of bottom-living invertebrates per unit area (numbers per square foot or per square meter) dropped to about one-quarter of normal.

The small invertebrates living on a riverbed have adapted to the flow speeds normally encountered over many years. Large-scale floods that happen only once in 50 or 100 years (see "Floods," pages 55–56) can take a massive toll on bottom-living invertebrates by dislodging them and reshaping the river channel. In one study of the Glenfinnish River in Ireland during the 1980s, a massive flood in 1986 caused the density of large bottom-living invertebrates to crash by more than 90 percent, and by 1989 densities had returned to only about 25 percent of the original. This was a natural event, but human activities, such as stripping trees from the vicinity of a river, could massively increase runoff and produce a similar effect by accident.

Some fish species, such as salmon and freshwater eels, migrate between rivers and the sea. Many more species migrate up and down river systems but do not enter brackish water or seawater. Migrations can have a profound effect on the ecology of a river system. Spawning salmon, for example, provide a massive injection of nutrients into headwaters. Salmon mature in the sea but spawn in the headwater streams where they themselves hatched as fry many years before. In North America, returning Pacific salmon spawn in the headwaters of rivers from Alaska to California. The adults die after spawning, and their decaying bodies represent a massive transfer of energy and nutrients from the Pacific Ocean (where the fish grew to maturity) into the upper reaches of rivers. This transfer upstream is in the reverse direction to that normally associated with rivers—where nutrients travel downstream.

## Predation

In field studies of lakes and rivers, predation—animals consuming other live animals—has emerged as a major factor determining the structure of a biological community. Fish have always received a lot of attention from freshwater scientists, in part because of commercial interest in sportfishing and because some species have high food value. Additionally, fish are large and obvious members of the freshwater community. The findings of research on fish as predators is quite extensive compared to that on invertebrate members of freshwater communities. The findings from fish studies hint at the complexity of interactions likely to be found at lower trophic levels in food webs should they be studied as extensively.

The responses of prey species to predation are not straightforward. Prey species often respond to intense predation pressure by evolving morphological (to do with body form or structure), life cycle, or behavioral responses that reduce their likelihood of being consumed. At the margins of lakes, grazing zooplankton have evolved to hide in dense weed beds during the day and emerge at night to graze, when predators cannot rely on eyesight to find their zooplankton prey. However, zooplankton that live in the open water do not have the same opportunity to hide.

Cladocerans, such as the water flea *Daphnia,* are often major members of the grazing zooplankton community in the open waters of temperate lakes. Field studies and laboratory experiments reveal that young *Daphnia* adopt a different body shape, depending on whether they are being heavily

## *The trophic cascade*

When the abundance of one organism clearly affects the success of other organisms at more than one other trophic level, the effect is called a *trophic cascade.* It is so called because the impact of the feeding behavior of one species in the local community is "cascading" through the food web. In the open water of ponds and small lakes, three-level food chains are quite common. Small fish (as secondary consumers) eat zooplankton, and zooplankton (as primary consumers) graze upon phytoplankton (producers). The small fish check the growth of the zooplankton population, which in turn means that, if nutrient availability, light penetration, and temperature are favorable for photosynthesis, phytoplankton can grow abundantly without being overgrazed.

Theoretically, if larger predatory fish were introduced into the lake, this would have a domino effect through the existing food web. The larger fish would occupy a fourth trophic level (tertiary consumers). In consuming smaller fish, larger fish would have the effect of reducing the check on the zooplankton population. The zooplankton population would increase and therefore graze the phytoplankton population more heavily. Other factors aside, in this situation a four-level food chain would support a smaller phytoplankton population than a three-level chain.

predated by midge larvae (genus *Chaoborus*) or not. In a population under heavy predation, young *Daphnia* develop an elongated spine on their "tail" and a sharp "tooth" at the back of the head—deterrent features that make predation by *Chaoborus* less likely. These features develop in response to chemicals released by the predators. In the absence of *Chaoborus,* young *Daphnia* do not develop the spine and tooth, because to do so is expensive in terms of energy consumption and reduces growth rate.

Cladocerans have a range of predators, including small to medium-size fish as well as predatory invertebrates such as midge larvae. Fish tend to prefer large *Daphnia,* while invertebrates tend to consume *Daphnia* at smaller sizes. Selection pressure on the growth of *Daphnia* therefore varies depending on whether fish or invertebrates are their main predators in a given situation. In the absence of fish, medium-size *Daphnia* are at high risk of predation and selection pressure encourages *Daphnia* to reach a large size as soon as possible. In the presence of fish, there is an advantage to *Daphnia* remaining small and so avoiding the attentions of fish. Under these conditions, *Daphnia* tend to mature and reproduce at smaller sizes.

Just as zooplankton in lake margins have evolved behavioral strategies to avoid predation, so, too, have open-water species. Most fish hunt zooplankton by sight and do so in the upper levels of the water column during the day. Some zooplankton species avoid their fish predators by migrating vertically in the water column, descending to deeper, darker waters during the day and rising to near the surface at night to feed. In Babine Lake, British Columbia, the copepod crustacean *Heterocope* rises to near the surface at night to feed on smaller zooplankton, while at the same time avoiding the attentions of predatory sockeye salmon. At the same time the cladoceran, *Bosmina,* a favorite prey of *Heterocope,* descends at night and rises near the surface during the day to avoid *Heterocope. Bosmina* are too small to interest sockeye salmon as food.

Manipulation of food webs, by stocking lakes with larger predatory fish, is currently being considered by environmental managers as a means of controlling unwanted algal blooms (see "Restoring overenriched lakes," pages 221–223). However, stocking lakes and rivers with novel predators can have unintended effects. The impact is likely to be most detrimental where the introduced predators are "exotic"—that is, they are not native to the region and so have not coevolved with potential prey species they are encountering for the first time (see sidebar "Coevolution," page 144).

Classic studies on the effect of introducing an exotic fish species into streams (see the sidebars "Trophic cascade" and "Coevolution") took place in the 1980s and 1990s in New Zealand. Galaxiids are small troutlike fish native to streams in southern South America, New Zealand, and Australia. The abundance of these fish in Australia and New Zealand has declined dramatically since the 19th century, following the widespread colonization of the territories by Europeans. Two factors were blamed for the galaxiid decline. One was change in freshwater habitats due to altered land use, such as removing native bush and tussock grasslands and replacing them with conifer forest or sheep pasture. The other factor was the introduction of European and North American trout; trout were not native to Australasia. But which of these two factors—changing land use or trout introductions—was most likely responsible for the decline? Or were both factors responsible and, if so, which was more important? New Zealand researchers undertook a series of elegant investigations to find the answer.

Their studies began with plotting the distribution of the common river galaxias (*Galaxias vulgaris* and related species) and the brown trout (*Salmo trutta*) in relation to land use. It might be expected that galaxiids would thrive better in streams passing through native landscapes containing indigenous vegetation, while brown trout would do better in the freshwaters of landscapes that had been altered. No such link was revealed. However, the study results clearly showed that galaxias and trout were hardly ever found in the same place. A stretch of stream containing a wide variety of habi-

## Coevolution

Where organisms have had a long history of coexistence stretching back many thousands or millions of years, many have coevolved. Coevolution is the process by which two or more distantly related species that interact closely evolve in tandem. Classic examples occur among predators and their prey. If there is selective pressure on predators to become better swimmers with faster reactions to successfully intercept their prey, the prey have to respond accordingly with appropriate strategies to avoid or outswim their predators; otherwise they will be hunted to extinction. Predator and prey become locked in an evolutionary "arms race." As the predator evolves more effective hunting strategies, so the prey evolves more successful defensive strategies.

In situations where predator and prey are brought together for the first time, without a long history of coevolution, prey have not yet evolved suitable defensive strategies to outwit the novel predator. There is a high likelihood, in the short term, that the prey can be hunted to extinction locally. This is what happened when trout and galaxiids were brought together in the streams of New Zealand.

tats, including pools and riffles, would contain either trout or galaxias, but hardly ever both.

Further study revealed that galaxias tend to be found upstream of trout and often separated from them by waterfalls at least 10 feet (3 m) tall. Three obvious explanations for this distribution spring to mind. According to the first, galaxias might prefer shallow, upstream sections of rivers while trout favor deeper, downstream sections; these differences could be due to feeding or breeding preferences. Alternatively, one species may be excluding the other through competition for resources; they might both have similar food preferences. Finally, one species could be eating the other.

The accumulating evidence points to trout eating galaxias, and it is this predatory interaction that has reduced the distribution of galaxias. The distribution of trout in New Zealand has increased since the 19th century, while that of galaxias has decreased, and in many cases galaxias no longer live in downstream, deepwater sections of the river where they did before. They survive in upstream reaches because trout cannot leap high waterfalls to reach them. Later studies from Australia also showed trout eliminating galaxias from localities after trout were introduced. In the original New Zealand study, trout and galaxias only coexisted in a few places where the stream was shallow and braided, and there was plenty of stream cover in which galaxias could hide from the trout.

So trout are eliminating the galaxias in many situations, but does this affect the rest of the local freshwater community? To find out, the New Zealand group continued their research by setting up a dozen artificial stream channels in an otherwise natural stream. These channels contained mesh to constrain the fish, but smaller invertebrates could move freely into and out of the channels. In four channels they placed galaxias, in four they placed juvenile trout, and four contained no fish. After 10 or 11 days they collected all the larger bottom-living invertebrates in each channel and scraped a sample of algae from cobbles in each. Their results showed that the highest numbers of invertebrates were in the "no fish" channels, slightly fewer in the galaxias channels, and considerably fewer in the channels containing trout. The best explanation was that trout were consuming the most invertebrates and galaxias substantially fewer. Along with these differences in invertebrate numbers went changes in the standing crop (the living biomass) of algae. Standing crop is estimated from the amount of chlorophyll, the alga's photosynthetic pigment, in a sample scraped from a given area of rock. The trout channels contained the most algae and the "no fish" channel the least. Such results can be explained in terms of the number of grazers left to consume the algae. Trout channels contain fewer grazers than the other channels because trout have eaten a larger proportion of them, so algae have had greater opportunity to grow without being cropped. Later studies compared the density of algal biofilm in trout streams with that in galaxiid streams. These studies confirmed the earlier experimental results, showing more algae in trout streams than in galaxiid streams.

These experiments explored fairly simple interactions in comparatively small streams. Many river systems have much more complex food webs than those explored in these studies, and the complexity of species interactions is correspondingly greater. Studies on these more complex systems produce less clear-cut results because so many factors need to be taken into account. Even so, the findings from simpler studies suggest that influencing the abundance of a single key species is likely to have repercussions that can resonate through a river's food web in complex ways, resulting in many adjustments in the abundance of various species at more than one trophic level.

## Wetlands

A wetland is an area of land with surface soil that is covered in water for at least part of the year. There are many kinds of wetlands—both freshwater and saltwater—but they all share in common certain ecological similarities because of the high water table and the water-saturated soil at or near the surface.

Wetlands are not a main focus of this book. They are considered in another volume in the series, but their relevance to lakes and rivers cannot be ignored, because some forms of wetlands are intimately connected with the open water of lakes and rivers and they strongly influence each other.

Among the various kinds of freshwater wetlands, marginal wetlands are of particular relevance because they border rivers and lakes. They fall into two main types: Fringe wetlands and

*A marginal wetland dominated by reeds, sedges, and cattails in the Okavango Delta, Botswana, Africa. This delta is unusual, as it is an inland one, forming where the Okavango River empties into a low-lying region.* (Frans Lanting/ Minden Pictures)

flood wetlands. Fringe wetlands have a more or less continuous connection with open water and are typically found at the edges of lakes and slow-flowing rivers. They are rich in emergent vegetation such as reeds and cattails. Flood wetlands, on the other hand, are not directly connected to open water, except at times of high water. Unless fed by groundwater sources, when not flooded such wetlands gradually lose their water through drainage or evaporation. In temperate climates of Europe, trees such as alder, ash, poplar, oak, sallow, and willow grow on such floodplains.

Freshwater marginal wetlands perform a number of useful functions for adjacent lakes and rivers. These functions can be broadly categorized into three groups: hydrologic functions concerned with the movement of water, maintenance and improvement of water quality, and the provision of wildlife habitats.

Marginal wetlands perform several hydrologic functions. They intercept and store water that runs off the land and, acting in the reverse direction, they "soak up" floodwaters from adjacent lakes and rivers. In this way they moderate the rise and fall of water levels in adjacent water bodies. Without marginal wetlands, the water levels in many lakes and rivers would rise and fall even more than they do at present. Wetlands also reduce erosion of riverbanks by water flow and that of lake margins by waves. Additionally, wetlands contribute to the collection and gradual release of groundwater. These hydrologic functions of marginal wetlands benefit humans and wildlife alike. They reduce flood damage, minimize erosion, maintain groundwater aquifers, and can help sustain water input into lakes and rivers during the dry season.

But wetlands not only store water; they also clean it. Wetlands act as a "sink" for inorganic and organic nutrients and toxic (poisonous) materials—a place where these substances are stored or degraded. Various physical, chemical, and biological processes remove potentially harmful materials from the water column and immobilize them, storing them or transforming them into nontoxic substances. Toxic ammonium ions and the nutrients nitrate and phosphate are examples of potential pollutants that these wetlands processes affect.

The gas ammonia ($NH_3$), which dissolves in water to form ammonium ions ($NH_4^+$), is a common waste product of animals, including fish, and is a product of decomposition in oxygen-poor conditions. In high concentrations, it is toxic to most life-forms. In aquariums, the buildup of ammonia is a common cause of fish fatalities in poorly managed systems.

Although the soil in wetlands is often oxygen-poor because of high rates of decomposition and the presence of stagnant water, oxygen is transported through the stem to the roots of emergent plants such as reeds (genus *Phragmites*) and cattails (genus *Typha*). From there, oxygen diffuses into the surrounding soil and encourages nitrifying bacteria to convert ammonium ions to nitrates. Nitrates—also associated with water that is eutrophic (nutrient-rich)—are, in turn, broken down into nitrogen gas by denitrifying bacteria. Thus wetland functions break down both toxic ammonia and excess nitrate into harmless nitrogen, which escapes into the atmosphere.

Phosphate, another nutrient commonly associated with eutrophic conditions and pollution from agricultural fertilizers, is absorbed by wetland microbes or is retained in the sediment. The tangle of plant roots acts as both a net, trapping suspended sediment, and as a latticework with an enormous surface area for the attachment of microbes. The activities of reeds and their associated microbes are a potent force in purifying water. Studies of the Rhine River floodplain in eastern France in the late 1980s demonstrated that heavily polluted river water shed its excess nitrates and phosphates as it passed through reedbeds and became groundwater. The groundwater was significantly less polluted than the river water that fed it. This effect also works in reverse, in that polluted runoff or groundwater can be cleansed by reedbeds before the water enters a river. Wetlands that contain extensive reedbeds are, in effect, natural water treatment works. So effective are mixed reedbeds at cleansing water that artificial reedbeds are now constructed by some building developers in Europe and North America to clean the wastewater of small housing settlements.

Lastly, wetlands provide feeding and breeding areas for a wide variety of wildlife. Many wetlands are inaccessible to larger land animals, which would flounder in the shallow water and waterlogged soil beneath. In many cases, wetlands also provide only limited access to larger fish; many of the shallower and more densely weeded areas are inaccessible to them. Wetlands can therefore provide a relatively safe haven from predators for nesting waterfowl and for young fish. For example, the papyrus beds at the edges of Lake Victoria in Africa provide a refuge for some fish species from the ravages of an introduced predator, the Nile perch (*Lates niloticus*). (See "Alien invasions," pages 199–205.) At the same time, the wetlands are also highly productive, providing an abundance of plant material at the base of food chains. In Africa, more than one-third of the continent's freshwater fish catch comes from floodplains and fringe wetlands.

Wetlands that border lakes and rivers provide many important resources for people. They also strongly influence people's access to open water, encouraging it in some instances and preventing it in others, with important consequences for both people and these wetland environments. Highlights of the historical connection between lakes, rivers, and people are considered in the next chapter.

# CHAPTER 6

# RIVERS AND LAKES IN HISTORY

The birth and growth of many major civilizations have depended upon the existence of major rivers, and many major cities rely on them to this day. Rivers provide supplies of freshwater for drinking and irrigation and then carry away wastes. Rivers have always provided routes to explore the interiors of continents, and later, served as avenues for the flow of commerce. Freshwater is vital as a raw material, a coolant, and a waste remover for industry. It also holds biological riches in the form of food fish, and its movement can be harnessed to produce hydroelectricity—electricity generated by moving water. (The benefits of lakes and rivers as freshwater ecosystems are considered in further detail in chapter 7.)

While irrigation projects, concrete riverbanks, and power-generating dams are among the most dramatic signs of human influence on freshwater systems, there is probably no river or lake of appreciable size on Earth's surface that has not been affected by the activities of humans. Even small rivers and pools in remote regions have doubtless been affected by humankind's influence on global climate (see "Climate change," pages 196–199). These freshwater systems also contain detectable traces of atmospheric pollutants released by human activities taking place thousands of miles away (see "Acid waters," pages 210–212). However, most rivers and lakes have been affected much more dramatically by human intervention.

Many of the challenges that beset today's rivers have a long history. On the other hand, many of today's rivers are rather different in their physical, chemical, and biological characteristics from those that existed only 200 years ago. Three of the most studied rivers in the world—the Nile in Africa, the Thames in Europe, and the Colorado in North

America—illustrate some of these differences, and the human-induced changes to each are described in detail later in this chapter. While these three examples are not necessarily representative of the vast diversity of river systems across the world, between them they illustrate many of the ways human activities have affected river systems, and the complexity of these interactions.

Clearly people have great impact on lakes and rivers. But lakes and rivers likewise influence people. Most notably they affect human health, particularly the spread of disease, and this has had important historic and present-day consequences.

## Rivers, lakes, and human health

According to recent estimates made by the World Health Organization (WHO), the United Nations agency with responsibility for promoting health and medicine, perhaps three-quarters of all illnesses in developing countries are water-related. Amebic and bacterial dysentery, cholera, and typhoid fever are transmitted from person to person by microorganisms living in water. People become infected by ingesting contaminated food or water. Such diseases cause potentially life-threatening diarrhea and vomiting, conditions that affect some 4 million people each year in developing countries and contribute to the deaths of more than 1 million of them, especially children. These conditions dehydrate and malnourish the individual, weakening them and making them more likely to succumb to other medical complaints.

(opposite page) *Mosquito larvae in the water-filled bract of a Heliconia plant* (Heliconia wageriana). *Notice the larvae's breathing tubes that puncture the water surface to obtain air. Adult female mosquitoes of the genera* Aedes *and* Anopheles *can transmit the human diseases yellow fever and malaria respectively. Public health personnel may drain standing waters or spray still waters with oil in efforts to prevent mosquito larvae from hatching into the adults that can spread these diseases.* (Michael & Patricia Fogden/Minden Pictures)

Other human diseases are transmitted by larger organisms that spend part or all of their lives in freshwater. The two most prevalent of these diseases are malaria and schistosomiasis. Malaria is the disease condition caused by the protozoan parasite *Plasmodium,* which enters the human body when an infected female of some species of *Anopheles* mosquito bites a person. Mosquitoes lay eggs that hatch into larvae in standing water—puddles, ponds, lakes, canals, slow-moving stretches of river, and the like. Malaria is most prevalent in tropical and subtropical regions wherever there are suitable conditions for the host mosquitoes to breed and plenty of human victims to bite.

The malarial parasite has a complex life cycle, much of it taking place inside the human body, where the parasite enters the red blood cells of its host, multiplies, and then ruptures the cells. The cell damage generates periodic bouts of high fever and violent chills in the sufferer. An infected

## *The arrival of two water-related diseases in the Americas*

*Anopheles* and *Aedes* mosquitoes, transmitters of malaria and yellow fever, respectively, arrived in the Americas in the 17th century C.E., carried on slave ships from Africa. The mosquitoes introduced the diseases first to the Caribbean region, then to mainland Central and South America, and finally to North America. Such was the spread of these diseases that during the 1880s the construction of the Panama Canal ground to a halt because more than 5,000 workmen died of either yellow fever or malaria.

individual loses, on average, 10 working days for each bout of fever, and without successful malarial treatment, the fever may return regularly for the rest of the person's life. Malaria affects some 300 million people worldwide of which more than 1 million die each year from the disease. In 2001, the WHO estimated 1.1 million human deaths from malaria, with more than 85 percent occurring in Africa. And malaria is not the only fatal mosquito-borne human disease (see sidebar)

The disease schistosomiasis, or bilharzia, is caused by the parasitic blood fluke *Schistosoma,* a type of flatworm. Its larvae enter people who come into contact with contaminated water. *Schistosoma* larvae emerge from infected freshwater snails and bore through a person's skin or gut lining. Then they migrate through blood vessels, where they develop into adult flatworms and release eggs that travel to the bladder or intestines. Eggs released into the person's urine or feces (solid waste) can complete the life cycle if they are unharmed and come into contact with freshwater containing suitable host snails. Bilharzia is therefore most prevalent in places where there is poor sanitation and infected feces or urine enters freshwater. The eggs hatch into larvae that enter host snails, thus completing the life cycle.

Schistosomiasis is most debilitating to those people who are regularly reinfected by contact with water containing *Schistosoma* larvae. Their bodies' immune reactions to the parasite's eggs, which can become lodged in various parts of the body, produce inflammation and scar tissue that can damage the brain, liver, and lungs as well as the bladder or intestines. Schistosomiasis can cause mental and physical disability, making the person no longer a productive worker and shortening his or her life. More than 200 million people worldwide have the disease.

Malaria and schistosomiasis place a massive financial burden on affected communities. Worst off are the poorest communities that are least able to gain access to medical care for treatment. Malaria alone has profoundly shaped human history, influencing the places where humans have been able to settle and thrive.

The malarial parasite and the nature of its transmitting host or vector, the *Anopheles* mosquito, were not identified until the 19th century C.E. Despite this, malaria has long been associated with swamps and stagnant water, hence its name, which comes from the Italian *mal aria,* meaning "bad air." The Roman scholar Marcus Terentius Varro (116–27 B.C.E.) warned against settling in swampy areas where mosquitoes thrived. In warm regions of the Americas, Africa, and Eurasia, wherever there is uncovered standing water, mosquitoes flourish and the possibility that malaria or other mosquito-transmitted diseases will gain hold is increased. Some scholars of ancient history consider malaria a major contributing factor in the loss of vitality of classical Rome. As late as the early 20th century, malaria remained prevalent in some marshes lying within 100 miles (160 km) of Rome.

Malaria control campaigns have proved highly successful in North America and Europe, where malaria-transmitting *Anopheles* mosquitoes tend to be at the northern edge of their range and where there are considerable financial resources to combat malaria. By the 1920s malaria had been eliminated from almost all North American towns by a combination of control methods: Mosquito-control personnel used copper sulfate or copper arsenic to kill mosquito larvae in ponds and spread kerosene on the water surface to prevent mosquito pupae from hatching. People living nearby installed window screens and slept under nets to keep mosquitoes away from them at night. Similar methods brought malaria under control in southern Italy by the early 1940s. In 1947 the U.S. National Malaria Eradication Program began spraying the insecticide DDT in households to kill mosquitoes, and by 1951 the federal government declared malaria eradicated in the United States.

Malaria has proved intractable in many developing countries, however. In the early 1960s the World Health Organization (WHO) sought to eradicate malaria from many tropical countries by spraying DDT into dwellings and onto the surface of all standing waters in many malaria-infected regions (but not in much of sub-Saharan Africa, where malaria is most prevalent today). The WHO campaign coupled this approach with treating people with antimalarial drugs such as quinine to kill the parasite within their bodies. The plan failed, in part because not all malarial waters could be located and, in any case, the mosquitoes gradually became resistant to the insecticide. Today some strains of the *Plasmodium* parasite itself are resistant to antimalarial drugs.

Campaigns to reduce the incidence of schistosomiasis using molluscicides, to kill the snail vectors, like campaigns that used insecticides to control malaria-carrying mosquitoes, have also had only limited success in developing countries. The disease can be effectively treated with oral

## Dam-building and disease

Dams built to raise local living standards can also unintentionally encourage the spread of bilharzia and malaria. For instance, the construction of the Aswān High Dam in the early 1960s has reduced water flow rates both above and below the dam. This has massively increased the acreage of Nile water where conditions are suitable for bilharzia larvae and their snail hosts to survive. In northern Senegal the Diama Dam was completed in 1986. By 1994 a large proportion of the local population had succumbed to bilharzia in what was previously a bilharzia-free area. Small dams built in Ethiopia since about 1975 have subsequently led to a several-fold increase in the incidence of malaria among local people. Water management schemes aimed at improving quality of life can have unexpected consequences in terms of public health.

medication, but people at risk need improved sanitation and access to clean water to avoid becoming reinfected. Educating local people about safe hygiene is a vital component of any successful schistosomiasis control campaign.

Developments such as dams, built to provide hydroelectric power, prevent floods, and control irrigation, can unfortunately increase the incidence of malaria and bilharzia locally if they are planned and operated without sufficient regard to potential health hazards (see sidebar).

## The historic Nile

The Nile River has arguably played as great a role in the early development of human civilization as any other river. Menes, the first pharaoh or ancient king of Egypt, reputedly funded the damming of the Nile River to provide land on which to build the ancient city of Memphis, Egypt, in about 3100 B.C.E. Since then, many successors have sought ways to tame the river and harness its annual flood to irrigate the land (see "The Nile River," pages 72–75).

For some 6,000 years, until the 19th century C.E., systems of embankments and gravity-fed canals were the main form of irrigation and water resource management on Egypt's Nile floodplain. Floodwaters were directed into flood basins that were inundated to a depth of about six feet (1.8 m) at the peak of the annual flood in August and September. The floodwaters left behind a layer of nutrient-rich silt that fertilized the sandy soils, making the land highly productive. Cotton and various cereal grains have been harvested at high yields from the Nile floodplain and delta for more than 5,000 years.

Throughout this great expanse of history, the Nile was a major thoroughfare between what is now Sudan to the south and the Mediterranean Sea to the north. Boats are recorded in Egyptian friezes dating back to before 3500 B.C.E., and in about 2330 B.C.E., local people cut a channel through the first Nile cataract, near present-day Aswān, to allow boats to pass through safely. At about the same time, slipways were constructed to allow boats to be dragged around the obstacle of the second cataract farther south. Within the past 5,000 years, climate change has brought drier conditions to the

Nile floodplain, and engineers constructed more sophisticated systems of embankments and canals to harness the smaller and more erratic annual flood. Forests alongside the Nile succumbed to drought or were felled and did not regrow because people used the land to grow crops.

Human activity over thousands of years has undoubtedly caused great alterations to the Nile River's biological community, but these changes are difficult to trace. Changes in the distribution of large vertebrates offer some clues. The African elephant (*Loxodonta africana*) disappeared from Egypt sometime in the third millennium B.C.E., hastened by the disappearance of the Nile floodplain forests. The Nile crocodile (*Crocodylus niloticus*) was still abundant at this time, but today it has almost entirely disappeared from Egypt. Human hunting of the animal for both its skin and meat and to remove it as a dangerous competitor, has reduced its numbers to the extent that breeding populations in Egypt are no longer viable. In the 20th century the Nile crocodiles in Sudan were systematically hunted to virtual extinction to make the waters safe for bathing. Crocodiles select larger fish as food. In the absence of crocodiles, the Nile's population of predatory fish has probably increased, with domino effects for other fish in the food chain (see "Predation," pages 141–146).

The human impact on the Nile has increased massively within the past 200 years. By the 1840s, with the human population expanding rapidly in Egypt's capital city, Cairo, and in the delta to the north, planners sought ways to better utilize the Nile's water for agriculture. Their approach was to "smooth out" the water supply during the year, between the excess in late summer and fall and the drought during the rest of the year. Water managers constructed small dams in the delta region and along the Lower Nile to control flooding and to store water from the months of excess for use in the months of scarcity.

The Nile River and its major tributaries flow through 10 countries—Egypt, Sudan, Ethiopia, Uganda, Democratic Republic of the Congo (DRC), Tanzania, Kenya, Rwanda, Burundi, and Eritrea—many of which are water-starved. Each country draws water from the Nile or its tributaries and discharges wastewater back into them. Egypt and Sudan are the two largest users of Nile water, and they lie downstream of all the others. Thus the quality and abundance of the Nile water they receive is affected by the activities of the countries upstream. By the early 1900s it was clear that effective utilization of Nile waters would require agreement between the countries along the Nile. In 1929 Egypt and Sudan (both then under British colonial rule) signed an agreement for their use of Nile waters. The pact effectively vetoed countries nearer the headwaters using Nile water in amounts that might threaten Egypt and Sudan's water supplies.

In 1902 the first Aswān Dam was completed on the Nile's lowest cataract. It stored water for controlled release throughout the year for irrigation purposes. Additional construction raised the dam's height in 1912 and 1934, and much of its function was replaced in the 1960s by the Aswān High Dam. Of all human interventions, the Aswān High Dam has had the greatest environmental impact on the Nile River.

The Aswān High Dam was designed to expand on the irrigation, flood control, and hydroelectric functions of the earlier Aswān Dam. Work began in 1960, the dam was finished in 1969, and its hydroelectric functions became fully operational in 1971. The dam is 364 feet (111 m) high and nearly 2.5 miles (4 km) wide, and it holds back a huge reservoir, Lake Nasser, which extends up to 298 miles (480 km) upstream and into Sudan.

The Aswān High Dam has brought undoubted benefits to Egypt. The country largely recouped the dam's building costs within two years of operation, through increased agricultural production and new hydroelectric power generation. The dam smooths out highs and lows in water supply, ensuring that land downstream does not flood excessively in wet years or become parched in dry ones. The years 1972 and 1973 were dry years, with reduced river flows arriving in Sudan and Egypt. Egyptian rice and cotton were grown successfully in these dry years and in those that have occurred since. Before the construction of the dam, dry years had a devastating effect on crop production.

Since the construction of the dam, land bordering more than 500 miles (800 km) of the river's length has been converted from an annual one-crop system to a three-crop rotation, with irrigation water supplied year-round. Also, an additional 1,545 square miles (4,000 sq km) has been brought under cultivation. More than 50 percent of the dam's financial benefit comes from increased agricultural production. The hydropower from the Aswān High Dam provides more than half of Egypt's electrical power and nearly 40 percent of the dam's financial return.

The benefits of the Aswān High Dam, however, have been offset by a wide range of problems, with some revealing themselves only decades after construction. About 100,000 Nubians, a group of local people in Egypt and Sudan, had to move away from their drowned villages when Lake Nasser began to fill. Although government authorities planned for this displacement and provided newly built villages, this caused great disruption to the local people's traditional way of life. Many chose to stay close to Lake Nasser and suffer hardship rather than move to distant newly created villages.

Another problem is that water losses by evaporation and seepage from Lake Nasser, and from irrigation systems downstream, are much greater than anticipated. Because of high rates of evaporation, the water passing through the dam and then later, irrigating the fields, is saltier than typical freshwater (when water evaporates its salt load is left behind). Before the dam was constructed, floods flushed salts out of the irrigated soil, but this no longer occurs, and in some areas crop yields are declining due to salt stress.

The water held back by the dam has also caused unexpected problems. When Lake Nasser was at its highest level in the early 1980s (levels have since declined), its water reached geologically unstable rock, which shifted slightly under the high water pressure. This caused, in November 1981, an earthquake classed as strong (5.3 on the Richter scale), followed by a series of smaller quakes. Lake Nasser levels are now kept lower than originally planned to prevent such seismic events from recurring.

In addition, the Aswān High Dam holds back astonishingly large volumes of sediment—an estimated 110 million U.S. tons (100 million metric tons) a year—that would otherwise flow down to the Lower Nile. These sediments are gradually filling Lake Nasser, reducing its water-storage capacity. At the same time, the drastically reduced levels of sediment being deposited downstream of the dam are having a major impact on the Nile Delta. Starved of its regular supplies of Nile silt, the delta is gradually eroding. This is having significant economic impact. The encroaching sea is threatening agriculture and tourism in some parts of the delta. Egypt's government is considering building sea barriers to address the problem, but these will prove very costly and may not prevent saltwater intrusion from spoiling some currently productive agricultural lands.

Lake Nasser is retaining nutrients as well as sediment, and this is curbing the productivity of not only the agricultural land on the Nile River's former floodplain but also the waters of the southeastern Mediterranean Sea, into which the Nile discharges. Without its annual soaking in nutrient-rich floodwater, Egypt's agricultural land maintains its productivity by the application of costly commercial fertilizers. The decline in nutrients discharged into the Mediterranean Sea has had a marked effect on local marine fisheries. Within a few years of the dam's construction, sardine catches in the vicinity of the Nile delta had fallen by some 95 percent. Egypt's mackerel, shrimp, and lobster fisheries suffered as well, with a loss of some 3,000 fishing-related jobs in all. Mediterranean catches did increase in the 1990s, perhaps due to increased inputs of nutrients from open drains carrying sewage and agricultural runoff. But neither this nor the small fishing industry created in Lake Nasser has compensated for the overall losses.

Finally, the dam has had health implications for the Nile Valley. The incidence of waterborne diseases has increased both downstream and upstream of Lake Nasser. In particular, bilharzia (schistosomiasis) has become more widespread because of the much higher acreage of standing water where parasite-harboring freshwater snails can survive.

When such long-term negative impacts are accounted for, the benefits of such a large dam become much less clear. The lessons learned from the Aswān High Dam have informed current international policies on dam-building, which now tend to favor constructing many smaller dams rather than a few large ones.

In comparison to dam-building, freshwater pollution is a more recent threat to the Nile River, but an escalating one. Until the late 20th century, the Nile was relatively unpolluted, except for human sewage. With rising population levels in Cairo and in other major settlements on and near the river's former floodplain, levels of sewage input are rising substantially. The Nile is also receiving large inputs of pesticides and herbicides in the water running off agricultural land. As industrialization advances, a mix of heavy metals and potentially harmful synthetic organic substances is likely to add to the cocktail of substances entering the Lower Nile (see "Freshwater pollution," pages 205–207).

The Nile continues to supply Egypt with about 95 percent of its water resources. Egypt's agreement with Sudan over allocation of water, which has held since 1929 and was reinforced in 1959, is now coming under strain. In 1959 the Egypt-Sudan agreement allocated about 13 cubic miles (55 cubic km) of Nile water annually to Egypt and about four cubic miles (18 cubic km) to Sudan. Since then, the population of Egypt has tripled, and Egypt's agreed water allocation is no longer sufficient to irrigate its agricultural lands. Meanwhile, water-starved countries upstream of Sudan and Egypt, such as Ethiopia and Tanzania, are arguing for a new agreement that gives them a more equitable share in Nile's water (see "Putting the pieces together," pages 229–236).

A temporary solution to Egypt's water shortage problems could be the construction of a 224-mile (360-km) long watercourse, the Jonglei Canal, which would carry water from Sudan's southern swamp, the Sudd, to the Nile. Rates of water evaporation in the Sudd are high, and the canal is seen as one way of recouping water that would otherwise be lost. Work on the canal was begun in 1978 but abandoned in 1984 following a raid by southern rebels. The construction of the canal—which would divert water away from people living in the Sudd—was one of the triggers for Sudan's current civil war.

## The historic Thames

The Thames is Britain's most famous river but neither its largest nor its longest. The Thames meanders for about 147 miles (237 km) across the countryside of southeast England before meeting the tidal waters of the Thames estuary at England's capital city, London. The use and misuse of the river have a long written history. As early as the 11th century C.E. wooden weirs (small dams) diverted the river's flow to power water mills. The wooden barriers provided opportunities for setting fish nets and traps. As early as 1075 C.E. England's Norman king, William I (ca. 1027–87), ordered that "milles and fisheries be destroyed" because they were impeding the migration of spawning salmon. Sewage pollution affected the Thames wherever sizable settlements developed. By the early 17th century the city of Oxford had its own River Thames inspector charged with prosecuting the worst offenders who fouled the river with domestic sewage, rotten meat, and other unwanted matter.

Beginning in the late 18th century, engineers erected a series of weirs along the Thames every few miles, with associated locks that boats could navigate. The system of weirs and locks ensured a depth of at least six feet (2 m) through much of the river system, enabling cargo vessels of moderate size to navigate as far as Oxford, some 50 miles (80 km) from London. The weirs also served as a form of flood control. The large volume of water they held back served to raise the water table in the surrounding land.

By the mid-19th century the river's water quality was getting noticeably worse. Newly invented flush toilets now connected to sewers, which emptied the untreated waste straight into the Thames. By the 1850s the lower river's lock gates were becoming blocked with floating mats of sewage, and the Thames became popularly dubbed "The Great Stink." Nevertheless, most springs in the Thames Valley produced water of reasonable quality for drinking, having been largely cleansed on its passage through porous rock. Matters came to a head in 1858, when the Houses of Parliament—Britain's elected seat of government, located in London on the banks of the Thames—could not avoid the river's foul smell. The government rapidly passed the Thames Conservancy Act, which established a body, the Conservators of the River Thames, with power to prosecute polluters, whether private companies or public (municipal) organizations. By the early 20th century almost every town and village along the river had its own sewage treatment works. Many of these, and the network of sewers connected to them, still operate 100 years later.

The Thames no longer stank but nor was it clean. Enough sewage still entered the river to cause bacterial decomposers to strip the lower river's water of much of its oxygen. The only fish that survived were freshwater eels. So the situation remained until the 1950s, when in response to public indignation at the state of the river, the British government enacted regulations to limit the discharge of effluent (partially treated wastewater). Sewage treatment plants were systematically upgraded, with new treatments introduced to aerate the water (mix it with air) and remove nitrates and phosphates before the water was discharged into the river. All these practices gradually raised average oxygen levels in the lower river, from about 10 percent of saturation to more than 50 percent. By the mid-1970s the number of fish species in the Thames had risen from one (the eels) to more than 100 in the space of only 20 years. Fisheries staff began restocking the river with Atlantic salmon (*Salmo salar*), a clean-water species, in 1979.

Today the Thames River receives the effluent from some 12 million people living in the Thames Basin, and yet the river supports more angling and pleasure boating than any other river in the United Kingdom. Some people even swim in its middle and lower reaches. Such is the intensity with which Thames water is utilized for domestic use that a single drop of Thames water typically passes through the bodies of six people on its journey from source to estuary.

Since the 1990s there have been signs that the 100-year-old system of sewers and upgraded treatment works are no longer coping effectively with London's wastewater. In 2004 summer storms overloaded sewerage systems with runoff. Millions of tons of untreated sewage were discharged into the Thames in and around London. These discharges killed hundreds of thousands of fishes and posed a health hazard to river users such as anglers and boaters. Studies are now under way to evaluate the health risk of such sewage release and to devise ways of preventing it. Latest studies suggest that

### *The Thames Barrier*

The Thames Barrier, a series of giant gates positioned across the river downstream of London, was completed in 1982. It holds back estuarine floodwaters that would threaten London should high tides coincide with strong onshore winds (breezes blowing from sea to shore). The gates are raised to allow water and boat traffic through and lowered to hold them back. Because sea levels are probably rising due to global warming (see "Climate change," pages 196–199), the barrier may need to be strengthened within the next 25 years.

installing new sewage works and upgrading sewers to prevent the worst discharges is likely to take about 10 years. Meanwhile, climate change is increasing the unpredictability of local weather conditions, including precipitation, and is heightening the risk of the Thames overflowing its banks and flooding parts of London (see sidebar).

## The Colorado River's disputed water

The Colorado River flows southwest from the Rocky Mountains of the state of Colorado to the Gulf of California (Sea of Cortés) in Mexico. The river is notable because, among U.S. rivers, it is probably the most physically controlled and legally disputed river system of all. Water usage has reduced the flow of the lower Colorado from that of a mighty river to a comparative trickle in less than 80 years. In some years the Colorado River runs dry before it reaches the sea. The historical impact of water management policy on the health of the Colorado River delta is clearly evident.

The flow of the Colorado River is largely driven by snowmelt in the Rocky Mountains. In the late 19th century, before a series of dams and diversions were constructed on the river, the flow of the lower Colorado—the lower river borders the states of Arizona, California, and Nevada—fluctuated enormously from one month to the next and from one year to the next. Irrigators began diverting water from the

Colorado River in the 1890s, but floods washed away most of their newly constructed dams and levees within a few years. So silt-rich was the river in those days that it was commonly described as "too thick to drink, too thin to plow."

The first large dam on the river, the Laguna Dam, was completed in 1909, but by 1910 its reservoir had become congested with silt. The Hoover Dam, a landmark achievement in civil engineering, was the first dam on the Colorado River to completely regulate the flow of the lower river. It was the world's first truly multiuse dam, providing domestic and irrigation water as well as hydroelectricity. Today at least 10 dams operate on the Colorado River system, with the Hoover and Glen Canyon Dams being by far the most important. The effect of these two dams has been to turn the once cloudy, turbulent waters of the lower Colorado into a clear, regulated stream. In the lower Colorado, levels of suspended sediment have dropped by more than 98 percent since the construction of the Hoover Dam in 1935 and the Glen Canyon Dam in 1963. The Colorado River no longer feeds its delta with silt-rich water to replenish the material that waves and sea currents remove. As a result, the delta is gradually being washed away.

Water management on the Colorado River is governed by a complex legal framework, known as the "Law of the River," that has evolved piecemeal over more than 80 years. Today the Law of the River operates at three levels. At the top level, Mexico is guaranteed 0.44 cubic miles (1.85 cubic km) of water of sufficient quality per year to be usable for irrigation and domestic supplies. At the second level, water is divided for use between the upper and lower basins, and then to the various U.S. states within each basin. At the lowest level, water is allocated within each state.

The U.S. Bureau of Reclamation controls the allocation of water to the lower basin through the operation of the Hoover Dam. The Law of the River allocates a fixed quantity of water to Mexico but none specifically to maintain the integrity of the Colorado River delta. In 1962 Mexico complained about the quality and quantity of water the U.S. states were passing on. Since 1973 the United States has been responsible for ensuring the quality of the water flowing to Mexico. To meet its obligations, the United States built and operates the Yuma Desalting Plant on the border between the United States and Mexico.

Until the early 1930s and the completion of the Hoover Dam, the Colorado River delta was a highly diverse and productive seasonal wetland, starved of water during the winter months and inundated in the late summer. It supported at least 200 species of vascular plants and a great diversity of waterfowl, fishes, and estuarine invertebrate species. When the Spanish arrived in the region in the 17th century C.E., they discovered some 20,000 Cocopah Native Americans inhabiting the delta region, coexisting with large mammals such as jaguars, beavers, deer, and coyotes. Until the mid-20th century some 3,000 Cocopah people continued a sustainable lifestyle by fishing in the freshwater lakes of the delta. Today fewer than 200 remain, and they fish in the sea because most of the lakes have disappeared.

In the mid- to late 1930s, when the Lake Mead reservoir behind the Hoover Dam was first filling with water, and then again between 1963 and 1981, when Lake Powell filled behind the Glen Canyon Dam, no freshwater reached the delta. In the years in between and since, much less than 1 percent of the river's annual flow has reached the delta in most years, and the water that does reach it is murky, salty, and high in pesticide residues.

Without freshwater to flush salts and heavy metals from delta soils, these potentially harmful substances can become concentrated in food chains through the processes of bioaccumulation and biomagnification to reach levels that impair animal reproduction (see sidebar "Bioaccumulation and biomagnification," page 207). In the late 1990s measured levels of the heavy metal selenium in delta water, sediment, and fish tissue were up to 14 times higher than the Environmental Protection Agency's (EPA's) limits for wildlife protection.

Lack of flowing freshwater in the Colorado River also affects marine animals in the upper Gulf of California. During the 1970s, when Lake Powell retained the freshwater that would have flowed into the delta, the upper gulf fishery for the totoaba fish (*Cynoscion macdonaldii*) collapsed, and the United States now classes the fish as endangered. Shrimp catches in the late 1980s and early 1990s dropped to about 50 percent of the average over previous years. The Colorado delta clam (*Mulinia coloradoensis*) is found only in the Colorado River delta and upper Gulf of California. Population densities have dropped by more than 90 percent over 40 years. The clam is now on the U.S. endangered species list.

The delta still sustains the largest remaining populations of an endangered bird, the Yuma clapper rail (*Rallus longirostris yumanensis*), and an endangered fish, the desert pupfish (*Cyprinodon macularius*). In most years the delta supports more than 60,000 resident birds and at least 40,000 migratory birds.

However, in years when freshwater flows into the delta have been well above average, wetlands containing cattails and other emergent plant species and bordering land containing cottonwood trees and willows have shown a remarkable capacity for recovery. And in 1993 local freshwater floods in the delta region caused a resurgence in the upper gulf's schools of corvina fish (*Cynoscion xanthalus*) after an absence of more than 30 years.

Until recently, the conservation of the Colorado delta and the lifestyles of its indigenous population had not been high on the agenda of the U.S. or Mexican governments. However, environmental groups such as the Living Rivers/Colorado Riverkeeper organization have raised international awareness of the plight of the delta's indigenous people and its endangered animal species. International environmental agencies estimate that only 1 percent of the lower river's average flow, allocated to the delta region, would be enough to help the delta flourish once again. Comparatively small changes to the allocation of water among U.S. states bordering the lower Colorado could have a big impact in restoring the delta ecosystem.

The lower basin of the Colorado River provides water for about 17 million people and irrigates more than 1 million acres (405,000 ha) in Arizona, California, and Nevada. Since 1929, the Colorado River Water Pact has sought to limit California's annual share to 1.3 cubic miles (5.4 cubic km). Since the construction of the Colorado River Aqueduct, however, the state has regularly overdrawn its quota. In October 2003 the U.S. Department of the Interior and four California water agencies agreed to a 14-year plan for California to reduce the amount of water it removed from the Colorado River, by more efficiently utilizing water for irrigation and reducing losses through seepage. This agreement, the Colorado River Quantification Settlement Agreement (QSA), honors the pact California signed in 1929 but has since failed to keep.

Scientific cooperation between the United States and Mexico governments is underway, alongside negotiations on institutional arrangements for allocating water. Consequently, international agencies and environmental groups now project with a degree of confidence that further degradation of the Colorado River delta could be halted within the next decade.

As the descriptions of the Colorado, Thames, and Nile Rivers illustrate, any river system serves a multiplicity of uses that impact on its biological communities. Moreover, the size and nature of these operations changes over time scales of only a few decades. As a result, any consideration of how freshwater ecosystems should be managed must take into account rapidly changing human priorities.

# CHAPTER 7

# USES OF LAKES AND RIVERS

Water is an invaluable resource. Adult humans need to consume at least 2.1 U.S. pints (1 L) of water a day to maintain the balance of water and salts in the body and prevent dehydration. In a hot, dry environment where water loss from sweat and breathed-out air is greater, individuals need a larger daily quota. The water—if drunk as freshwater—needs to be clean and safe, which in practice means that it does not harbor harmful organisms, high levels of injurious chemicals, or high concentrations of dissolved salts. In reality, many people across the world consume their daily intake of water in other beverages and in food, rather than by drinking clean, clear water.

People also need freshwater supplies for washing themselves, for cleaning clothes and other household items, and for disposing of human wastes. This is domestic water usage (see table on page 172). This usage does not take into account the large amounts of water used to produce the food and drink that people consume or to manufacture and operate items that people use daily, such as vehicles, clothes, electrical items, and so on. When these uses are also computed, people in highly developed countries such as Canada and the United States use in excess of 1,850 U.S. gallons (7,000 L) per day, while in stark contrast, those in developing countries such as Angola, Ethiopia, and Laos use less than 26 gallons (100 L) daily. In developed countries, access to clean, clear water is taken for granted by most people. In many communities of the poorest developing countries of Africa and Asia, clean clear water is considered a luxury, as yet unattainable.

Freshwater is used in such a variety of ways that one aquatic science expert aptly dubbed it a "pillar of our civilization." Freshwater bodies serve as mediums for transport and as political boundaries. People use freshwater to irrigate crops,

*Local girls obtaining water from a well beneath a dry riverbed on the African offshore island of Madagascar. Lack of clean freshwater threatens the lives of millions of people each year in developing countries.* (Frans Lanting/Minden Pictures)

prepare food, and wash themselves and their possessions clean. Freshwater environments store water, helping to prevent damaging floods, and disperse wastes. Rivers and lakes

## Typical water consumption for domestic use in Canada

| Water use | Percent of total |
|---|---|
| Bathing and showering | 35 |
| Toilet flushing | 30 |
| Laundry | 20 |
| Cooking, drinking, and dish washing | 10 |
| Household cleaning | 5 |

Data source: Environment Canada, 2004

provide edible items such as fish and aquatic plants and can be a source of hydroelectricity. They also provide some of the world's most scenic destinations and exciting boating experiences. The multiplicity of uses of lakes and rivers, not all of which can be easily costed, nevertheless reveals their very high value as resources.

### Highways and political boundaries

Rivers and lakes are natural highways. Today travel by inland waterway is, in most cases, slow compared to other modes of transport. However, it remains an inexpensive means of conveyance for freight. Canal construction and inland waterway improvement for transporting freight marked the first stage of the Industrial Revolution in Europe in the late 18th and early 19th centuries. Large inland waterways such as the Great Lakes–Mississippi system of the United States (see "Mississippi River," pages 69–72) and the Rhine and Danube in northwestern Europe (see "Danube River," pages 64–66) carry considerable freight traffic. Across the world, many large rivers have been straightened, dredged, and engineered to the extent that large sections are essentially canal-like in form, with gentle bends, steep concrete sides, and a flattened riverbed. Such intervention drastically alters the flow properties of the river and reduces the diversity of habitats within it together with the range of organisms it can support (see "Biodiversity," pages 187–190).

Besides altering natural watercourses to behave more like canals, people also cut canals between distant rivers or bodies of water. Cutting canals to connect different river systems for transportation purposes has unintended effects, however. Doing so destroys previous barriers to migration and allows species to enter rivers and lakes from which they were previously excluded. Classic examples of the unintended consequences of cutting canals are the entry and subsequent impact of the sea lamprey and zebra mussels in the Great Lakes of North America (see "Alien invasions," pages 199–205).

Shipping and boat traffic have a dramatic effect on the life of a river or lake. The noise, the wake, and the turbulence they create as they move through the water disturbs wildlife and lifts sediment from the river or lake bottom. The raised sediment can smother small bottom-living organisms as well as blocking sunlight penetration for photosynthesis. The waves produced by boat traffic erode soft banks unless they are artificially reinforced. Pollution—the alteration of physical or chemical factors in the environment to the detriment of organisms—also accompanies increased boat traffic unless strict controls on dumping waste matter are enforced.

Rivers and large lakes provide more or less permanent, ready-made physical barriers. In many cases nations have adopted these bodies of water as convenient boundaries to mark the borders of national or provincial territories. Often the boundary line runs approximately through the middle of the lake, as in the boundaries between the United States and Canada that run through Lakes Superior, Huron, Erie, and Ontario (see "Lake Superior," pages 84–87). A similar situation often applies to rivers, as in the case of the Danube River, which along its length forms the boundary for several countries, including Bulgaria in the south and Romania to the north (see "Danube River," pages 64–66). But problems can and do arise in the management and use of the resource, such as who has ownership of or access to fish stocks. And engineering developments and pollution incidents created by one of the bordering nations can affect the other one. The use of a water body as a political boundary can slow development of the region, but more often than not, it creates legal problems in the management and control of its resources (see "Putting the pieces together," pages 229–236).

## Agricultural, industrial, and domestic water supplies

People obtain their freshwater supplies by extracting it—the process is technically called *abstraction*—from water on the surface of the land or from groundwater. Today streams and rivers, natural lakes, and artificial reservoirs supply water that is abstracted through intakes, whether by pumping or under gravity. Groundwater supplies are collected from natural springs or artificial wells. Removing the salt from sea water, a process called *desalination,* is an expensive method of obtaining freshwater, but it is important in affluent, water-poor regions of the world such as parts of the Middle East and parts of the United States. As desalination technology becomes cheaper, its use is gradually spreading to less affluent countries.

Worldwide, international agencies calculate, at least two-thirds of all water drawn from surface resources and from groundwater is used to irrigate crops. The demand for irrigation has increased dramatically between 1800 and the early 2000s, from about 20 million acres (8 million ha) of irrigated land to more than 618 million acres (250 million ha) today. The demand for irrigation is greatest in arid countries. In Egypt, for example, nearly 90 percent of the nation's water consumption is used for irrigation. Across the world, water demand is usually quite seasonal, with more required in hot, dry seasons than in the cooler, wetter ones.

Much of the water used for irrigation eventually evaporates from the soil surface or from the leaves of plants. Applied inappropriately, irrigation can cause soils to become too saline, as the water evaporates leaving salts behind. Once irrigation water is applied to the land, its composition may rapidly change. As a result, the water draining from irrigated land may be carrying high loads of nutrients, sediment, and pesticides. The physical and chemical properties of agricultural runoff can harm biological communities in the watercourses into which the water discharges (see "Freshwater pollution," pages 205–207). Irrigation ditches filled with standing water can also provide ideal habitats for the mosquitoes and freshwater snails that are vectors of malaria and bilharzia (see "Rivers, lakes, and human health," pages 152–157).

As the table below reveals, the amount of water abstracted per person varies dramatically from country to country, being highest in developed countries and lowest in water-deficient countries of Africa with low rates of runoff. The low rate of abstraction for the United Kingdom can be accounted for, in part, by its wet climate, which provides water for crops without the need for large-scale irrigation.

The allocation of abstracted water to different economic sectors also varies enormously from nation to nation. Within a country, the amount and quality of freshwater required depends on the nature of the service or process for which it is needed. Domestic supplies, for example, require moderately small amounts of safe drinking water, while power stations require large volumes of water for cooling, where water quality is of much less importance and water can be used

## Rates of water abstraction in selected countries and percentage by economic sector

| Country | Water abstraction* | Domestic use (percentage) | Industrial use (percentage) | Agricultural use (percentage) |
|---|---|---|---|---|
| Brazil | 86 (324) | 21 | 18 | 61 |
| Canada | 378 (1,431) | 11 | 81 | 8 |
| China | 114 (431) | 10 | 21 | 69 |
| Egypt | 213 (809) | 6 | 8 | 86 |
| Ethiopia (& Eritrea) | 8 (31) | 11 | 3 | 86 |
| France | 156 (591) | 16 | 69 | 15 |
| India | 131 (497) | 5 | 3 | 92 |
| Russian Federation | 139 (527) | 19 | 61 | 20 |
| United Kingdom | 53 (201) | 20 | 77 | 3 |
| United States of America | 446 (1,688) | 12 | 46 | 42 |
| Zambia | 49 (187) | 16 | 7 | 77 |

Data source: Gleick, Peter H., et al. *The World's Water 2002–2003: The Biennial Report on Freshwater Resources*. Washington, D.C.: Island Press, 2002.

*Per person in thousands of U.S. gallons per year (thousands of liters per year)

with little or no pretreatment. Small industrial plants often obtain their water supplies from domestic networks, while larger industrial plants, such as automobile factories or plastics manufacturing plants, may obtain their own supplies directly from a lake or river.

In many developed countries, people have access to large supplies of clean water. In these places, the water used for drinking and for other domestic purposes, from washing to toilet flushing, is of the same high standard. Where freshwater supplies are more restricted, water used for drinking and for other domestic purposes may come from separate supplies and be of different quality. Water used for drinking and washing should be clean and clear, without an objectionable odor or taste and without potentially dangerous levels of disease organisms or harmful chemicals. It should meet minimum acceptable criteria for clean water set by the World Health Organization (WHO).

Water abstracted from headwaters, from mountain springs, and from some wells, usually meets the high WHO standards without treatment. Water taken from most lowland rivers, however, must be treated to achieve a sufficiently high standard for domestic use. This treatment involves most or all of the following processes: sieving to remove large debris, coagulation of salts, allowing sediment to settle, fine sand filtration, and finally sterilization using chlorine, ozone, or ultraviolet irradiation. Specific problems may call for additional treatment. "Hard" water—water with a high bicarbonate or sulfate content—is sometimes "softened" through the addition of slaked lime and soda ash to remove calcium ($Ca^{2+}$) and magnesium ($Mg^{2+}$) ions. Acidic water that could corrode metal pipes may be partially neutralized by adding lime. High levels of nitrate in abstracted water can be lowered by diluting the water with low-nitrate supplies or, more expensively, by using reverse osmosis or distillation methods.

The effect of abstraction on the ecology of a river or lake depends upon the volume of water taken—whether it is a large or small proportion of the supply source—and the quality and quantity of used water that is subsequently returned to the river (see "Freshwater pollution," pages 205–207).

## Flood control and water storage

The high fertility of soils that are regularly enriched with sediment from floods has encouraged farmers to settle on floodplains, and in their wake large settlements have grown. However, destructive floods pose a threat to the settlements they originally encouraged. To counter the perceived flood problem, a wide variety of constructions and in-stream modifications, ranging from dams and levees (flood banks) to deep channels and river straightening projects, now constrains water to river channels rather than allowing it to spill over the banks regularly. Such flood control works tend to reduce the diversity of habitats within the river channel, while making seasonal variations in volume flow and water depth more extreme. On heavily constrained river channels, floods that spill over the banks may occur less often than they did before, but when floods do occur, they can be all the more destructive (see "Floods," pages 55–56).

Regional and seasonal differences in the volume of water runoff mean that local water resources are not always able to meet consumer demand. It is common for some parts of a country to have excess rainfall while other parts have insufficient rainfall to meet local water consumption demands. Water managers may have to divert water from other watersheds or store water for long periods. The desert lands of southern California, for instance, obtain most of their water supply from farther north along the 242-mile-long (390-km-long) Colorado River Aqueduct. In the United Kingdom most rainfall occurs in winter, and most falls in the north and west. Water demand is greatest in the summer, and industrial and domestic demand is highest in the northwestern, middle, and southeastern regions of England. Water is stored in large artificial reservoirs close to such major cities as Manchester, Liverpool, Birmingham, Bristol, and London, often being piped from locations tens of miles away. For example, the water supply to Manchester and Liverpool largely comes from the Lake District, more than 50 miles (80 km) to the north. Clearly, water diversions and water storage facilities create widespread changes to freshwater ecosystems, as well as creating new ecosystems (see sidebar).

## Waste disposal

Lakes and especially rivers are employed worldwide for the cheap removal of waste products. The assumption is that the freshwater system will dilute the wastes, transporting them downstream (in most cases, ultimately to the sea) and along the way breaking down much of the waste into less hazardous forms by physical, chemical, and biological processes. This assumption holds true only to a limited extent. The heavily polluted state of so many rivers across the world reflects the fact that many river systems are overloaded by the amount and types of wastes they receive (see "Freshwater pollution," pages 205–207).

The most obvious waste entering freshwater systems is sewage, or general wastewater. This is used water of primarily household, agricultural, and small-scale industrial origin. It contains a very wide variety of particulate matter and dissolved substances. Perhaps the most important of these components—from the public health viewpoint and the impact on the ecology of freshwater systems—are those originating from the excrement of people and farm animals. Disease organisms may survive in the sewage water and, if discharged untreated into open watercourses, could come into contact with people and infect them (see "Rivers, lakes, and human health," pages 152–157). Sewage also contains high levels of organic materials that enrich the water. The action of bacteria in decomposing the organic material removes oxygen from the water (deoxygenates it), posing a threat to aquatic organisms that require oxygen for respiration.

Another source of waste in freshwater is surface runoff. Chemical fertilizers added to fields produce nutrient-rich runoff that enters watercourses. Runoff of organic material and chemicals from fertilizers into lakes and rivers increases the likelihood that these freshwater ecosystems will become *eutrophic,* or overenriched (see "Too many nutrients," pages 207–210). Often farmers spray their fields with pesticides and herbicides. Through runoff, the more persistent of these find their way into lakes and rivers where they may accumulate in organisms and become concentrated in food chains (see "Bioaccumulation and biomagnification," page 207).

Finally, effluent (partially treated water) containing wastes from industrial and mining activities may enter a freshwater system. Effluent can contain toxic substances such as heavy metals, ammonia, and a range of organic substances, including phenols and some substances that have estrogenic properties—they mimic estrogen and other closely related female sex hormones. Estrogenic substances can reduce the fertility and reproductive success of male fish.

Apart from the chemical properties of wastewater, its physical properties are often enough to harm the lakes and rivers it enters. Many sources of wastewater are sediment-rich. Added sediment not only smothers some bottom-living organisms, but also blocks sunlight penetration, thus depriving some phytoplankton and attached plants the opportunity to photosynthesize.

## Biological products

Among the most valuable "services" freshwater systems provide are a range of biological products, ranging from fish to plants and microbes, that are an important source of income for local communities.

Fish are the most obvious and most valuable biological product from rivers. People harvest fish through capture fisheries and by fish farming—raising fish in enclosures within or alongside lakes and rivers. Rivers and lakes can be highly productive, both in terms of fish yield and value per unit area, because they often utilize the nutrient-rich runoff from a large catchment. Also, high-value species, such as salmon, shad, sea trout, and some sturgeon species, mature in the sea and return to rivers to breed, and on their spawning migration they are often intercepted by fishers.

Fish farming, a form of aquaculture (the water-based counterpart to agriculture on land), has been practiced for at least 3,000 years in the Far East. It has proliferated in many parts of the world in the last 30 years. Members of the carp family (Cyprinidae) remain the most commonly farmed species in Asia. They are often raised as part of other farming practices, such as growing rice in paddy fields. Catfish are predators that are able to survive in waters of moderately poor quality.

Various catfish species are caught or farmed in the Americas, Africa, and parts of Asia such as Thailand and Vietnam. In the Middle East, tilapia—perchlike cichlid fishes—are commonly farmed in ponds. Members of the family Salmonidae (salmon and trout) are favored in Europe and North America. Modern methods for farming them often involve raising the fish at high densities and feeding them high-protein pellets laced with vitamins and antibiotics. Under such crowded conditions fish are susceptible to disease. The medication added to food helps prevent or control outbreaks of bacterial infection in the fish population. Fish farmers commonly abstract water from rivers to supply their fish enclosures. High levels of waste may then exit from farms and impose a high nutrient load on the parent river into which they are discharged (see "Freshwater pollution," pages 205–207).

Sport and commercial fishing can have a dramatic effect on the health of fish populations (see "Overharvesting," pages 212–216). Also, the traps and weirs used to capture fish, and the constructions used to raise fish, alter the flow pattern of rivers.

Freshwater's contribution to world nutrition is substantial. The Food and Agriculture Organization for the United Nations (FAO) calculated the 2001 yield of freshwater fish and shellfish from capture fisheries to be 9.7 million U.S. tons (8.8 million metric tons) and from aquaculture, 24.6 million U.S. tons (22.4 million metric tons). This compares with marine yields of 90.8 million U.S. tons (82.5 million metric tons) and 16.6 million U.S. tons (15.1 million metric tons), respectively. Inland aquaculture is more significant than inland catch fisheries or marine aquaculture. But even these large numbers probably greatly underestimate the true catch from freshwater capture and aquaculture sectors, particularly in developing countries. Many fish-harvesting activities are carried out on a subsistence basis in remote places for which no catch statistics are recorded. Many fisheries experts suspect that the caught and farmed yields of freshwater fish may, in reality, be about twice that of the recorded estimates.

In many countries the recorded freshwater fish harvest is lower in total mass, but not necessarily in commercial or nutrient value, than plant or animal produce from land-based farming. Freshwater fish provide an important source of protein in the diet of many communities. People in land-locked African countries such as Malawi and Zambia obtain more than 50 percent of their animal protein from freshwater fish. Of the 30 countries with the highest per-person consumption of inland fish, about two-thirds are classified as low-income, food-deficient countries (LIFDs) by the FAO. In these countries freshwater fish make a major contribution to otherwise meager diets.

Fish are not the only freshwater animals people exploit. Trappers in the cooler regions of the Northern Hemisphere capture beaver, muskrat, and mink for their fur. Hunters take waterfowl, such as ducks and geese, for human consumption as well as sport. And fishers harvest crustaceans, such as crayfish and large freshwater shrimp, and mollusks, such as mussels and clams. Among reptiles, freshwater turtles are hunted and farmed for their shells, meat, and to provide medicinal products in the eastern Asian market. Crocodiles, alligators, and caimans—whether wild or farmed—provide leather and meat.

People also harvest aquatic plants, and these are a significant resource in many parts of the world. For instance, reeds of the genus *Phragmites* are still harvested in parts of Europe and North America as a source of cellulose for paper and textiles and as thatch for roofing. And farmers in the United States, Europe, and in Asia in countries from India to Japan cultivate freshwater algae of the genus *Spirulina* for use as a vitamin and mineral supplement, particularly for those who have vegetarian diets. *Spirulina* is particularly rich in the vitamins A, B-12, and E, and in the mineral iron. Taro plants (*Colocasia esculenta*), grown at the flooded margins of lakes and rivers, are important food crops in West Africa, South Pacific islands, and the Caribbean. Taro tubers are starchy roots comparable to potatoes and used in cooking, while the leaves can be eaten as greens. Another freshwater food plant, watercress (*Rorippa nasturtium-aquaticum*), is a favored green salad leaf that is farmed across Europe. Finally, rice (genus *Oryza*) is a cultivated wetland plant and a staple food for about half the world's population.

## Water power

Hydroelectric power (HEP), or hydropower, is currently the world's most abundant source of renewable energy. It is a renewable resource because the power generated by water flowing under gravity is replenished when water evaporates and later falls as rain on higher ground, so recharging upland water sources. Water's potential energy—its stored energy by virtue of its position—is transformed into kinetic energy (energy of movement) when water flows through narrow watercourses in the HEP system and drives turbines, thereby generating electricity. In the early 2000s hydropower provided about 19 percent of the world's annual electricity supply.

Hydropower systems are most appropriate in landscapes where there is high relief (hills or mountains) and rates of water flow are high. Hydropower accounts for about 65 percent of Canada's electricity and nearly 100 percent of Norway's. Hydropower is now emerging as a major energy source in rural China.

Hydropower has many positive aspects. First and foremost, the energy source for HEP is continuously renewable. Once the construction phase is over, HEP plants produce little, if any, greenhouse gases. These are gases released into the atmosphere, such as carbon dioxide and methane, that trap outgoing infrared radiation and have a warming effect (see "Climate change," pages 196–199). Nor do HEP systems produce other atmospheric pollutants, such as oxides of nitrogen and sulfur, which are released when fossil fuels are burned in conventional power stations (see "Acid waters," pages 210–212). Once established, HEP plants have a very long working life (often in excess of 50 years), low operating costs, and extremely high energy conversion efficiencies—commonly in excess of 90 percent—making them the most efficient of all energy conversion technologies. Overall, HEP electricity is cheap and clean. And many hydropower systems can respond almost instantaneously to changes in consumer demand. Often the reservoirs associated with many HEP projects provide water supplies for communities, farms, and industries in the region.

Stacked against the benefits of hydroelectric power are its negative impacts, particularly those associated with larger

HEP systems. The dams used in large projects hold back vast reservoirs of water that flood the landscape, destroying land that previously had other uses and at the same time displacing communities of people. Worldwide, the total area of dammed water for HEP systems is greater than the area of the state of California. More than 70 million people have been forced to move to create space for these reservoirs. The ecology of the river system both above and below the dam is usually radically altered, often to the detriment of both (see "Altering the flow," pages 190–193).

Although some massive HEP projects are going ahead (see "Yangtze River," pages 75–77), internationally the move is toward smaller HEP projects that have a lesser impact on river systems (see sidebar "Dams and channelization," page 191). Small hydropower plants can generate 10 megawatts (10 million watts) of electricity—enough energy to power a small town in a rural area. Small schemes need not dam an entire river, but may harness just a small proportion of its flow. In rural China, for example, 45,000 small HEP plants—many containing machinery that fits into a small hut—are providing power for 300 million people.

## Leisure and recreation

Many rivers and lakes in developed countries have considerable economic value as places where people spend their leisure time. In England, for example, 3 million freshwater anglers (sport fishers) form a significant lobby group that presses for improvements in freshwater quality. As regular visitors to the waterside, they are in a good position to monitor environmental change. Sport fishers' observations of the decline of fish catches in rivers such as the Trent in England have prompted scientists to investigate issues such as the presence of estrogenic substances (substances that mimic female reproductive hormones) affecting the reproductive success of freshwater fish. On the other hand, management for angling has resulted in the introduction of exotic species for sport fishing purposes, and these fish have sometimes threatened native species (see "Alien invasions," pages 199–205). And some forms of angling prompt managing agents to defoliate the banks of the river or lake to allow anglers easier access to the waterside. This is bad news for birds and other wildlife that nest in the vegetation of the riparian zone (see "On two or four legs," pages 117–127).

Apart from angling, freshwater venues draw other leisure activities, such as duck shooting, boating, sailing, swimming, scuba diving, and waterskiing. Clearly, not all these activities are compatible with one another. For instance, many forms of boating, swimming, or diving are unsuitable alongside angling in the close vicinity. And shooting is incompatible with the others in the same place at the same time. Those managing lake and river access usually schedule activities so that shooting occurs at different times from the other pursuits.

Of course, many lakes and rivers have great natural beauty. Features such as the tumble of water in a river, the tranquility of a lowland lake shrouded in early morning mist, or the mirrorlike reflections of a mountain lake give freshwater ven-

## *The true value of freshwater ecosystems*

Only by evaluating the economic worth of the full range of resources and services that inland waters provide can one appreciate the real value of freshwater ecosystems. These include so-called ecosystem services, such as improving water quality and flood control, as well as more tangible benefits, such as water for irrigation or fish for consumption.

In 1997 a multidisciplinary team led by the environmental scientist Robert Costanza published an article in the scientific journal *Nature* that attempted to give a financial value to ecosystem services provided by the world's biomes. Their conclusion? Of nonmarine ecosystems, lakes and rivers have an average value of $3,440 per acre ($8,498/ha), and freshwater wetlands, $7,924 per acre ($19,580/ha). They are many times more valuable per unit area than terrestrial ecosystems such as forests ($392 per acre; $969/ha) or grasslands ($94 per acre; $232/ha). In fact, the total value of ecosystems services provided by freshwater ecosystems and brackish water wetlands (nearly $6.6 trillion per year) was similar to that of all other nonmarine ecosystems combined (some $5.7 trillion per year). Inland water ecosystems, although only occupying about 3.5 percent of the land surface, contribute as much as and possibly more than the rest of the land surface.

*A wilderness experience by canoe in Minnesota* (Jim Brandenberg/ Minden Pictures)

ues a very high amenity value for aesthetic enjoyment. Besides this, freshwater is essential for human survival and well-being. Lakes and rivers thus remain of singular importance in religion, culture, and the arts, as well as having great wildlife and scientific interest. All these factors combine to encourage tourism to many localities that are rich in lakes and rivers, which in turn provides a significant economic contribution to the region (see sidebar).

# THREATS TO LAKES AND RIVERS

The freshwater biome is a fragile one. Lakes and rivers have the capacity to "self-clean" (see "Waste disposal," pages 178–179). However, the demands of a rapidly expanding human population coupled with industrial development have strained freshwater ecosystems such that their capacity to recover from stress has been compromised. In the last two centuries the spread of industrialization, urbanization, and intensive agriculture has markedly changed the quality and quantity of water cycling through lakes and rivers.

Aquatic communities are immersed in a watery medium that, for most inhabitants, is the source of everything they require, including living space, food, and oxygen. Changes in the quantity and quality of the water affect most or all aspects of the lives of residents. Many of them—unlike flying birds and insects that frequent freshwater—do not have the opportunity to escape should the conditions of their watery environment change for the worse.

The network of lakes and rivers connects all other biomes, acting as a major thoroughfare between land and sea. As such, the freshwater biome of lakes and rivers is susceptible to harm from almost any direction, whether polluted air, contaminated runoff from the land, tainted groundwater, or migrating animals swimming upstream from the sea. In fact, destructive changes to a water body are rarely due to a single effect. Typically they combine, as in the case of the Aral Sea, where both water abstraction from feeder streams and inputs of a wide range of pollutants devastated this lake ecosystem (see sidebar "The Aral Sea disaster," page 194).

Many freshwater ecosystems are undergoing radical change because their inputs, outputs, and the channel that contains them are being altered, and many of these changes are likely to be harmful to at least some of the organisms living there.

## Biodiversity

Biodiversity, short for "biological diversity," is a measure of the richness and variety of life. Biologists measure biodiversity at different levels of organization, such as the amount of genetic variation in a species (genetic diversity), the range of species or groups of species within a locality (species diversity), and the diversity of ecosystems within an area (ecosystem diversity).

Biologists and environmentalists regard loss of biodiversity as important for several reasons. First, biodiversity is important in maintaining ecosystem functions. For example, microbes in lakes, rivers, and marginal wetlands break down organic matter and release nutrients, so helping to purify water. Through photosynthesis, phytoplankton and attached plants in lakes and rivers replenish the oxygen in air and reduce its carbon dioxide load. The diverse community of organisms works together to perform ecosystem functions, and not enough is understood about how ecosystems work to know which organisms might be most important to the health of the community. Microscopic organisms that play vital roles may be overlooked. The fact that most freshwater ecosystems have evolved to be highly complex, with thousands of different kinds of organisms operating at several different trophic levels, suggests that biodiversity is, in itself, important in maintaining these ecosystem functions.

Second, there is a strong economic argument against destroying life-forms. Individual species have properties that might be useful in the future. Some freshwater plants are rich sources of dietary supplements (see "Biological products," pages 179–181). Medically useful substances such as the blood-thinning agents (anticoagulants) found in the saliva of leeches might be lurking out there in aquatic animals, plants, and microbes that have yet to be studied.

Last, some argue for the moral and aesthetic merits of preserving lakes and rivers. The moral argument is that humans do not have the right to damage habitats and endanger

## The Earth Summit

In 1992 representatives of 172 nations met in Rio de Janeiro, Brazil, at the United Nations Conference on Environment and Development (UNCED), or the "Earth Summit." At this meeting, the issue of biodiversity and its loss was high on the agenda. One major outcome of the Earth Summit was Agenda 21, a plan of action that seeks to halt further global environmental degradation while improving the quality of life for the world's poor. In addition, two major treaties emerged from the conference that continue to have a strong influence on actions to curb biodiversity loss in freshwater ecosystems. The first, the Framework Convention on Climate Change (FCCC), seeks to stabilize levels of greenhouse gases in the air and so help counter global warming. The FCCC asks industrialized countries to make plans and take action to reduce emissions of greenhouse gases (see "Climate change," pages 196–199). The second, the Convention on Biological Diversity (CBD), requires nations to develop plans for protecting habitats and their resident species. Together these treaties seek to tackle two of the most pressing environmental issues facing humanity today—habitat loss and global warming.

species simply to make bigger profits. A more person-centered view is that removing life-forms and the beautiful places where they live means denying future generations the opportunity to see nature's masterpieces. Since the early 1990s the issue of biodiversity has risen to public awareness in developing countries. A key influence was the United Nations Conference on Environment and Development (UNCED), popularly known as the Earth Summit (see sidebar).

One way to track biodiversity at the species and ecosystem levels is to monitor species or groups of species and see whether their populations are changing in abundance or in their geographic distribution. Such changes can be linked to shifts in land use, water flow, and other environmental impacts such as pollution. Done properly, this would involve experts in a wide range of specialties gathering samples from the study area; identifying the species; and recording the numbers of individuals of each, their distribution of sizes, and their biomass. This process would need to be repeated at intervals of decades. Such studies are expensive and time-consuming, however, and at present, there is a shortage of experts who can identify small organisms to species level. As a result, biodiversity studies tend to be much narrower in scope. Typically only a few key indicator species are studied, and it is assumed that if these organisms are changing, so are many others. In practice, the biodiversity of fish or larger invertebrates is commonly used as an indicator of water quality (see "Freshwater pollution," pages 205–207). If the distribution and abundance of these indicator species are changing, so, too, are many less obvious components of the ecosystem, such as phytoplankton and zooplankton.

What, then, is the current state of freshwater biodiversity? Recent data have been compiled by the United Nations Environment Program (UNEP), the World Conservation Union (IUCN), and the World Wide Fund for Nature (WWF) in conjunction with the World Conservation Monitoring Center (WCMC). These surveys suggest that worldwide about 30 percent of freshwater fish species are threatened, along with

## Classifying risk

The World Conservation Union (known as IUCN, despite a name change in 1990) assesses the extent to which a species is at risk of becoming extinct in the near future. It allocates a given species to one of several categories—such as "extinct in the wild," "critically endangered," "endangered," or "vulnerable"—on the basis of various kinds of evidence. Such evidence includes the extent to which the population is localized or fragmented (broken into small populations) and how its abundance and distribution have changed historically. It also takes into account the species' favored habitats and the pressures on them, as well as the habits and life cycle of the species concerned. A "critically endangered" species faces an extremely high risk of extinction in the wild within the next few decades. An "endangered" species faces a very high risk of extinction over a similar timescale, while a "vulnerable" species faces a high risk of extinction over a slightly greater length of time. During the 20th century, 39 extinctions of species or subspecies of freshwater fish were reported in North America. Nonnative fish were implicated in at least two-thirds of the extinctions (see "Alien invasions," pages 199–205).

25 percent of amphibians and an astonishing 65 percent of freshwater mammal species (see "Classifying risk," page 189). In addition, many land-living birds and mammals are at risk when marginal wetlands, lakes, and rivers are altered or removed and breeding and feeding areas are lost. According to the WWF, a higher proportion of animal species is threatened in freshwater ecosystems than in tropical rain forests.

Overharvesting, pollution, and the introduction of exotic species—intentionally or by accident—all take a toll on freshwater biodiversity, but the most important threat to freshwater biodiversity is habitat loss or alteration. When a section of river is straightened, its channel dredged, and its banks cemented over so that marginal vegetation can no longer grow, the habitats in the river are radically altered. Many water-loving plants and animals no longer have a suitable habitat in which to live. When dams are built, they break the river into separate sections through which migrating species such as salmon and sea trout may be unable to travel (see "Dams and channelization," page 191). Dams may also level out seasonal flow patterns and reduce river flow overall. Fish such as trout that require fast-flowing, cool, and oxygen-rich water may gradually die out in the main river, and the wetlands found on the floodplain at the edges of rivers may disappear.

## Altering the flow

The throughput of water in a lake or the changing pattern of flow in a stretch of river is technically called its *water regime.* Environmental impacts such as new dams, irrigation systems, and flood defenses change the water regime of a river. They cause the river to flow on average faster or slower, to behave with more or less predictability, or to change flow dramatically in a short space of time. These changes in water regime affect the community of organisms in the river, causing the structure of the biological community to shift.

In an ideal world, scientists might monitor a river's water regime and the nature of its biological community before a specific shift in its water regime occurred. Because of the cost

## Dams and channelization

Dam-building and channelization (the straightening and deepening of a river channel for navigation) remain the two most widespread threats to freshwater ecosystems. Between 1950 and 2000 the number of large dams worldwide rose from about 5,000 to 45,000; "large" dams are those taller than 50 feet (15 m) or holding back more than about 105 million cubic feet (3 million $m^3$) of water. Fewer than 10,000 major waterways had been channelized by 1900, but by 2000 the number had risen to more than 500,000. The Mekong River, along with its tributaries, is a biodiversity "hot spot" in Southeast Asia that was largely unaffected by channelization and dam-building until the 1990s. In the early 1990s the construction of the Pak Mun Dam on a major Mekong tributary, Thailand's Mun River, shows just how fragile the situation has become. Many of the 150 fish species in the Mun underwent a catastrophic decline following the construction of the dam.

Following the guidelines published by the World Commission on Dams (WCD) in 2000, the World Bank and other development banks now require a more thorough examination of the benefits and costs of dam construction and other major water projects. The WCD report highlighted that more than 60 percent of large dam projects caused significant disruption to fish migrations. In many cases, obstacles to migration occurred even when devices such as fish ladders have been installed. (Fish ladders help salmon, sea trout, sturgeon, and other migratory species ascend channels alongside dams.) More than 300 very large dam projects are still going ahead in developing countries (see, for example, "Yangtze River," pages 75–77). Once a dam is constructed, how it operates has a substantial impact on the survival of aquatic species downstream. For example, guaranteed minimum flow rates can help maintain the stock of flow-loving fish and ensure that important spawning shallows remain submerged. In 2001, following lobbying by local Thai people, water managers altered the operation of Pak Mun Dam to ensure higher rates of flow downstream. Populations of some of the 150 fish species that had previously declined showed rapid signs of recovery. However, despite continued pressure from those downstream who had their livelihoods threatened, the dam's operation in 2002 was less favorable, and the survival of healthy fish populations in the lower river remains precarious.

and effort involved, however, this often does not happen, and commonly dams are built or flood defenses constructed before scientists have a good understanding of the river's water regime and how organisms in the river will respond to any shifts in the regime. Another approach is for scientists to compare rivers flowing through catchments similar in geology, bankside vegetation, and gradient, and sharing a similar range of aquatic species. If one river has an altered flow regime and the other does not, differences between the two should highlight the impact of changing the water regime.

U.S. freshwater biologists carried out such a study on two Alabama rivers in the late 1980s. They sought to find out whether daily fluctuations in river flow associated with the discharge from a hydroelectric dam in one river, the Tallapoosa, altered the fish community relative to the nearby Cahaba River, which had a natural water regime. Variation in discharge from the dam on the Tallapoosa River causes the river downstream to fluctuate on an almost daily basis between still, lakelike conditions and turbulent flow. The scientists discovered that flow-loving river fishes were scarce just downstream of the dam but after several miles rose to levels comparable to those found throughout the Cahaba. Generalist fish species (those that are found in both rivers and lakes) were distributed similarly along the length of both rivers. The dam and its operation appeared to alter the structure of the fish community locally by disadvantaging flow-loving fishes.

Though successful, this two-river study did not reveal precisely how the flow-loving fishes are disadvantaged. The operation of a dam could affect these river fishes in a variety of ways. For instance, the fish may require a continuous supply of well-aerated water to maintain normal activity; the lack of water flow at certain times each day might stop the flow of drifting invertebrates on which the fishes feed; or flowing water may be critical for the fishes to breed successfully. Or some other factor involving competition with generalist fish species may be operating. Detailed experimental studies would be needed to establish the precise reasons why flow-loving fishes are displaced from the vicinity of the dam.

In a study of northern California rivers in the early 1990s, researchers showed experimentally how a dam's effect on water flow could have unexpected consequences on the structure of the biological community downstream. They chose to study a predator-resistant caddis fly, *Dicosmoecus gilvipes*. This caddis fly avoids being eaten by predatory fish such as trout and by larger invertebrates as well. It does so by growing to a large size and building a robust protective case made of small stones sewn together by silk, in which it lives. This protection comes at a cost, however. Because the case is bulky and heavy, the caddis fly lives on the riverbed and cannot retreat to narrow crevices when the river is in flood and flowing fast. In flood conditions a high proportion of *Dicosmoecus* get swept away.

The study team noted that *Dicosmoecus* increased in abundance during periods of reduced water flow. *Dicosmoecus* grazes attached algae, and at such times this caddis fly is likely to take a larger share of available algae because it is predator-resistant. Meanwhile other algal grazers, including less well-protected species of caddis fly, would be susceptible to predators such as trout and are eaten.

Using artificial stream channels constructed on the riverbed, the team went on to show that at high densities *Dicosmoecus* did avoid being eaten by trout. At the same time *Dicosmoecus* grazed the algae and consumed some other bottom-living invertebrates. This reduced the food available to trout. In the absence of *Dicosmoecus,* but in the presence of other algal grazers, the algal turf was less heavily grazed, in part because a proportion of these invertebrates were eaten by the trout. The presence or absence of *Dicosmoecus* had an effect on algal cover, the abundance of other algal grazers, and on the food available to trout.

All in all, the study shows that the influence of water flow on the abundance of *Dicosmoecus* can have domino effects throughout a food web, from producers such as algae to predators such as trout. The effects of changes in water flow, such as those created by dams, are many and complex.

## Changes in land use

Changes in land use in a river or lake's catchment area can profoundly alter the nature of a freshwater system within a very few years (see sidebar "The Aral Sea disaster," page 194). In the 19th century, tree felling in the vicinity of Lake Ontario on the U.S.-Canada border radically altered the nature of some streams that flowed into the lake. In vegetation-cleared areas, nutrients and soil particles ran into the streams, making the water quality unsuitable for migratory Atlantic salmon (*Salmo salar*) that spawned there. Clear-felling of trees reduces river flows in summer because more water than usual evaporates off the land before it enters the streams. In addition, the lack of tree shade allows more sunlight to reach the stream and warm the water. In the last few decades attempts to reestablish the salmon fishery in many of these rivers have failed because the water is now too warm and the flow too sluggish to maintain cool, oxygenated water flowing over gravel beds. This is a basic requirement for salmon to spawn successfully.

## The Aral Sea disaster

The Aral Sea in Central Asia was, until the 1960s, a massive inland sea. Then between 1960 and 1990 the water level in the lake fell by some 48.6 feet (14.8 m). At the same time the lake's area declined by nearly 51 percent and its volume by 69 percent. The cause? A massive increase in water abstraction for irrigation from the Aral Sea's two main feeder rivers, the Syr-Dar'ya and Amu-Dar'ya. This followed a Soviet plan to make the Central Asian republics self-sufficient in cotton production. By 1987 the area under intensive cotton cultivation had reached 19 million acres (7.6 million ha), and much of the water for this expansion came from Syr-Dar'ya and Amu-Dar'ya. The Aral Sea was being starved of water. As a result, the sea's thriving fishing industry had been destroyed. Few fishes were left to be caught, and fishing villages were left high and dry many miles from the shores of the now shrunken sea.

Apart from the sea's massive loss of water, two other factors played key roles in altering the structure of the biological community in this once-giant sea: salinity and nutrient content. Though the sea's volume declined, it contained the same overall amount of dissolved salts, so its salinity (the concentration of dissolved salts) rose from about 10 parts per thousand (brackish) to 29 parts per thousand (nearly that of average seawater). At the same time the sea became starved of nutrients. By 1990 all Aral Sea fishes, whether native or introduced, were practically extinct except close to where rivers flowed into the sea. Only four of the 24 fish species present in the early 1960s were still present in 1990. As if this were not enough, today many pollutants also contaminate the region's river water and threaten the health of local people. Pesticides sprayed on the intensively farmed land are among these.

*Sediment-laden runoff from deforested hills has stained Madagascar's Ikopa River brown with silt.* (Frans Lanting/ Minden Pictures)

Field studies carried out in and around Hubbard Brook, New Hampshire, during the 1960s showed that when trees in the catchment area were clear-felled, chemicals that were originally incorporated into the vegetation became flushed into the river, radically altering its chemical composition. Levels of nitrate in the river rose more than fiftyfold following several seasons of clear-cutting and, along with other released chemicals, this made the water quality less favorable for the survival of trout.

## Climate change

In the 1990s the average annual temperatures in the Northern Hemisphere were the highest since detailed climatic records began to be compiled in the first half of the 19th century. This could be a sign of global warming—a trend showing a rise in average temperatures across the globe. Global warming is too complex a process for many scientists to be readily convinced that it is actually happening and, if it is, what is the best way to combat it. Assessing whether global warming is taking place depends on decades of measurements to ensure that any rise is not just a temporary anomaly. Moreover, global climate is the sum total of regional climates across the globe. Even if some regions are becoming warmer, others are becoming cooler as climate patterns shift. It is necessary to work out average temperatures across the globe, month by month, year by year, to see whether there is a trend.

The Intergovernmental Panel on Climate Change (IPCC), a group made up of hundreds of scientists from across the globe, has been meeting regularly since 1990 to evaluate whether global warming is taking place and, if it is, to determine both the cause and what can be done about it. On balance, the IPCC is convinced that global warming is taking place and that rising levels of greenhouse gases in the atmosphere are the most likely cause. Currently, carbon dioxide levels in the global atmosphere are increasing, probably caused by humans burning more fossil fuels. Carbon dioxide is a greenhouse gas implicated in global warming (see sidebar). Any process that slows, halts, or reverses rising atmospheric carbon dioxide levels might help counter global warming.

The Earth's surface appears to be warming. Between the years 1900 and 2000, the Earth's surface temperature rose by about 1°F (0.6°C) overall. In 2001 the IPCC estimated that the global surface temperature will probably rise by 2.5°F to

10.4°F (1.4°C to 5.8°C) between 1990 and 2100, with a best guess in the region of 5.4°F (3°C). Warming of about 9°F (5°C) since the last great ice age, some 15,000 years ago, was sufficient to transform the entire landscape of Canada from a wilderness deeply covered in snow and ice to the rich mixture of landscapes seen today. The predicted changes in global climate in the current century are clearly a cause for concern.

A 5.4°F (3°C) global temperature rise in the time span of little more than a century would affect freshwater systems in numerous ways. For example, the timing and distribution of precipitation and runoff would change, but the effect would vary from region to region. In tropical Africa and in temperate regions of the Northern Hemisphere, for instance,

## The greenhouse effect

The greenhouse effect is a natural feature of Earth's atmosphere that has been operating for billions of years. It is caused by certain atmospheric gases—dubbed "greenhouse gases"—most notably water vapor, carbon dioxide, and methane.

When sunlight strikes the Earth's surface, some of the absorbed energy is emitted back into space as infrared radiation. Greenhouse gases absorb some of the outgoing infrared radiation, thus trapping heat in the atmosphere. During Earth's history, the greenhouse effect has been vital in sustaining a rich variety of life on Earth. Without the greenhouse effect, the planet would probably be, on average, at least 54°F (30°C) cooler than it is.

The name "greenhouse effect" comes from the superficial similarity between the operation of greenhouse gases and the glass in a greenhouse. On a sunny day in winter, the inside of a greenhouse is noticeably warmer than the air outside. The effect is due to the greenhouse glass, which helps prevent infrared radiation from leaving the greenhouse and so has a pronounced warming effect.

The problem with the atmospheric greenhouse effect is not that it is happening, but that human activities appear to be "enhancing" the natural greenhouse effect. Globally, people are burning more fossil fuels—in particular, petroleum oil products, coal, and natural gas—than ever before. This activity is releasing additional carbon dioxide into the atmosphere, which is enhancing the greenhouse effect, trapping more heat energy in the atmosphere and contributing to global warming.

precipitation would be likely to increase during the winter, while in Australia, Central America, and southern Africa, winter rainfall would be likely to decrease. Higher winter precipitation would increase water flows in rivers and make flooding more likely. Lower winter rainfall would make droughts and water stagnation more likely. Both effects are likely to alter zonation patterns in rivers (see "How freshwater communities function," pages 133–139).

According to the IPCC, sea level, averaged across Earth's surface, would probably rise by some 3.5 inches (0.09 m) to 34.6 inches (0.88 m) between 1990 and 2100. This is because seawater expands slightly as it warms and because polar ice caps would melt marginally, adding freshwater to the sea. The rise in sea level will vary with latitude (because sea level bulges slightly at the equator due to the rotation of the Earth). The overall effect might well be to reduce the drop between source and the sea and to increase the incursion of seawater into rivers and its seepage into land that drains into rivers. The tsunami of December 26, 2004—a series of giant ocean waves generated by an offshore earthquake in the eastern Indian Ocean—provides a foretaste of what saltwater intrusion can do. In coastal regions across a wide area, saltwater contaminated aquifers and their associated wells and entered rice paddy fields. This deprived local people of both food crops and drinkable freshwater.

Other factors aside, a 5.4°F (3°C) rise in the average annual temperature of a freshwater system might well alter the community of animals and plants that live there, favoring some and leaving others at a disadvantage. For example, in many temperate regions of the Northern Hemisphere, a rise in summer peak water temperatures from, say, 59°F (15°C) to 64.4°F (18°C) would reduce dissolved oxygen levels and thus favor the survival of panfish such as bass and perch over salmonids such as trout and salmon.

As inland waters warm, the species mix of lakes and rivers is likely to change. Taking the rivers and lakes of Canada's conifer forest belt as an example, aquatic species from the south are likely to invade inland freshwaters. Present freshwater species of this cold forest belt (called boreal forest or taiga) include cold-water fish such as lake trout, grayling, and dolly varden. These could be replaced by warmer-water species, including pike and walleye. Meanwhile, some freshwater taiga species could be displaced northward into what is now treeless tundra territory. In addition, climatologists suspect that thousands of boreal forest lakes and wetlands might dry up in the next 100 years as levels of precipitation decline.

Although shifts in Earth's climate occur regularly, at different scales of magnitude and at timescales ranging from decades to thousands of years, the current concern is that human-induced climate change is producing a massive climate shift within a century. This short period of time may be too abrupt to allow species to disperse successfully from their existing distributions to new ones. Without further human intervention—such as people helping to facilitate the transfer of species to new locations—many populations could be wiped out and the survival of aquatic species threatened.

Most atmospheric scientists agree that a substantial proportion of the global temperature rise during the last century—at least half—can be accounted for by a rise in atmospheric levels of greenhouse gases produced by human activities. The obvious way to halt global warming is for governments to work together to cut down the release of greenhouse gases. This means reducing the amount of fossil fuels being burned. The Kyoto Protocol, an international agreement on reducing greenhouse gas emissions, seeks to lower greenhouse gas release by about 5 percent before 2012. Canada has ratified the treaty and hopes to make the cuts by offering incentives to people to make their homes more energy efficient. The Canadian government is also encouraging the use of cleaner gasoline and biodiesel, made from vegetable oil, as fuels that burn to produce fewer oxides of nitrogen (some forms of which are greenhouse gases). As of March 2005 the United States had declined to sign to the protocol although Russia, following the example set by more than 140 countries, had recently done so.

## Alien invasions

One of the most damaging forms of ecological impact is the introduction of "exotic" species from one geographical location to another. Exotic species are also called alien, nonnative, or nonindigenous species. They are introduced to new locations deliberately or accidentally by human activities. This distinguishes them from native species that have lived in a locality since at least prehistoric times. Many exotic species do not survive for long in their new locality, but among those that do, a small proportion are highly disruptive of the new habitat they have entered. Biologists call exotic species *invasives* when they become locally abundant and dramatically affect native species. Because they are part of watersheds receiving water from a wide area, lakes and rivers are particularly vulnerable to invasions by alien species. Artificial waterways have connected aquatic systems that were hitherto separate, and boat traffic disperses organisms from one watershed to another in ballast water or attached to ships' hulls.

Many scientists estimate that invasive species are the second-greatest cause of freshwater extinctions after major forms of habitat alteration such as channelization or interrupting the river's flow by constructing a dam. Invasive species may harm native forms by competing with them, consuming them, or modifying the habitat physically or chemically.

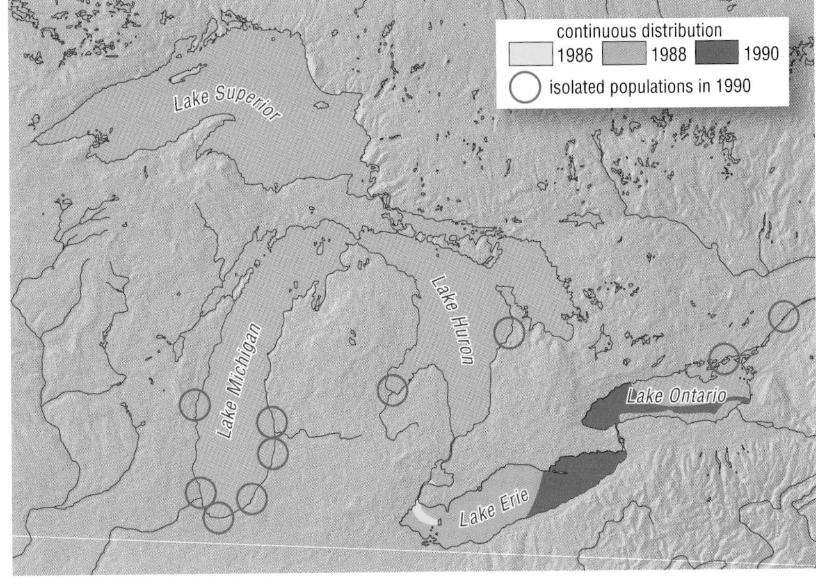


*The rapid spread of the zebra mussel* (Dreissena polymorpha) *through North America's Great Lakes between 1986 and 1990. Today the mussel is prevalent in all the Great Lakes.*

Accidental introductions of invasive species into the Great Lakes of North America provide examples of all three major types of ecological impact: competition, predation, and habitat alteration. The most pervasive of recent invaders is the zebra mussel (*Dreissena polymorpha*). The first sighting of this mollusk in North America was at Lake St. Clair, a small lake connecting Lake Huron and Lake Erie, in 1988. The mussel probably found its way there from ballast water picked up by an oceangoing ship in a European freshwater port. After its transatlantic voyage this ship must have entered the Great Lakes system through the St. Lawrence Seaway and discharged its ballast water. The water contained the mussel's microscopic planktonic larvae, which grew and rapidly established themselves in their new surroundings. Their spread across the Great Lakes and beyond has been astonishingly rapid. By 1990 (see figure on previous page) the mussel had entered all the Great Lakes. By 2002 the mussel had spread through the Mississippi watershed to New Orleans and the Gulf of Mexico. The high rate of dispersal and establishment can be partly explained by the mussel's high rate of reproduction. One female can produce 40,000 planktonic larvae in a season. At present, there appear to be insufficient parasites, diseases, or predators to keep the mussel numbers in check.

The impact of the zebra mussel on other organisms of the lake community has been dramatic. The mussels attach to almost any hard surface and crowd out other attached mollusks such as clams. Carpets of zebra mussels can reach densities well in excess of 2,000 animals per square foot (22,000/$m^2$) in some places. They will even settle and grow on the surface of plants and animals, including crayfish and clams.

In Lake St. Clair, native clams have been ousted by zebra mussels. These mussels filter the water to consume phytoplankton. Although this activity improves water clarity, it deprives other filter feeders of food. By blocking inlet pipes, attaching to ship's hulls, and otherwise disrupting facilities, zebra mussels are costing water suppliers and other lake users well in excess of U.S.$60 million a year. The zebra mussel is one in a list of more than 140 invasive species that have entered the Great Lakes since the 1800s, including the sea lamprey (*Petromyzon marinus*), a predator on valuable freshwater fish such as the trout (*Onchorhynchus* and *Salmo* species). Keeping lamprey numbers in check using chemical treatments to kill their larvae still costs some U.S.$12 million a year.

While many of the worst invasives in North America's Great Lakes were introduced by accident, arguably the worst invasive of Lake Victoria—the Nile perch (*Lates niloticus*)—was introduced by design. Lake Victoria is Africa's largest lake by surface area (see "Lake Victoria," pages 87–89), and its biological communities have been radically transformed by introductions of exotic species within the past 50 years. In the 1950s Lake Victoria supported a remarkable fish population containing more than 300 species of haplochromine fish (a type of cichlid fish), of which more than 90 percent were endemic (that is, found in the locality but nowhere else in the world).

The Nile perch is a large predatory fish that often reaches weights in excess of 80 pounds (36 kg). It was first introduced into Lake Victoria in the late 1950s. At this time lake stocks of larger cichlid fish had been depleted by overfishing, and some people viewed the introduction of the Nile perch as a way of making good the shortfall with a high-value food fish. Between the early 1960s and late 1970s, stocks of the Nile perch remained relatively low, perhaps because fish-eating haplochromines ate their young. When overfishing further reduced the populations of predatory haplochromines, more Nile perch were able to survive to maturity and breed.

In the early 1980s the population of Nile perch exploded in numbers and biomass. The perch consumed haplochromine fish in vast numbers, and the abundance and diversity of these fish plummeted. Haplochromines and other cichlids have relatively low rates of reproduction and so cannot rapidly replenish their populations. Many of the haplochromine species were algal grazers and detritus feeders, and when their numbers crashed, the growth of phytoplankton and attached algae went largely unchecked. Decaying phytoplankton and attached algae made the deep water of Lake Victoria nutrient-rich and oxygen-poor, forcing deep-water species into shallow water. There they more easily fell prey to Nile perch.

Two species have conspicuously benefited from changes in Nile perch abundance and the decline in Lake Victoria's water quality. A small fish, the dagaa (*Rastineobola argenta*), a zooplankton feeder and member of the carp family, has increased in abundance to occupy the niche left by zooplankton-feeding haplochromines. And a species of freshwater prawn that is tolerant of low-oxygen conditions, *Caridina nilotica,* now thrives in the oxygen-poor hypolimnion where most fish cannot survive.

Today the community of fish living in Lake Victoria is much less diverse than it was only 30 years ago. In the early 1970s the upper waters of Lake Victoria supported a diverse fish population, of which about 40 percent of the biomass were algal-grazing or detritus-feeding haplochromines and 40 percent fish-eating or zooplankton-consuming haplochromines. By the 1990s Nile perch accounted for 90 percent of the fish biomass. The perch now resort to feeding on invertebrates as well as fish. The upper waters of Lake Victoria support only half the biomass of fish they did 30 years ago, and much of the phytoplankton production goes uneaten. About 200 of the 300 species of haplochromines have been driven to extinction or are so scarce that they do not reveal themselves in attempts to sample the fish population. It is possible that some of the missing species may be eking out a living in wetlands close to the lake. Nevertheless, the decline of Lake Victoria fish species probably represents the single largest 20th-century extinction event among vertebrates.

Added to this remarkable change in fish diversity—largely accounted for by Nile perch predation—are other problems. In 1989 the water hyacinth (*Eichhornia crassipes*), a floating aquatic plant from Central and South America and now widespread in Africa, entered Lake Victoria from feeder rivers. By the late 1990s the plant had spread to cover more than 50,000 acres (20,000 ha) of Lake Victoria. At low densities, the plant can provide safe habitats for small fish to breed, but at high density it blocks almost all sunlight penetration. This prevents phytoplankton and attached algae from growing in the water beneath, where they could enrich the water with oxygen. As a result, the water becomes oxygen-depleted.

Apart from crowding out native plant and animal species, beds of water hyacinth block boat traffic. The plants also increase rates of debilitating human diseases such as malaria and schistosomiasis (see "Rivers, lakes, and human health," pages 152–157). This is because the plants create patches of near-stagnant water where schistosoma-carrying snails and the larvae of malaria-carrying mosquitoes can thrive. In 1997 lake authorities introduced two species of plant-consuming South American weevil (*Neochetina eichhorniae* and *Neochetina bruchi*) to control the weed. While this did massively reduce plant densities temporarily, there are signs that the weed density is increasing again.

Unwanted introductions are very difficult to prevent because they can come about through the thoughtless actions of only one or a few people. And once alien species have established themselves in a new locality, it can prove impossible to dislodge them. The World Conservation Union (IUCN) has developed a global strategy for the prevention and management of invasive alien species, and it is seeking to implement the strategy across the world through international conventions. There are four major stages to tackling invasions by alien species: prevention, early detection, eradication, and, failing eradication, control. Once alien species are established, the eradication or control options are usually expensive and difficult to apply; prevention is usually the cheapest and most effective option.

As for North America's Great Lakes, various agencies seek to limit the invasives problem through a combination of biological monitoring and control, public education programs, and enforcement of national and regional legislation. For example, vessels entering the Great Lakes and St. Lawrence Seaway are now required to empty and refill their ballast water beforehand at sea. This minimizes the likelihood of unwanted freshwater organisms being transferred to the Great Lakes system through ballast water. Involving the general public in identifying invasives and taking action to control their introduction and spread is a vital part of any invasives control program. Boaters can be encouraged to clean the hulls of their vessels to remove attached animals and plants before they take their craft from one watershed to another. Anglers can be educated to not transfer water or release fish from one watershed to another, without expert guidance.

## Freshwater pollution

Pollution can be defined as human alteration of specific physical or chemical factors in the environment that are not ordinarily present at such levels. If it happens to an extent that is likely to harm living organisms, it is called pollution. Pollutants are those substances or factors that enter the environment at levels believed to be harmful.

There are a multitude of freshwater pollutants, ranging from more or less "natural" substances, such as human or animal feces that enter lakes and rivers in large quantities, to entirely artificial substances such as chlorine-based organic pesticides and industrial cleaning agents (see the table below). Worldwide, industries develop hundreds of new

### Major types of freshwater pollution

| Type of pollutant or effect | Description |
|---|---|
| Microbiological | Pollution containing microorganisms such as bacteria that are harmful to humans or other forms of life |
| Eutrophication | Caused by high levels of plant nutrients such as nitrates and phosphates |
| Acidification | From atmospheric pollution that causes acid deposition |
| Thermal | Raised water temperatures such as those from warm-water discharges from electricity-generating power stations |
| Radionuclides | Radioactive substances |
| Solid waste | Fairly inert solid objects such as plastics or concrete blocks |
| Suspended solids | Particles suspended in the water column that block light penetration and could smother bottom-living organisms |
| Heavy metals | Metals such as copper, iron, and zinc that can enter watercourses from mining operations |
| Pesticides | Synthetic substances such as DDT. Many are persistent and accumulate in food chains |
| PCBs | Polychlorinated biphenyls: stabilizers previously found in a wide range of products including plastics, adhesives, inks, and lubricants. Like many pesticides, they are persistent and accumulate in food chains |

Note: Based in part on a classification used by the United Nations Environment Program and the Global International Waters Assessment chemical substances each year, and at least some of these find their way into lakes and rivers.

Pollutants are often classified according to their means of entry into aquatic systems. *Point sources* are localized entry sites such as pipes or drains. *Diffuse sources* are those that enter a river or lake across a broad front, as in the case of runoff from an agricultural field next to a river or acid rain falling on a lake. As a general rule, pollutants from point sources are easier to manage, because their input is more easily located, sampled, and, if necessary, cut off.

In practice, to demonstrate that a given chemical produces a specific effect on organisms in the environment is difficult and costly. Typically, the danger posed by a chemical is calculated based on laboratory studies in which organisms, or cultured tissues from organisms, are exposed to the chemical in question to see its effect. From such studies, scientists estimate acceptable levels of such chemicals in the environment. They err on the side of caution, usually setting the acceptable levels quite low. But the complexity of interactions in the environment makes such simple estimates difficult to translate to the real-world situation.

Some organisms concentrate chemicals in certain tissues in their body, so the toxic effect of the pollutant is greater than anticipated based on analyzing samples of water or sediment. Also, traces of some pollutants accumulate as they pass from one organism to another through a food chain, so the pollutant becomes concentrated in the tissues of consumers at higher trophic levels (see sidebar). Finally, the environment contains a rich cocktail of chemicals that may interact with one another, so the combined effect of two different substances may be much worse than one chemical on its own.

By the 1990s more than 500 kinds of toxic pollutants had been identified in the waters of the Great Lakes of North America. They entered the lakes through the atmosphere, from streams and rivers flowing into the lake, and from direct discharge into the lakes. Among the most worrying groups of these pollutants were PCBs (short for polychlorinated biphenyls). These are synthetic organic substances that have great stability—they do not break down rapidly. Until the late 1970s PCBs were in widespread use by North Ameri-

## *Bioaccumulation and biomagnification*

Pollutants can enter organisms through the foods they consume or simply by contact with some part of the body surface. The gills, those thin-walled structures that fish and many invertebrates use to exchange gases with their watery surroundings, are a common route of entry. Once a pollutant enters the body it may be broken down or excreted before it does harm, or it may accumulate in specific parts of the body, a process called *bioaccumulation.*

For example, PCBs tend to accumulate in body fat. Substances that bioaccumulate and are long-lasting (they remain undegraded for weeks, months, or years) tend to be passed on to consumers that eat the organism in which they bioaccumulated. If this occurs at each step of a food chain, consumers at upper trophic levels of a food chain will have received the bioaccumulated substances from many individuals lower in the chain. In effect, the pollutant has become concentrated as it rises up a food chain, a process called *biomagnification.* This is significant. In freshwater systems of North America and Europe, some top predators such as trout, salmon, and fish-eating birds of prey have accumulated toxic levels of PCBs by biomagnification.

can industries. The United States banned domestic production of PCBs in 1978, but by the 1990s levels of these substances were still worryingly high in some of the trout and salmon caught in Lake Michigan. The PCBs had bioaccumulated and their levels biomagnified as they were passed along food chains. The effects of high levels of PCBs include reproductive failure and skin and digestive disorders, as has been demonstrated in laboratory tests on mammals. In the 1990s local health officials recommended a combination of bans and restrictions on the consumption of Lake Michigan trout and salmon. This followed concern over high levels of PCBs, pesticide residues, and the metal mercury in fish flesh.

### Too many nutrients

Among the most widespread forms of freshwater pollution are those involving substances that serve as plant nutrients. Lakes and rivers near large human communities have, historically, often undergone dramatic changes in water quality (see "The historic Thames," pages 162–165). There are many pollutants that can cause this change but a common source is the input of large quantities of human sewage. Untreated sewage not only contains suspended sediment that clouds the water and blocks out light, but the particles contain organic material that is rich in the chemical elements carbon (C), nitrogen (N), and phosphorus (P). When this organic material decomposes, it enriches the water with nitrates and phosphates, which are plant nutrients. Their presence encourages the growth of phytoplankton and attached plants. Highly elevated levels of nitrates and phosphates tend to reduce aquatic biodiversity. Consider the case of phytoplankton, for example. At very high densities their photosynthesis saturates the water with oxygen during the day. But at night, when photosynthesis ceases, the respiration of phytoplankton and other organisms and the decomposition of detritus by bacteria rapidly deplete dissolved oxygen. Many animals cannot survive the low oxygen levels and die. The susceptibility of aquatic animals to low oxygen levels varies by animal group (see the table below). Clear,

## Sensitivity to oxygen-depleting organic pollution in freshwater invertebrates

| Category* | Invertebrate groups |
|---|---|
| 1 | Oligochaete worms |
| 2 | Chironomid (midge) larvae |
| 3 | Water louse (*Asellus*); most leeches; most pond snails |
| 4 | Alder flies; fish leeches; *Baetis* mayflies |
| 5 | Blackflies; crane flies; flatworms; most diving bugs and beetles |
| 6 | Freshwater mussels; *Gammarus; Viviparus* pond snails; some dragonfly species |
| 7 | Most caddis fly larvae; some mayflies; some stoneflies |
| 8 | Crayfish; most dragonfly species |
| 9 | Some dragonfly species |
| 10 | Most mayflies; most stoneflies; some caddis fly larvae |

*Category 10 denotes the most pollution-susceptible groups of animals; category 1 denotes the least.

## Zones of disturbance and recovery in a temperate North American river affected by sewage pollution

| Location relative to significant sewage discharge | Zone | Dissolved oxygen level | Typical members of the animal community |
|---|---|---|---|
| Upstream | Clean | Normal | Trout, perch, and bass. Mayfly, stonefly, and caddis fly larvae |
| Just downstream | Septic | Very low | Oligochaete (sludge) worms and chironomid (midge) larvae. No fish |
| A few hundred yards to a few miles downstream | Recovery | Moderate | Small fish such as mudminnows (*Umbra*). Chironomid (midge) and blackfly larvae |
| Typically several miles downstream | Clean | Normal | Trout, perch, and bass. Mayfly, stonefly, and caddis fly larvae |

oxygen-rich waters typically contain a rich variety of mayfly, stonefly, and caddis fly larvae. In the murkiest, most oxygen-depleted waters, segmented worms and midge larvae may thrive, but few other large invertebrates can survive.

When high levels of partially treated or untreated sewage are regularly discharged into a river, the stretch of river typically shows a characteristic pattern of disturbance and recovery (see table above). Just upstream of the sewage discharge point the water may be comparatively clean and oxygen-rich and harbor a wide variety of fish and other animal species. Just downstream of the sewage discharge the water becomes murky and oxygen-depleted. In this *septic zone* fish are absent and the dominant invertebrates are oligochaete worms plus mosquito and midge larvae. After a few hundred yards or a few miles (depending on the size of the river and the relative amount of sewage) the septic zone gradually gives way to the *recovery zone*. Here much of the sewage has decomposed and dissolved oxygen concentrations are rising to moderate levels. Small fish such as mudminnows (*Umbra*) survive here, as do blackfly larvae. The recovery zone eventually gives way to the *clean zone* downstream, where dissolved oxygen levels and the diversity of the biological community are similar to those upstream of the sewage discharge, provided that no other environmental factors intervene.

Phosphate, rather than nitrate, is often the major nutrient that causes overenrichment of freshwater systems. Apart from sewage, other potent sources of phosphates include the runoff from fields to which agricultural fertilizers have been applied and phosphate-active detergents (most of which have now been phased out in developed countries) that find their way into industrial and domestic wastewater. Several approaches are now used to reduce the problem of eutrophication, but in the case of some lakes it is too costly to undo the damage done in previous decades (see "Restoring overenriched lakes," pages 221–223).

## Acid waters

Acid rain became an internationally recognized problem in the early 1970s. In the course of burning fossil fuels (such as oil, coal, and natural gas), motor vehicles, power stations, and industrial processes release sulfur and nitrogen oxides. These oxides react with water, ozone, and other chemicals in the atmosphere to form sulfuric, nitric, and other acids. The droplets of moisture fall from the clouds as acid rain. This is rain with a pH of less than 5, compared with "normal" rain, which has a pH of about 5.5 (see "Freshwater's chemical composition," pages 18–21).

Acid rain is better called *acid deposition* because it is not just rain that causes the problem. Acid can travel through the air in snow, mist, fog, and even dry air. Air pollution drifts hundreds of miles on air currents, causing acid deposition in neighboring countries. The smokestacks and car exhausts of British and German cities affect the lakes and forests of Scandinavia. Air pollution released in Chicago and Detroit falls as acid rain by the time it reaches Ontario, Quebec, Labrador, and Newfoundland.

In June 1972 at the UN Conference on the Human Environment in Stockholm, Sweden, Swedish scientists claimed that acid gases released from countries in northwest Europe were drifting over Sweden and damaging lakes and forests. This claim triggered 20 years of research by European scientists that showed the Swedish scientists were largely correct but that the effects of acid rain were more complex than expected. The results prompted European governments to meet and establish international laws to combat air pollution that crosses international boundaries. It is not effective to treat the effects of acid deposition damage at their final destination. It has to be managed by reducing the release of the gases at their source (see "Dealing with acidification," pages 223–225).

The effect of acid deposition varies widely from lake to lake depending, in large part, on the nature of the underlying bedrock. In lakes with bedrock rich in carbonates, lake water typically contains high levels of dissolved calcium carbonate. Its presence counteracts the effects of acid deposition, a feature called a high *buffering capacity.* Lakes with granite bedrock, as are common in the central, conifer-forested regions of Canada and Scandinavia, contain very little dissolved calcium carbonate. These lakes have a low buffering capacity and are very susceptible to acid deposition. High levels of acid deposition can turn lake water quite acidic (pH less than 5.5) with the result that plants, invertebrates, and fish are killed or their reproduction is affected. The highly acid water also causes metals to dissolve out of the underlying ground, and some of these metals, such as mercury and aluminum, are toxic to people as well as other living organisms. Hundreds of lakes in Ontario have become so acidic (pH 4.5 or less) that they are now devoid of most animal life. How long they will take to recover is not known. Hundreds more lakes in Quebec, Canada, and in Sweden are pH 5 to 4.5 and are dangerously close to losing their entire fish populations and most of their invertebrates.

In lakes and ponds that had approximately neutral pH levels (pH 6.5 to 7.5) in the 1950s and 1960s, a reduction of pH to the range of 5 to 6 has had a marked effect on the nature of their plant and animal communities. Acidification favors some types of phytoplankton over others. Diatoms and blue-green algae that were abundant at near-neutral pH levels become replaced by dinoflagellates and chrysophytes. Both the biomass and biodiversity of phytoplankton tend to decline as acidification proceeds. Along with this goes a shift

## Lowest pH levels at which selected animals successfully breed in northern European waters

| pH | Animal |
|---|---|
| 4.8 | Most mayflies |
| 4.8 | Perch (*Perca fluviatilis*) |
| 5.0 | Most pond snails |
| 5.1 | Crayfish (*Austropotamobius*) |
| 5.2 | Roach (*Rutilis rutilus*) |
| 5.3 | Freshwater shrimp (*Gammarus*) |

in the composition of the animal community. Freshwater shrimp (*Gammarus*) and crayfish (such as *Austropotamobius*) die out when pH levels drop to between 5.5 and 5, and *Daphnia* become fewer; and only a few species of fish can reproduce successfully at pH 5 or less (see the table above). Crustaceans such as *Gammarus* cannot produce their chalky cuticle under highly acid conditions. The effects on phytoplankton and the animal community are due not just to the direct effect of acidification, but also to the indirect effect of the release of aluminum and heavy metals such as lead and cadmium. These remain chemically locked in sediments at higher pH levels but become liberated at lower pH levels. Fish, in particular, are very susceptible to metal poisoning. High levels of dissolved aluminum cause fish to produce excess amounts of mucus that clog their gills.

## Overharvesting

Overharvesting means removing more mass of living matter from an ecosystem than can be replaced by natural growth and reproduction. As a result, the population of the biological resource—whether a plant or animal—gradually goes into decline. Individuals in the population become less abundant and their average size decreases because larger members tend to be removed and do not survive to old age. In freshwater systems the most obvious form of overharvesting is overfishing (see sidebar "Standing stock, fish production, and maximum sustainable yield").

## Standing stock, fish production, and maximum sustainable yield

The average biomass of fish (or any other type of organism, for that matter) that survives in a lake or river year after year is called the *standing stock* for that particular ecosystem. The standing stock depends on many factors, such as the availability of food for that species, the existence of predators, how favorable the physical and chemical environment is, and so on. *Production* is the amount of biomass that is added to the fish population each year (and that is subsequently lost from it by predation and other factors) so that the population's biomass remains stable. Scientists estimate production for a fish species in a given ecosystem on the basis of food availability and rates of energy transfer through the food web (see "Energy flow, food chains, and food webs," pages 128–133).

Assuming a fish population remains relatively stable in terms of the number and size of fish in the population, then new fish join the population each year through breeding and perhaps by arriving from elsewhere by migration. This annual addition of fish is called *recruitment.* Fish leave the population when they are eaten by predators or die from other causes such as disease. These combined annual losses are called *mortality.* Fish might also leave the area by migration. Other factors aside, if recruitment is equal to mortality plus emigration, then the population remains stable in its number of individuals and in the size and age distribution of its members.

In a population subjected to fishing for food, fishing often forms a major part of the population's mortality. The *maximum sustainable yield* is the largest number of fish that can be taken by fishers from the population year after year without causing the stock to diminish. Since other predators are also taking their toll on the fish population, and enough of the fish must remain to reproduce to replace losses, the maximum sustainable yield is typically estimated to be in the range of 30 to 50 percent of annual fish production. However, because recruitment varies from year to year, fisheries scientists tend to err on the side of caution. They seek to set maximum sustainable yield estimates at some 20 to 40 percent of annual fish production unless the fish stock is boosted by artificial stocking (adding fish that have been bred in captivity).

In an unstocked fishery, if fishers exceed the maximum sustainable yield year after year, it becomes harder and harder to catch fewer and fewer fish. The fish that are caught are also smaller in size, and few survive to reproduce. The population goes into a precipitous decline from which it may not recover. To produce sound estimates of the maximum sustainable yield requires a good understanding of the reproductive behavior of the fish

*(continues)*

*(continued)*

stock, monitoring to check on the standing stock, and an understanding of how recruitment can vary from year to year (see "Managing freshwater fisheries," pages 225–229). Without such understanding to inform management decisions, it is easy for fishers to exceed the maximum sustainable yield.

In North America and northwest Europe, most freshwater fisheries are managed largely or entirely for recreational fishing. In parts of central and eastern Europe, recreational fishing often takes place alongside commercial fishing. Large freshwater systems in Africa and South America are fished commercially or on a subsistence basis, with fishers catching fish on a small scale to feed themselves and their families and selling any excess at local markets. Fish are a vital source of food and cash in these communities. Although wild-caught freshwater fish make up only some 9 percent by weight of the global fish catch, given that lakes, rivers, and wetlands cover only 3.5 percent of the land surface, the fishing pressure on many of them is intense.

There are numerous examples of fish stocks in freshwaters being harvested to commercial extinction, meaning that the effort involved no longer makes it worthwhile to harvest the few remaining fish. In Africa's Lake Victoria, for example, between the 1930s and 1960s, the fishery for one species of tilapia (*Oreochromis esculenta*) collapsed. Fishing became more intense as fishers hunted the dwindling stocks using nets with smaller and smaller mesh sizes. In the 1930s five-inch mesh nets were in common use, but by the 1960s these were replaced by four-inch and even three-inch mesh nets. Few fish were surviving to breed. In nets set overnight, the catch per net fell from six fish in the 1930s to less than 0.5 by the late 1960s. By this time fishing for *Oreochromis* was no longer worthwhile, and this was one of the reasons why local authorities encouraged stocking with the Nile perch (see "Alien invasions," pages 199–205).

There are also many examples of overfishing leading to actual extinction locally. Among North America's Great Lakes, for example, overfishing by sport and commercial fishers from the 1870s through to the early 1900s drove first the muskellunge (*Esox mosquinongy*) and then the lake sturgeon (*Acipenser fulvescens*) and Northern pike (*Esox lucius*) to extinction in Lake Erie.

Fishing affects not only targeted species but also other species in the food web. For example, fishers who use encircling purse seine nets to catch schools of fish often take other species as well. Although the unwanted fish might be returned to the water, if they are damaged during the catching process, they may well die soon after.

Selectively removing certain species of fish from a lake or river usually causes other elements in the food web to adjust. The predators of harvested fish may diminish because part of their food supply has been removed. In many cases, harvested species are predators at or near the top of food chains, and their removal alters the balance of organisms at lower levels, including the abundance of different species of zooplankton, bottom-living invertebrates, and phytoplankton (see sidebar "The trophic cascade," page 142). Fish species that compete with harvested fish for food may increase in abundance as the gap created by removed predators enables them to take a greater share of available food.

The act of fishing often causes damage to the physical environment itself. Nets that scrape the riverbed or lakebed disturb plants and bottom-living invertebrates and raise sediment that can smother organisms. In rivers disturbed invertebrates drift downstream and become easy prey for predators or may fail to settle at all and become swept away on the current until they are battered to death or enter unfavorable chemical conditions where they die. Sport fishers who use nylon fishing line and commercial fishers who use nylon mesh nets often leave broken tackle in the water, where it can snare animals for months or years before it decays. Nontarget species, including birds and aquatic mammals, amphibians, and reptiles, can also become entangled in the lost or discarded nylon tackle. Entangled animals often die a lingering death. So apart from its direct effects on a target fish population, fishing can have many other impacts on the biological community and the physical environment where it takes place.

In summary, habitat alteration, global warming, alien invasions, and pollution are the major threats to freshwater ecosystems. These impacts are accelerating the pace of environmental change in freshwater ecosystems. As the next chapter reveals, these threats do not act separately but combine to make the management of lakes and rivers a growing challenge.

# CONCLUSION: MANAGING LAKES AND RIVERS

Lakes and rivers serve a multiplicity of uses. They act as political boundaries and transport corridors. Water utilities take water from freshwater ecosystems to supply farms, industrial complexes, and offices and homes. Utilities regulate the flow of water in rivers using dams and flood defenses and by straightening and deepening natural water channels. Other utilities use rivers to dispose of wastewater. Some people harvest the biological resources of lakes and rivers, especially fish. And a wide variety of people spend their leisure time at the waterside, whether boating, fishing, shooting, or simply admiring the wildlife and its setting.

These various demands threaten the quantity and quality of freshwater in lakes and rivers. This happens mainly through altering the water regime and thereby changing aquatic habitats, through pollution and the introduction of exotic forms of animals and plants, and through overharvesting. How are these threats and conflicting demands to be resolved? How can lakes and rivers be used in a sustainable way for the benefit of people and wildlife? Achieving these aims on a global scale requires cooperation between people at all levels, from local to international, and this is the focus of the final chapter.

## Integrated management

The drainage basin—containing a main river and its network of tributaries—is a logical scale at which to undertake management of water resources. Such management encompasses both the river system's economic resources and its "natural environment." In any drainage basin, most of the water reaching the main river will have run across the land or percolated through rock and soil within the watershed, so managing the quality and quantity of this water is a realistic if challenging undertaking.

Modern approaches to the management of a river basin are moving in the direction of *integrated* management. This means taking into account all human activities that use or affect the freshwater in the river basin. This approach is called integrated river basin management (IRBM). For IRBM to work, some activities outside the watershed, such as air pollution on the global and regional scale that also affect the drainage basin, must be managed or at least taken into account (see "Climate change," pages 196–199, and "Acid waters," pages 210–212).

Management of freshwater ecosystems at all scales of magnitude, from the local to the international, is increasingly shifting toward *sustainable* management that will maintain the resources and the environment into the foreseeable future. This idea was promoted at the United Nations Conference on Environment and Development (UNCED) in 1992, which highlighted the concept of sustainable development (see sidebar "The Earth Summit," page 188). Sustainable development is the principle that progress that improves the lives of people today must not exhaust natural resources or increase environmental problems for future generations. It is enshrined in much international legislation relevant to freshwater ecosystems, including the Framework Convention on Climate Change (FCCC), the Convention on Biological Diversity (CBD), and especially the Ramsar Convention on Wetlands.

The Ramsar Convention's full title is "The Convention on Wetlands of International Importance especially as Waterfowl Habitat." Since being adopted in the Iranian city of Ramsar in 1971, this intergovernmental treaty has extended its scope far beyond a focus on waterfowl (waterbirds dependent on wetland habitats). The convention now recognizes all aspects of wetland conservation and wise use, in recognition of the key role of wetlands in biodiversity conservation and their importance in maintaining the well-being of human communities. The Ramsar Convention adopts a wide definition of wetlands as "areas of marsh, fen, peatland or water, whether natural or artificial, permanent or temporary, with water that is static or flowing, fresh, brackish or salt, including areas of marine water the depth of which at low tide does not exceed six m (19.7 feet)." Those countries who join the convention contract to deliver their commitments through "three pillars" of action that include:

- working toward wise use of their wetlands through water allocation, sustainable wetland management, and through integrated river basin management
- devoting particular attention to developing the List of Wetlands of International Importance (the Ramsar list). A country that joins identifies at least one site to describe and add to the list and agrees to promote this site's conservation. In addition, the convention obliges the country to continue to "designate suitable wetlands within its territory." Selection for the Ramsar list is based on the wetland's significance in terms of ecology, botany (plant biology), zoology (animal biology), limnology, or hydrology.
- cooperating internationally in the delivery of wetland conservation and wise use

Countries join the Ramsar Convention because it provides a framework for international as well as national and local action. It gives nations a voice in international forums that deal with wetland conservation issues. It increases publicity and prestige for their own wetlands. It also gives them access to the latest information, advice, and training, and guidance from international experts that can be applied to their own circumstances. And finally, it brings the prospect of funding for their wetland projects, either through the Ramsar Convention or through international agencies such as the United Nations Educational, Scientific and Cultural Organization (UNESCO) and the United Nations Development Program (UNDP).

Countries that contract to the convention, take requisite action, and gain support, can halt the degradation of specific wetlands and even occasionally restore them to something like their former condition. However, as the River Dniester example at the end of this chapter reveals (see "Putting the pieces together," pages 229–236) doing so is often quite problematic and progress is comparatively slow. This is partly because of the wide diversity of stakeholders involved, and their conflicting interests, and the necessity to set up management and enforcement frameworks at local and regional levels. However, there are success stories, particularly where the water body involved is comparatively small and well defined, there are endangered species threatened, there are relatively few stakeholders, and there is strong local political will as well as international support.

The Srebarna Nature Reserve in Bulgaria contains a 2,224-acre (900-ha) freshwater lake that is supplied by seasonal floods from the River Danube. It is both a Ramsar site and a World Heritage Site. In 1992 authorities placed Srebarna on the World Heritage in Danger List because its bird populations were declining. Of the 99 waterbird species that breed there, 24 were particularly threatened, including the colony of the vulnerable Dalmatian pelican (*Pelecanus crispus*), representing up to about 10 percent of the world's population. The pelican colony had dropped to about one-third of its previous numbers. The cause of the bird decline was habitat alteration due to changes in the operating regime of the Danube's Iron Gate Dam, which interrupted Srebarna's normal flooding regime. The lake began to dry into a marsh. In addition, runoff from adjacent agricultural land threatened the quality of Srebarna's remaining water. Scientists, nongovernmental organizations (NGOs), and local naturalists brought the problem to international attention, and through funding from Ramsar and UNESCO the reserve has been restored almost to its previous condition. Authorities cut two canals to improve the water supply, put pressure on Romania's operation of the Iron Gate Dam, curtailed farming activities in Srebarna's locality, and extended the size of the reserve to provide further protection. By 2000 the reserve had appointed a manager, two guards, and four scientific staff. By 2002 the breeding population of the Dalmatian pelican had risen to its former numbers, and in 2003 Srebarna was removed from the World Heritage in Danger List.

As of early April 2005, more than 140 countries had contracted to the Ramsar Convention. Ramsar's List of Wetlands of International Importance contained 1,428 entries representing a total surface area of more than 304 million acres (123 million ha).

Moving from the international to the local level, the following sections consider the specifics of applying biological knowledge to maintaining or restoring freshwater habitats. Managing water pollution, for instance, like other aspects of environmental management, rests on good science. To convince politicians and public servants to take action to curb pollution, managers of freshwater systems need to have a wide range of information at their fingertips. They need to know the sources by which pollutants enter their lakes and rivers, the pathways of major pollutants as they pass through these systems, and the impact of these pollutants on people and wildlife. Only then can they marshal solid arguments to justify taking action to curb pollution.

Two examples—restoring overenriched lakes and reversing acidification—serve to illustrate that, as is usually the case in environmental management, it is better to prevent the problem in the first place rather than trying to control or treat the problem once it has occurred. Today managers of freshwater systems are often, at one and the same time, seeking to prevent new pollution incidents while trying to restore a freshwater system to something like the condition that existed several decades ago.

## Restoring overenriched lakes

Highly eutrophic lakes—those that are too rich in nutrients—invariably have less biodiversity than moderately nutrient rich lakes. In highly eutrophic lakes the dense population of phytoplankton blocks sunlight penetration, and dead plankton drift to the lake bottom. As bacteria break down these remains they strip the water of much of its oxygen and make it difficult for other organisms to survive (see "Too many nutrients," pages 207–210). Blooms of phytoplankton and bacteria containing toxins that can harm humans and wildlife—so-called *red tides*—also become more common. Highly eutrophic lakes are generally less suitable for wildlife than those with lower nutrient levels. They are also less suited for human needs, such as water supplies and leisure activities.

Since the 1970s, governments in Europe, North America, and other developed regions have recognized the importance of treating sewage before discharging it into lakes and rivers. Treatment can remove much of the phosphate content of wastewater before it is discharged into lakes or rivers. Sewage treatment has helped reduce eutrophication, but it has not totally eradicated the problem. This is because nutrient-rich deposits had built up on the lakebed over many decades. Although wastewater treatment massively reduced the discharge of nutrients into the lake, the sediment at the bottom of the lake continued to liberate nutrients and thus keeps the water overenriched.

This release of nutrients from sediment continues for many decades unless steps are taken to halt the problem. One solution to the difficulty is to physically remove nutrient-rich sediments by dredging. In this process, a dredging device scoops sediment from the lakebed and dumps it into a truck or barge for transport away from the site. For technical and economic reasons, dredging is most suitable for fairly small, shallow lakes.

A second method of dealing with nutrient-rich sediments is to treat the lake with a cocktail of chemicals that include the elements iron (Fe) and calcium (Ca) and the ions nitrate ($NO_3^-$) and hydroxide ($OH^-$). The overall effect is to encourage the growth of denitrifying bacteria in the sediment on the lake bottom. These bacteria convert nitrate to nitrogen gas ($N_2$), which dissolves in the water and escapes into the atmosphere. If encouraged successfully, the denitrifying bacteria form a layer on the lake bottom that converts any nitrates rising from the lake sediment into harmless nitrogen gas.

A third strategy involves manipulating different parts of the food web so as to maximize the removal of phytoplankton as they grow and multiply and thus prevent harmful algal blooms from developing. This approach is called *biomanipulation.* Typically, it works best in shallow lakes. The process starts when fishery managers extract most of the fish that feed on zooplankton. They do this by capturing the zooplankton-eating fishes in nets and removing them from the lake. Other kinds of fish that are captured in the process are returned to the lake. The removal of fish is, in itself, a way of taking large amounts of nutrients out of the lake: The fish themselves are nutrient stores. They discharge nutrients in their urine and feces (solid waste) and when they die, the nutrients in their bodies are recycled. But elimination of certain fish is meant to be only the first step in the process of nutrient removal.

Once their predators, plankton-eating fishes, have been removed, the zooplankton population has a chance to build up to large numbers that can crop the phytoplankton effectively. The water then stays reasonably clear, or, if it becomes clouded by a dense bloom of phytoplankton, it soon clears because as fast as the phytoplankton multiply they are cropped by zooplankton. The clearer water means that submerged plants and bottom-living algae have the chance to photosynthesize and grow, and they take in nutrients that would otherwise become available to the phytoplankton.

The success of biomanipulation is far from guaranteed. Sometimes the approach will only work in combination with other methods, such as dredging or encouraging the activity of denitrifying bacteria. Sometimes the approach fails completely. In some cases managers top up the lake's fish community by adding predators that will consume zooplankton-eating fishes. However, introducing predators can pose a new set of problems (see "Alien invasion," pages 199–205). The use of biomanipulation in freshwater ecosystems remains in its infancy, and it does not yet yield predictable results, particularly in larger lakes.

## Dealing with acidification

Like eutrophication, acidification is a major outcome of chemical pollution that affects freshwaters. Reversing acidification requires a simpler approach than countering eutrophication.

The acidification of many temperate lakes in Canada and northern Europe since the 1960s can be explained in terms of air pollution resulting in acid deposition (see "Acid waters," pages 210–212). Lake managers can return some acidified lakes to something like their former pH condition by adding lime (calcium carbonate, $CaCO_3$). However, the process is costly and works best with relatively shallow lakes. Once the lime has raised the lake water's pH to near neutral, the water becomes more acceptable to fish, and the diversity of phytoplankton, zooplankton, and bottom invertebrates usually increases. The biomass of the lake system typically increases too. Of course, liming a lake is really only worthwhile if the source of acid deposition—pollution by released oxides of nitrogen and sulfur upwind—is curbed. Otherwise the acidification problem will simply recur.

In Europe and North America most power stations and metal smelting facilities now incorporate devices to remove oxides of sulfur and nitrogen from the fumes they discharge. Coal can be processed to remove much of its sulfur content before it is burned. Many cars now have combustion-efficient engines and run on low-sulfur fuels that produce lower levels of sulfur oxides in exhaust fumes. Such changes cut European releases of sulfur gases in half between 1980 and 1999 and slightly lowered levels of nitrogen oxide release. In the late 1990s the United States and Canada were between them still releasing about 35 million U.S. tons (nearly 32 million metric tons) of sulfur dioxide into the atmosphere each year. These two countries have now agreed to reduce their sulfur dioxide emissions by one-third by 2010.

## The partial recovery of Whitepine Lake and Whirligig Lake

Whitepine Lake and Whirligig Lake, two fairly small lakes lying in northeastern Ontario, Canada, are the original homes of the aurora trout (*Salvelinus fontinalis temagamiensis*). This is a spectacularly colored subspecies of the brook trout (*Salvelinus fontinalis*). In the 1960s the aurora trout disappeared from these lakes, and the subspecies was only saved because fishery staff had kept nine specimens for captive breeding. From these nine ancestors the subspecies has been kept alive.

Acid precipitation caused the demise of the trout in their original habitats. The pollution came from the smokestacks of Sudbury's smelting plants, which lay upwind of the lakes. As late as the mid-1980s this precipitation kept the pH of Whitepine Lake below 5.5. As a result, many fish in the lake were failing to breed successfully, and there was a marked reduction in the diversity of the invertebrate population. Over the next decade, however, the sulfur dioxide emissions upwind of the lake were approximately halved. In addition, water entering the lake from nearby wetlands was treated with lime. By the early 1990s the lake water's pH had risen above 6, the diversity of the invertebrate population had increased, and some of the fish stocks were recovering. Aurora trout were reintroduced into Whitepine Lake, but, although they survived, they failed to reproduce. In Whirligig Lake, which was lime-treated in a similar manner to Whitepine, the restocked aurora trout have successfully bred.

## Managing freshwater fisheries

Fishing, whether for sport or for livelihood, is an important generator of income in most lake and river systems. But managing a freshwater fishery can be challenging. First, each freshwater system is unique, with its own set of physical and chemical conditions and its own biological community. For example, trout may breed more readily in one lake than another very similar one. Management options need to take into account these unique circumstances. Second, it is rare to manage a fishery for just one species of fish, and in any case, affecting the abundance of one fish species influences other species (see, for example, "Alien invasion," pages 199–205). Last, water quality and quantity strongly affect the success of a fishery. Altered land-use practices in areas managed for other resources, such as farming and logging, can change the quality of runoff water (see "Altering the flow," pages 190–193, and "Too many nutrients," pages 207–210). Physical developments that change the water flow, such as dams or flood defenses, often impact upon the survival of fish species (see sidebar "Dams and channelization," page 191). A fishery depends on water that has arrived from elsewhere, and the quantity and quality of the water a fishery receives may be difficult to guarantee.

To maintain a healthy fishery, managers need to find ways to protect the quality and quantity of their source water, to restore the physical and chemical environment if degraded, and to manage the biological community that lives within and alongside the freshwater resource. In addition, managers need to control fishing activities. Managing all aspects of a fishery requires a sound understanding of freshwater science as well regular monitoring to track environmental and other changes and see how these influence one another.

There are three aspects to managing a freshwater fishery. First is managing the chemical and physical aspects of the freshwater habitat in which the fish and other components of the food web live. Second is managing the fish stocks and other important elements of the food web. Third is managing the activities of human fishers. All three approaches are important, which is why fishery management can be so challenging. Despite the challenges, many lakes and rivers in North America and Europe are successfully managed for sport fishing. However, this results in freshwater ecosystems that often are a far cry from "natural" systems.

As already discussed it is sometimes desirable and occasionally possible to alter water chemistry (see "Restoring overenriched lakes," pages 221–223, and "Dealing with acidification," pages 223–225). But often fisheries managers must simply accept water chemistry as a given and respond in other ways. In many North American lakes and rivers, less eutrophic waters are managed for trout fishing, with more eutrophic waters managed for larger predatory nonsalmonid species such as largemouth bass (*Micropterus salmoides*), northern pike (*Esox lucius*), and muskellunge (*Esox mosquinongy*), as well as smaller fish such as bluegill (*Lepomis macrochirus*) and green sunfish (*Lepomis cyanellus*).

The physical, rather than chemical, aspects of a freshwater habitat are often simpler to manage. In trout rivers, ways of enhancing the stream habitat include ensuring good water flows to maintain high oxygen levels and low water temperatures, and plentiful water depth. Cattle grazing can be prohibited alongside the river so that high vegetation can grow in the riparian zone. This not only reduces silt-laden runoff and nutrient input, but provides shade over the water, which helps keep water temperatures down. Vegetation growing over the water from the banks and in the water margins provides greater security for fish against predators such as otters, mink, fish hawks, and herons. Marginal vegetation also provides numerous sites of attachment for a host of invertebrates, including insect larvae, crustaceans, and snails, which in turn provide food for fish. The physical aspects of stream management can have a variety of beneficial impacts on resident fish.

Managing the fish stocks themselves means monitoring them to see whether the stock is healthy or in decline. A common method of monitoring fish stock is to estimate the biomass by practical measurement. Fisheries staff can make biomass estimates by removing all the fish in a sample area using nets, by applying chemicals that kill or stun the fish, or even by stunning larger fish using electrical devices. If the sampled areas are representative of the entire fishery, then the biomass in a small area can be multiplied to represent the whole. Another approach involves marking some of the fish with tags, releasing them, and then recapturing them. In subsequent catches, the proportion of tagged to untagged fish gives an estimate of the size of the fish population. Tagging also enables biologists to track the migration of individual fish.

Besides population size, another measure of the health of fish stocks is the growth rate of the fish. Fisheries biologists can use biological structures within the fish to estimate how fast the fish are growing. In a heavily fished lake or river—but one that is not overfished—the fish may grow quickly because any removed fish leave more food and space for the fish that remain. Fish scales and certain bones can be examined by scientists to reveal growth rings similar to those found in the trunks of trees. Each ring represents a season's growth, and several rings lying close together implies slow growth. Where rings are widely spaced, seasonal growth has been faster. By analyzing growth rings in catches from subsequent years, fisheries biologists can follow the growth of a fish population. They can see how changes in environmental conditions and fishing pressure affect the growth of the fish population.

Fishery managers monitor fish; they also monitor fishers. Managers commonly sample the catch of fishers or require fishers to keep detailed records of their catch. If fish become scarce in the face of greater fishing effort and those fish that are caught tend to be of smaller size than in previous seasons, these can be signs of overfishing.

Setting a maximum sustainable yield, the largest number of fish that can be taken from the fishery year after year without causing the stock to decline, is tricky (see sidebar "Standing stock, fish production, and maximum sustainable yield," pages 213–214). The reproductive success of a fish population varies from year to year based on factors such as weather, food availability, and the condition of spawning sites. Agreeing a maximum sustainable yield is also problematic because diverse interest groups have different motives. Scientists and environmentalists are likely to press for low estimates of maximum sustainable yield. They do this to help ensure the long-term survival of the harvested stock and to minimize the impact on the physical environment and on other components of the food web. Commercial fishers, fishery managers, and politicians, on the other hand, are more likely to be influenced by arguments for short-term financial gain, and they tend to seek higher estimates of maximum sustainable yield.

There are many approaches to curbing the activities of fishers for the benefit of the fish stock in the long term. If nets are used, the mesh can be limited to a large size so that smaller fish can escape capture. If fishers are using rod and line a catch limit (a maximum number of fish that can be caught and removed each day) may be set, together with a minimum size at which fish can be removed; smaller fish must be returned unharmed. A closed season policy involves closing down the fishery for part of the year, and especially when fish are likely to be breeding. Fishers may need to be licensed, so that a check can be kept on their numbers and so that their activities can be monitored. All these options will only work if there is adequate enforcement. Unregulated fishers tend to catch all they can with little regard for the long-term sustainability of the fishery.

In developing countries, where fishing is for food and not for sport and where the success of fishing affects the health and even survival of local communities, the challenges of fisheries management are that much greater. Here, many of the approaches used in developed countries are not viable because the fishery is mixed and difficult to regulate. In traditional fisheries, more than 20 different fishing methods may be used, including traps, hooks and lines, spears and harpoons, and natural plant poisons, as well as nets. However, fishing in developing countries tends over time to become more intensive and centered on a narrower variety of fish. Although this trend can lead to a loss of biodiversity (see "Alien invasions," pages 199–205) it is opening up the possibility of managing the fisheries in ways more similar to those found in developed countries.

One approach that is being tested in developing countries is the inclusion of "no-take" zones—parts of the ecosystem where fishing is prohibited—as a means of helping to protect overfished stocks. These safe areas provide habitats where adults can breed and fish larvae can grow undisturbed and then migrate into the surrounding area. Some initial findings in southern and eastern African lakes show that no-take areas can increase the yield from adjacent fisheries, provided that the areas are carefully chosen with respect to the life cycle and breeding habits of the fish. But most importantly, the no-take areas act as a safe haven for fish to thrive regardless of what is happening elsewhere in the lake. As such, incorporating no-take areas is a useful precaution in heavily fished and otherwise poorly managed fisheries.

But there is no quick fix to managing fisheries whether in developed or developing countries. One of the major problems facing those who manage freshwater ecosystems is that the environmental, social, and political context is changing at an increased pace. Those who manage freshwater ecosystems must be skillful if they are to preserve these resources for the future.

## Putting the pieces together

Many of the world's lakes and rivers are in a rapid state of change. Many freshwater systems have altered more in their physical, chemical, and biological characteristics in the last

200 years than they did in the previous 2,000. The global climate is changing, with likely effects that are, as yet, poorly understood. In the face of such change what needs to be done to manage freshwater systems sustainably for the benefit of people and wildlife?

First, scientific knowledge and understanding is vital. At the moment, there are surprisingly large gaps in information about freshwater systems in both industrialized and developing countries. For example, even in well-studied rivers of the United States, scientists find it challenging to estimate minimum water flows that will support high biodiversity. In developing countries, massive river systems such as the Mekong (which flows through Vietnam, Cambodia, Laos, and Thailand) contain some of the world's largest freshwater fish, yet knowledge of the existing habitats and the distribution of species within them is sorely lacking. In the mid-1990s, consultants who were assessing 10 proposed sites for dams and their hydroelectric installations in the Mekong River Basin could not decide among the sites. There was insufficient environmental data to make a judgment (see sidebar).

Besides the Mekong, other rivers where the world's largest freshwater species are at risk include the Amazon in South America, the Yangtze in China, and the Tigris in the Middle East. By raising public awareness of such "charismatic" fishes, a WWF–National Geographic Society project hopes to establish urgent conservation priorities for these little-studied species.

New technological approaches are available to make scientific assessments of the physical, chemical, and biological characteristics of freshwater systems easier. Satellites armed with remote sensors can track changes in water level in lakes and rivers. By detecting the color of surface waters, satellite-mounted sensors can monitor a range of environmental factors. Pollution incidents often show up as discoloration of the water or as changes in the reflectiveness of the water surface. The intensity of green pigments in the surface waters offers a measure of phytoplankton production.

Meanwhile, at ground level, studies of the genetic material obtained from a few fish in a river basin can tell investigators the degree to which populations in different parts of the river

## Charismatic freshwater fish

"Charismatic" animal species on land include the elephants, rhinos, and lions of Africa's savanna and the tiger of Asia's forests. These giant creatures capture the imagination of the public and have come to symbolize and draw attention to the threatened ecosystems where they live. In a similar way, the world's giant freshwater fishes—those that grow to at least 6.5 feet (2 m) in length or 220 pounds (100 kg) in weight—may soon serve to highlight the plight of rivers across the world. Launched in 2004, a project funded by the World Wide Fund for Nature (WWF) and the National Geographic Society is under way to raise awareness about the world's largest freshwater fishes.

In the Mekong River, for example, the giant catfish (*Pangasianodon gigas*) is classed as Southeast Asia's most endangered fish and is officially the world's largest freshwater fish, weighing in at more than 660 pounds (300 kg). It is threatened with extinction because of overfishing, dam construction, and the straightening and deepening of sections of the Upper Mekong for navigation. Channelization of the Upper Mekong will involve dredging and blasting areas where the catfish spawn. Two other gigantic Mekong species, the giant carp (*Catlocarpio siamensis*) and the giant stingray (*Himantura chaophraya*), are also threatened with extinction or are vulnerable. In the case of the stingray, experts believe that specimens reaching 16.4 feet (5 m) and weighing 1,100 pounds (500 kg) may exist. If this is confirmed, the stingray would displace the Mekong catfish as the world's largest freshwater fish.

system interbreed. A fish population flourishes only when there are enough members to maintain reasonably high genetic diversity. Estimating the genetic diversity of a fish population enables scientists to assess its vulnerability to extinction and therefore the degree of urgency in taking conservation measures.

Scientists can track the movements of large fish and freshwater mammals by tagging individuals with radiotransmitters or similar devices. Through such studies scientists can tell where fishes are feeding and breeding, and therefore which habitats and thoroughfares need to be protected to ensure the fish population's long-term health.

The second condition needed to successfully manage freshwater systems is cooperation at many levels of human organization, from the international down to the local. Already various international treaties with application to freshwater ecosystems are in place, including the Convention on Biological Diversity (CBD), the Framework Convention on Climate Change (FCCC), and the Ramsar Convention on Wetlands (see "Integrated management," pages 217–221). Taken together these provide a framework for action that can help governments manage freshwater ecosystems sustainably. However, when several countries draw upon the same water source, the potential for conflict is great (see, for example, "The historic Nile," pages 157–162). Although the Convention on International Watercourses provides guidelines for states to share the nonnavigational use of a river system, few nations have so far committed to it. In the absence of broad cooperation to protect them, freshwater ecosystems and the local human communities that depend upon them suffer.

The third factor needed to ensure that freshwater ecosystems are sustainably managed is public awareness of their worth. It is only when consumers appreciate the true value of water, and the many services that freshwater ecosystems provide, that they will support politicians and water resource managers who make the sustainable management of lakes and rivers a priority. For example, in North America and Europe until the late 1990s, government policies encouraged the draining of wetlands and the intensification of agriculture by giving farmers grants, subsidies, and tax incentives. In many cases, water runoff became much more variable in volume and poorer in quality as a result, with higher nutrient and pesticide levels. Networks of scientists and environmental lobby groups made governments recognize the damage this policy has done to freshwater systems. European agricultural policy, for example, is now encouraging farmers—through subsidies, grants, and tax incentives—to set aside a proportion of land *not* to be used for intensive agricultural production.

Another strategy is to charge consumers the true value of freshwater supplies rather than subsidizing them. Charging users more for their water encourages them to appreciate the resource and become more efficient in its use. Brazil, Mexico, and South Africa are among the countries spearheading moves in this direction. South Africa, for example, is increasing water charges to cover not only the setup, operation, and maintenance costs of irrigation schemes, but also to fund background scientific research, environmental monitoring, and water conservation and management initiatives. In other countries, these other activities are usually funded by the government, which means they may be poorly financed and that water users may remain unaware of the importance of these services.

The complexities of integrating management at different levels of organization, with stakeholders that have very different interests, can be illustrated with an example from Europe.

The Dniester River is a major watercourse of the former Soviet republics of Moldova and Ukraine. The Dniester rises in the Carpathian Mountains in Ukraine, in its lower section flows through Moldova, and then discharges into the Black Sea through Ukraine. The lower Dniester's open water and riverbed provides key spawning sites for migratory fish from the wider northeastern Black Sea region. The river's shallow-water margins are also vital nursery areas for young fish. The lower river contains 76 local fish species, including three that are endangered and two that are vulnerable based on IUCN classification.

An array of factors has degraded the lower Dniester's biodiversity during the last 50 years. Two dams have disrupted the migration patterns of the endangered star sturgeon (*Acipenser stellatus*), the vulnerable sterlet (*Acipenser ruthenus*), and several members of the carp family. A hydroelectric power station has been discharging cooled water into the Dniester, which has prevented several fish species from breeding locally, including the sterlet and the vulnerable European mud-minnow (*Umbra krameri*). Runoff from intensively farmed land continues to cause agricultural fertilizer and pesticide pollution (worse when the region was under Soviet control). The river's banks have become severely eroded due, in part, to illegal and over-intensive livestock rearing in the riparian zone, with animals damaging the river's banks as they clamber down to the river to drink. Authorities have drained some wetland areas. They have also encouraged prospectors to extract gravel from the

## Eight actions to help lakes and rivers

- On or beside freshwater venues, clear up any trash you see and don't leave any of your own.
- Consider eating less meat and more vegetables. A year 2000 study of the efficiency of water use in California revealed that to provide a given amount of protein or energy in the human diet, beef production uses at least six times more water than vegetable or cereal products such as potatoes, corn, wheat, and pulses (the edible seeds of leguminous plants such as beans and lentils).
- Find out what your local water and wastewater utilities are doing to monitor and reduce water leakage from their systems of pipework. What are they accomplishing to keep local lakes, reservoirs, and rivers clean? What are they doing to encourage their consumers to conserve water?
- Ask your local politicians what action they are taking to improve the quality of local freshwaters. What are their opinions about global warming? Are they doing anything to reduce the burning of fossil fuels?
- At home, reduce water wastage and use water more efficiently. Use water-efficient devices, such as modern showers and washing machines. Make sure your garden contains plants that are appropriate for the local climate and so require little additional water. Capture rainwater in butts or tanks for use in the garden. Water plants sparingly and in the early morning or late evening, when rates of evaporation are lower.
- Almost everything you buy uses water in its manufacture. Recycle old products rather than always buying new ones. Use fuel-efficient vehicles: it takes 18 gallons of water to manufacture one gallon of gasoline.
- Join an environmental group that campaigns for wildlife protection and organizes action to monitor local environmental conditions and clean up lakes and rivers.
- With friends and fellow students, find out more about the freshwater environment by subscribing to natural history magazines, reading the environment section of national newspapers, and researching books and Web sites (see "Bibliography and further reading," pages 246–247 and "Web sites," pages 248–251, for some examples). Deepen your understanding of environmental issues by discussing and debating what you discover.

riverbed, altering the river's flow and disrupting fish spawning sites. Commercial fishing is poorly regulated, and some fishing groups operate with mafia-style aggression.

In the face of all these problems, two nongovernmental organizations (NGOs)—Moldova's Biotica and a coalition of NGOs, Eco-TIRAS International Environmental Association of River Keepers—turned their attention to the lower Dniester in the 1990s. Their research revealed that both subsistence fishers and larger, well-organized gangs were illegally overfishing. They lobbied Moldovan and Ukrainian authorities to establish an integrated river basin management (IRBM) approach for the lower Dniester. Biotica proposed establishing a national park in the region and in the period 2000–03 this NGO restocked the lower Dniester with European mud-minnow fry and set up 400 artificial spawning structures for river fishes to use. Due in large part to the efforts of Biotica and Eco-TIRAS, parts of the lower river and its marginal wetlands are now designated as Wetlands of International Importance (Ramsar sites).

In 1999 Biotica drafted a convention for promoting the rational use of the water and biological resources of the Dniester River Basin alongside the conservation of landscape and biological diversity. It proposed the establishment of a joint river commission to involve principle stakeholders from Moldova and Ukraine in developing workable policies and management plans for the river basin. In 2003 Moldova supported the convention but Ukrainian authorities rejected it. The Organization for Security and Cooperation in Europe (OSCE) and the United Nations Economic Commission for Europe (UNECE) stepped in to fund a project to seek agreement. The project, called Transboundary Cooperation and Sustainable Management of the Dniester River, will define priorities to implement IRBM with the assistance of the ministries of environment and the water agencies of Moldova and Ukraine, and Eco-TIRAS. The project began in 2004 and should report its findings by 2006.

Meanwhile, Biotica has been assisting Moldova's Ministry of Environment in establishing fishery quotas and closed seasons. In 2004 Eco-TIRAS organized an IRBM-related conference focusing on the Dniester River system, which brought together more than 150 scientists and NGO representatives. Eco-TIRAS and its member NGOs raise awareness of the Dniester River's IRBM approach through newspaper and magazine articles, educational material for teachers, and lessons and educational events for local schoolchildren.

As the Dniester example helps illustrate, in order for lakes and rivers to be sustainably managed for the long-term future, all the different pieces of the water-management jigsaw puzzle need to fall into place: Authorities must apply scientific knowledge and understanding and undertake environmental monitoring. Workable water management and policy frameworks must be established at all levels from international to local. And the public must be made aware of the true value of freshwater ecosystems so they can play their own part as well as exert pressure on politicians and water and wastewater managers (see sidebar on page 234). Only then will lakes and rivers and their associated wetlands remain beneficial to people, resident wildlife, and the wider biosphere.

Finally, humankind's most pressing role as stewards of freshwater ecosystems is to ensure that everyone on the planet has at least the minimum requirement for clean water and sound sanitation to maintain health and well-being. More than 1.1 billion people in the developing world today face the daily risk of dehydration or disease because they lack reasonable access to safe drinking water. The United Nations defines "reasonable access" as the availability of at least 5.28 U.S. gallons (20 L) of clean water per person per day from a source within 0.62 miles (1 km) of the individual's home. With so many people still at risk, the United Nations' declaration of the decade 2005–15 as the "International Decade for Action 'Water for Life,' " with an emphasis on water-related actions that can help alleviate poverty and hunger, has come not a moment too soon.

# GLOSSARY

**abrasion** the wearing away of soil or rock by friction, as when a river drags stones along its bed and erodes the river bottom

**abstraction** the extraction of water supplies from groundwater or from surface water, such as lakes and rivers

**acid rain** rain made more acidic by oxides of nitrogen and sulfur added to the atmosphere by some forms of air pollution

**algae** simple nonflowering plants. They include single-celled phytoplankton (plant plankton) and attached algae

**alluvium** sediment deposited by a river in its channel or on the surrounding floodplain

**anadramous** having to do with fish that migrate between freshwater, where they breed, and seawater, where they grow to maturity

**aquifer** a water-saturated layer of rock that is sufficiently porous and coarse to enable the water to move freely to supply wells

**archaebacteria** bacteria that live in extreme environments and have structure and chemistry that are different from other forms of bacteria

**bacteria** simple, single-celled organisms that lack a nucleus

**bed load** The total amount of material carried along the bottom of a section of a stream or river as distinct from that which is suspended in the water

**benthic** having to do with organisms that live in or on the lakebed or riverbed

**bilharzia (schistosomiasis)** a human disease caused by the parasitic blood fluke *Schistosoma*. Freshwater snails release *Schistosoma* larvae that can enter the human body through the skin or gut lining

**bioaccumulation** the accumulation within the body of potentially harmful substances ingested in food or absorbed from the environment

**biodiversity** the variety of life-forms in a locality

**biofilm** the layer of small organisms that grow on the surface of objects in the water

**biomagnification** rise in the concentration of a bioaccumulated substance at successive trophic levels in a food chain

**biomanipulation** the process of applying the trophic cascade model to alter the abundance of particular organisms in a biological community

**biomass** the combined mass of life-forms in a locality

**blue-green algae** *see* CYANOBACTERIA

**braided stream** a shallow stream or river that has become choked with sediment, causing it to break into several channels that divide and recombine many times

**capacity** the maximum load of particles a given section of a stream or river carries. It is usually measured in grams per second

**cascade** a waterfall that tumbles through several levels rather than as a single drop; *see also* CATARACT

**catadramous** having to do with fish that migrate between seawater, where they breed, and freshwater, where they grow to maturity

**cataract** a waterfall with a single long drop; *see also* CASCADE

**channelization** the process of straightening and deepening the channel of a natural watercourse for navigation or other purposes. Usually channelization involves artificially reinforcing the riverbanks

**coevolution** the process of two or more distantly related but closely interacting species evolving in tandem

**collector** an invertebrate that consumes fine particulate organic matter such as the feces of other invertebrates

**competence** a stream or river's ability to transport debris. It is measured in terms of the size of the largest particle it can move

**consumer** an organism that consumes other organisms or organic matter derived from them

**continental drift** the slow movement of continents over Earth's surface

**convection current** the vertical circulation of a gas or liquid due to warm regions rising and cool regions sinking

**corrosion** the wearing away of soil or rock by chemical action or the solubility of its constituent substances in water

**crust** the solid, rocky outer layer of the Earth on which the land and sea lie

**cyanobacteria** photosynthetic, single-celled organisms related to bacteria, in the past incorrectly called blue-green algae

**dam** an embankment or similar construction across the current of a stream or river that holds back water

**delta** a triangular or fan-shaped deposit of low-lying land formed at the mouth of a river

**dentritic drainage** a drainage pattern that resembles the branches of a tree. It typically develops on gentle slopes where the underlying rock is fairly uniform in its properties and is not strongly folded or faulted

**desalination** the process of removing salt from salt-rich water, especially seawater

**dissolved (solute) load** the total amount of dissolved material carried by a section of a stream or river. It is usually assessed by filtering a known volume of river water and then evaporating it and weighing the dry residue that remains

**distributary** a branch of a river that flows away from the main channel and does not return to it, as in a delta

**drainage basin (watershed or catchment)** the area of land drained by a river system

**drainage divide** the high boundary that separates one drainage basin from another

**ecological succession** the development of an ecosystem in a distinct series of stages, in which the biological community at one stage produces conditions suitable for the development of the next

**ecosystem** the system comprising a community of organisms and their habitat, found in a particular locality

**ecotone** the edge of a biome, where one biome merges into another

**effluent** partially treated sewage

**epilimnion** the top layer in a lake that lies above the thermocline. It contains currents set up by winds or convection (the rise and fall of liquid due to differences in temperature and therefore density)

**epineuston** those organisms that inhabit the upper side of water's surface layer

**erosion** the breakdown and removal of rock by the action of wind, temperature change, or moving water or ice

**estuary** the locality where a river meets the sea and freshwater mixes with seawater

**eutrophic** having to do with a lake that is rich in plant nutrients

**eutrophication** the enrichment of water with plant nutrients. Eutrophication is commonly caused by the entry of nutrient-rich runoff from agricultural land or the discharge of sewage that is rich in organic matter

**exotic** having to do with species that are nonnative to the region where they arrive

**flood** the inundation of normally dry land when a river or lake overflows its banks

**flood pulse concept (FPC)** a modification of the river continuum concept that applies to some tropical rivers where flooding is an important and regular seasonal event. It takes into account that a significant part of nutrient input comes from flooded land

**food chain** the sequence of organisms in which each is food for the next organism in the chain

**food web** the interconnections between food chains in a community of organisms

**freshwater** the water found in most lakes and rivers and in groundwater. It has a salinity of less than 1 or less than 3, depending on authority

**global warming** a sustained rise in average surface temperatures across the world

**grazer** in the River Continuum Concept this refers to an invertebrate that consumes biofilm

**greenhouse effect** the warming effect caused by greenhouse gases in the atmosphere, such as carbon dioxide, trapping some of the infrared radiation emitted from Earth's surface

**groundwater** water that saturates the rocky layer below the surface of the ground

**habitat** the place where a specific organism or community of organisms lives

**hard water** freshwater that contains relatively high concentrations of dissolved calcium and magnesium. Soap does not readily form lather in hard water

**hydrologic cycle** the cyclical movement of water between land, sea, and air

**hydrology** the scientific study of the properties of water on Earth's surface, including its distribution and utilization on and beneath the land

**hypolimnion** the deep layer in a lake that lies beneath the thermocline. Its circulation is poor and in deep lakes it may be oxygen-deficient

**hyponeuston** those organisms that inhabit the underside of water's surface layer

**ice age (glacial period)** a cold period in Earth's history, lasting thousands of years, when glaciers and ice sheets are more extensive than usual and sea levels are lower. The most recent ice age ended about 15,000 years ago

**ice sheet** an extensive, thick layer of ice covering a major landmass. Ice sheets cover most of Antarctica and Greenland

**invasives** nonnative species that multiply and displace native species

**invertebrate** an animal without a backbone (vertebral column)

**ion** an atom or molecule with an overall positive or negative electrical charge

**laminar flow** nonturbulent flow of a fluid as found in water in shallow streams moving over a smooth flat surface. There is no mixing between adjacent layers of water

**latitude** a measure of angular distance in a north-south direction. The equator lies at zero degrees latitude, the North Pole 90°N, and the South Pole 90°S

**lava** molten rock (magma) on Earth's surface

**lentic** having to do with freshwater systems, such as lakes and ponds, which are not flowing

**limestone** sedimentary rock containing mostly calcium carbonate

**limnology** the scientific study of freshwater systems

**lithosphere** the outer rocky layer of the Earth comprising the crust and upper part of the mantle. About 20 plates make up the lithosphere

**longitude** a measure of angular distance in an east-west direction. The Greenwich Meridian (an imaginary line passing north to south through Greenwich, London) is zero degrees longitude.

**lotic** having to do with freshwater systems, such as streams and rivers, which are flowing

**magma** molten rock beneath Earth's surface

**malaria** a human disease caused by a parasitic protist, *Plasmodium,* which is transmitted by adult female *Anopheles* mosquitoes when they bite. The disease causes intermittent chills and fever and can be fatal

**mass wasting** the mass movement of rock, soil, or sediment down a slope under the force of gravity

**maximum sustainable yield** the largest number or greatest biomass of an organism that can be harvested from a population year after year without causing the stock to diminish

**meander** a wide bend in a stream or river. The bend gradually widens as the water's flow erodes the outer edge of the meander and deposits sediment against the inner edge

**migration** the mass movement of animals from one region to another, usually to find food or a breeding place

**moraine** an accumulation of fragments of rock of mixed sizes that has been transported and deposited by a glacier or ice sheet

**nekton** aquatic animals that can swim powerfully against currents

**neuston** organisms that inhabit water's surface

**niche** an organism's role in a community. It arises from its structural adaptations and its physiological (body function) and behavioral responses to the environment, such as where it lives within a habitat and what it feeds upon

**nutrients** substances such as nitrates and phosphates that plants need in small amounts to make organic (carbon-based) substances by photosynthesis

**ocean** the continuous expanse of saltwater that covers 71 percent of Earth's surface

**oligotrophic** having to do with a lake that is sparse in plant nutrients

**overfishing** harvesting a fish population at a level beyond which its numbers can be replaced by natural breeding

**oxbow lake** a crescent-shaped lake formed when a river abandons a meander and takes a shorter path

**pelagic** having to do with organisms that live in the water column rather than on the lakebed or riverbed

**photosynthesis** the process by which plants, and some protists and bacteria, trap sunlight in order to make organic (carbon-rich) substances such as carbohydrates

**phytoplankton** plant plankton; plankton that photosynthesize

**plankton** organisms that float freely in water at the mercy of currents. They swim weakly, if at all

**plate (tectonic or lithospheric plate)** a segment of Earth's rocky surface consisting of crust and attached upper mantle. About 20 slowly moving plates make up Earth's surface

**plate tectonics** the modern theory that Earth's surface is divided into moving plates. Their movements generate continental drift and are responsible for phenomena such as earthquakes and volcanoes close to plate boundaries

**pollution** human alteration of specific physical or chemical factors in the environment, not normally present at such levels, to the extent that the change harms living organisms

**predator** an animal of one species that kills and eats individuals of another animal species (its prey)

**producer** an organism in the community that makes food by manufacturing organic substances from simple inorganic ones. In freshwater ecosystems the major producers are phytoplankton, attached algae, and larger plants

**prokaryotes** bacteria, cyanobacteria, and archaebacteria. They are single-celled organisms that lack a nucleus

**protists** single-celled organisms that have a nucleus. They include plantlike forms, such as diatoms and dinoflagellates, and animal-like forms, such as amoebas

**reservoir** a lake maintained for water supply, including purposes such as irrigation and hydroelectric power generation as well as the provision of water for domestic or industrial use

**respiration** the process inside cells by which organisms break down food molecules to release energy

**riffle** shallow water in a river where the current is fast flowing

**riparian zone** the area of land alongside a stream or river where deeper soils are saturated with water

**river** a large body of water that moves under the force of gravity along a channel

**river continuum concept (RCC)** an ecological model that proposes that the nature of a river's biological community gradually shifts in a predictable way from source to mouth. The changes reflect alterations in physical conditions and the nature of nutrient inputs

**salinity** a measure of the saltiness of water. Most seawater has a salinity close to 35, or 35 grams of dissolved salts in 1,000 grams of seawater. Freshwater has a salinity of less than 1 or less than 3, depending on authority

**satellite remote sensing** the use of satellites to detect features of Earth's surface

**sea** a named part of an ocean, such as the Caribbean Sea, or a large salty inland lake, such as the Caspian Sea. Also, an alternative name for the water in an ocean

**sewage** general wastewater

**shredder** an invertebrate that consumes coarse particulate organic material such as partially decayed plant fragments

**species** the world population of genetically similar individuals that interbreed to produce fertile offspring

**specific heat capacity** the quantity of heat required to raise the temperature of a unit mass of substance by one degree

**standing stock** the average biomass of a population of organisms present in an ecosystem year after year

**stream** a small body of water that moves under the force of gravity along a channel. The term also applies to any such moving body of water irrespective of size

**stream ordering** the classification of rivers or streams according to their relative position in the drainage system. First-order streams have no tributaries. Second-order streams form where two first-order streams unite. Second-order streams meet to form third-order streams, and so on

**substrate** the material on a lakebed or riverbed that provides a medium on or in which organisms live

**surface runoff** water that runs off the land surface into lakes, streams, or rivers

**suspended load** the total amount of suspended material carried by a section of a stream or river

**swim bladder** an air-filled sac in the abdominal cavity of bony fishes. Adjusting the volume of air inside the swim bladder enables the fish to maintain neutral buoyancy

**thermocline** a layer in the water column across which the temperature rapidly changes

**transpiration** the loss of water by evaporation from the surface of larger plants

**tributary** a stream or river that flows into a larger one

**trophic cascade** predator-prey interactions that result in the abundance of a consumer species at the third trophic level or higher affecting the abundance of producers at the first trophic level

**trophic level** the energy level in a food chain or food web. Organisms at the first trophic level are producers. Organisms at higher trophic levels are consumers

**tsunami (seismic sea wave)** a giant wave, or series of waves, produced by an earthquake, volcano, landslide, or other major water displacement

**turbulent flow** movement of a fluid in which swirls and eddies cause the fluid in different layers to mix. Turbulent flow is typical of most parts of streams and rivers

**vertebrate** an animal with a backbone (vertebral column) or similar structure

**water column** the vertical expanse of water from surface to lakebed or riverbed

**waterfall** an abrupt discontinuity in the gradual slope of a river that causes water to fall downstream. Waterfalls commonly form where a river flows from hard to soft rock

**water table** the level below which pores in rock strata are saturated with water. Where the water table rises above ground level a spring, lake, stream, or river forms

**wave** a vertical disturbance that travels along the water surface

**weathering** the breakdown of rock into fragments or dissolved substances by a combination of physical, chemical, or biological processes

**wetland** a flat, low-lying area of land that is covered in water or has water-saturated soil

**zooplankton** animal plankton

# BIBLIOGRAPHY AND FURTHER READING


Brönmark, Christer, and Lars-Anders Hansson. *The Biology of Lakes and Ponds*. Oxford: Oxford University Press, 2005.

Claudi, Renata, and Joseph H. Leach, eds. *Nonindigenous Freshwater Organisms: Vectors, Biology, and Impacts*. Boca Raton, Fla.: CRC Press, 1999.

Cowx, Ian G., ed. *Management and Ecology of River Fisheries*. Oxford: Fishing News Books, 1999.

Cushing, Colbert E., and J. David Allan. *Streams: Their Ecology and Life*. San Diego, Calif.: Academic Press, 2001.

Dobson, Mike, and Chris Frid. *Ecology of Aquatic Systems*. Harlow, Essex: Prentice Hall, 1998.

Giller, Paul, and Björn Malmqvist. *The Biology of Streams and Rivers*. Oxford: Oxford University Press, 1998.

Gleick, Peter H., with Nicholas L. Cain, Dana Haasz, Christine Henges-Jeck, Catherine M. Hunt, Michael Kiparsky, Marcus Moench, Meena Palaniappan, Veena Srinivasan, and Gary H. Wolff. *The World's Water 2004–2005: The Biennial Report on Freshwater Resources*. Washington, D.C.: Island Press, 2004.

Gloss, Gerry, Barbara Downes, and Andrew Boulton. *Freshwater Ecology: A Scientific Introduction*. Malden, Mass.: Blackwell Publishing, 2004.

Goudie, Andrew. *The Human Impact on the Natural Environment*. Malden, Mass.: Blackwell Publishing, 2000.

Karr, James R., and Ellen W. Cru. *Restoring Life in Running Waters: Better Biological Monitoring*. Washington, D.C.: Island Press, 1998.

Maitland, Peter, and N. C. Morgan. *Conservation Management of Freshwater Habitats: Lakes, Rivers and Wetlands*. London: Chapman & Hall, 1997.

Moss, Brian. *Ecology of Fresh Waters: Man and Medium, Past to Future*. 3d ed. Oxford: Blackwell, 1998.

Paxton, John R., and William N. Eschmeyer, eds. *Encyclopedia of Fishes*. 2d ed. San Diego, Calif.: Academic Press, 1998.

Voshell, J. Reese, Jr. *A Guide to Common Freshwater Invertebrates of North America*. Blacksburg, Va.: McDonald and Woodward Publishing Company, 2002.

Wetzel, Robert G. *Limnology: Lake and River Ecosystems*. 3d ed. San Diego, Calif.: Academic Press, 2001.

Woodward, Susan L. *Biomes of Earth: Terrestrial, Aquatic, and Human-Dominated.* Westport, Conn.: Greenwood Press, 2003.

Worldwatch Institute, ed. *Vital Signs 2003: The Trends That Are Shaping Our Future.* New York: W. W. Norton & Co., 2003.

# WEB SITES

**American Association for the Advancement of Science**

URL: http://www.aaas.org

An international nonprofit organization dedicated to advancing science around the world.

**AQUASTAT**

URL: http://www.fao.org/ag/agl/aglw/aquastat/main

The global information system for water and agriculture developed by the Food and Agricultural Organization of the United Nations.

**FAO Fisheries Department**

URL: http://www.fao.org/fi

The Fisheries Department of the Food and Agricultural Organization of the United Nations.

**IUCN Red List**

URL: http://www.redlist.org

The World Conservation Union's Red List of threatened species.

**International Rivers Network**

URL: http://www.irn.org

A U.S.-based independent nonprofit organization committed to supporting local communities in protecting their rivers and watersheds.

**National Oceanic and Atmospheric Administration**

URL: http://www.noaa.gov

The U.S. federal government agency specializing in atmospheric and oceanographic sciences.

**NationMaster.com**

URL: http://www.nationmaster.com

An independent Web site that compiles statistics from international agencies and displays them in chart form.

**UNEP World Conservation Monitoring Center**

URL: http://www.unep-wcmc.org

The branch of the United Nations Environment Program that compiles and publishes data on the state of the world's biodiversity.

**UNESCO Water**

URL: http://www.unesco.org/water

The Web site of the United Nations Educational, Scientific and Cultural Organization, which provides information on the sustainable development and conservation of freshwater resources.

**United Nations Environment Program (UNEP)**

URL: http://www.unep.org

The UN agency with a focus on environmental conservation and sustainable development.

**USGS Office of Surface Water**

URL: http://water.usgs.gov/osw

The office of the U.S. Geological Survey that monitors and reports on surface water conditions in the United States.

**The World Conservation Union**

URL: http://www.iucn.org

The world's largest organization that brings together nongovernmental organizations, governments, and international agencies to foster wildlife conservation alongside sustainable development.

**World Health Organization**

URL: http://www.who.int/en

An agency of the United Nations aimed at raising standards of health worldwide. Its site includes up-to-date information on waterborne diseases.

**World Lakes Network**

URL: http://www.worldlakes.org

A global network of people and organizations working for the conservation and sustainable management of lakes.

**World Resources Institute**

URL: http://www.wri.org

An independent, nonprofit environmental research and policy organization based in Washington, D.C.

**The World's Water**

URL: http://www.worldwater.org

A site set up by the U.S.-based Pacific Institute, an independent think tank that studies development, environment, and security issues. The site provides up-to-date information on the world's freshwater resources.

**WWF**

URL: http://panda.org

The World Wide Fund for Nature, still called the World Wildlife Fund in North America, is an international nongovernmental organization that carries out promotional and practical conservation work, including field projects and scientific research in many countries.

# INDEX

Note: *Italic* page numbers refer to illustrations.

## J



## K



## L



## M



## N



## O

## U



## V



## W



## Y



## Z